unreal

Phil McDonald

unreal

ADVENTURES

OF

A FAMILY'S GLOBAL LIFE

NORTH LOOP BOOKS

Minneapolis

North Loop Books
2301 Lucien Way #415
Maitland, FL 32751
407.339.4217
www.northloopbooks.com

NORTHLOOP
BOOKS

Printed in the United States of America.

ISBN-13: 9781545657218

North Loop Books

unreal

Phil McDonald is president of Leader Empowerment And Development, Inc. (LEAD), an American nonprofit that empowers leaders in the developing world through education and social entrepreneurship.

With work experience in thirty-eight countries, the author has helped set up or empower over 150 overseas development projects on five continents. Projects included hospitals, clinics, orphanages, community centers, schools, businesses, farms, plantations, and factories. His current priority is helping social enterprises, bringing hope and dignity to his field partners.

Phil earned a PhD in International Education from Michigan State University and specialized in national planning, policy analysis, and development economics. His wife Rebecca is founder and CEO of Women At Risk International, Inc. (WAR), a leader in the fight against human trafficking. The McDonalds live in Michigan, have four adult children and seven grandchildren. A portion of this book's proceeds will be donated to both LEAD and WAR.

DEDICATED TO:

Our overseas field partners, who amaze us
Our generous financial partners, who made our careers possible
Our children, who lived this rich journey with delight
Rebecca, whose love, commitment, and passion are truly inspiring

CONTENTS

PART I

LIFE CHOICES

PART II

LEARNING THE ROPES

PART III

ROAD TO EMPOWERMENT

PART IV

UNLEASHING POTENTIAL

FOREWORD

This is an unusual, informative, and endlessly fascinating book, offering the reader an enjoyable and ultimately inspiring perspective on how one person can make a big difference in a complex and increasingly globalized world.

As Phil McDonald acknowledges at the outset, it was an unusual challenge from a college basketball coach in the spring of 1972 that launched his journey into the wider world: come to Africa, the coach said, and spend the summer working in the Central African Republic. Phil did go, and his life was changed forever.

This book describes that journey, starting with two summers spent in the Central African Republic and continuing through a series of other assignments, including Bangladesh, Philippines, Myanmar, Nepal, and Uzbekistan. By his calculation, he clocked more than two million air miles over the next four decades as part of his international service, the equivalent to eighty trips around the world.

In each case, Phil was far more than simply another tourist passing through. He had a mission and purpose, focused primarily on working closely with diverse populations in ways that might help them help themselves. While contributing in multiple ways, he approached each country with a strong sense of partnership, encouraging local ownership as a way to ensure that the programs he supported would continue long after he departed.

Unusually, the book combines a pragmatic description of the challenges and opportunities of development work with deep insights into the emotional responses—and sometimes internal conflicts—that he experienced at various steps along the way. Early on, he reflects on the lingering legacy of colonialism that he witnessed in his first trip to Africa. At the same time, he is skeptical about aspects of American university life that he experienced while working towards his PhD, noting in particular the self-satisfied smugness that is often all too apparent in contemporary academia.

He also provides important insights into his own decision-making process, one in which he repeatedly took the "less traveled" path. For example, early on he chose to work at a grassroots level rather than enter the highly paid world of the development bureaucracy. In doing so he forged close and enduring personal friendships with a variety of people from all walks of life and all parts of the world, contributing to the rich and revealing set of stories that recur throughout this narrative. He experienced the world as a private citizen, not a government employee.

Phil was also a risk-taker and development entrepreneur in the best sense of the word, challenging received wisdom in ways that resulted in more creative and ultimately more successful programs. He seemingly expected to learn something new from each challenge, suggesting a strong inclination to learn from failure as well as success. Indeed, the candid "lessons learned" gained from Phil's experience—partly embedded in his narrative and partly highlighted through a series of succinct "principles" that appear throughout the book—represent one of the most informative aspects of his presentation. Readers who have launched their own global journey will find this aspect of the book especially useful.

Phil's candor and honesty about his experience also figure prominently throughout the narrative. Perhaps more than anything, I was struck by the resilience that he demonstrated in critical situations, even in the face of disappointment, including the searing experience of being "fired" from a senior position. Yet Phil responds to these and other challenges with courage, fortitude, and spiritual depth, offering important empathy to those experiencing something similar.

Most notably, this book combines the personal with the professional in an unusually effective way, capturing both the external adventure of a life well lived with the internal reflections that were also part of Phil's life work. The interplay between that "inner journey" and "outer journey" makes for a powerful narrative, at times implicitly encouraging the reader towards similar intro-spection of their own.

Finally, this book represents a tribute to what Phil would undoubtedly describe as possibly the best decision of his life: his decision to meet and marry Rebecca while both were still students in Michigan. Unlike Phil, Rebecca had spent most of her childhood in Pakistan and Bangladesh, providing an international dimension to their marriage from the very beginning. Together, they forged a mutually beneficial partnership, drawing strength from each other in ways that also made a difference in the lives of countless others. That too is part of this story, a story that will inspire readers in their own varied journeys through life, journeys that can learn from, and be inspired by, the one that Phil and Rebecca embarked on long ago.

Jonathan Addleton, PhD

Former US Ambassador to Mongolia

Former USAID Mission Director in India, Pakistan,

Cambodia, and Central Asia

AUTHOR'S NOTE

The names of people are changed to protect their privacy or identities. Other than my family, or those who passed on, most names are altered. Several live in oppressive societies where freedom of speech or religion is not valued. Many have suffered enough for one lifetime. Revealing their names, and their organizations, could put their lives at risk.

In writing this book, I relied on personal correspondence and passport stamps, researched facts when available, and called upon my memory or the memory of others. Most of the conversations in this book between my wife and me are verbatim quotes.

Throughout the book, as patterns were recognized, principles emerged. Stands to reason, the lack of experience at the beginning of my career yielded few principles. Towards the end of the book, decades of experience produced more principles.

Contrary to the title of the book, all that is written is real. Events happened in the actual locations cited, and dates are correct.

Situations, incidents, and described actions are accurate and true to the events that occurred, to the best of my memory.

There are no composite characters or combined events in this book. Some events are compressed for the sake of maintaining continuity in the story but have no impact on the substance or veracity of the story.

Why I Wrote the Book

DO YOU EVER WONDER what it's like to live and work overseas in the developing world? I never wondered until I spent a summer in the Central African Republic. The exciting trip turned my world upside down. I was hooked by the opportunity that hid in the shadow of potential danger.

My career path changed from becoming an attorney to earning a PhD in international educational planning. I started out an overseas professor and ended up helping social entrepreneurs. For my family, life overseas was really cool. Any day could be an epic adventure. Crises became normal, fun, and exciting.

Many of our overseas experiences were unusual, bizarre, and unreal. Unreal means something so good or so bad, so incredible, amazing, and fantastic, that it doesn't seem real.

Make no mistake, don't let the word "unreal" fool you. Trust me, personal experiences with lions, rhinos, riots, war zones, rebel fighters, coups, pirates, terrorists, traffickers, cyclones, and deadly tropical disease were all very real.

While this book might read like a thriller, *unreal* is more than an adventure story. As a genre, *unreal* is a "journey memoir," a group of personal stories of my inner journey and how my life changed over my career. But I didn't stop there.

When people find out I have worked in thirty-eight countries, they often ask, "How do you do what you do?" With an earned doctorate, the professor in me could write an academic book. But who wants to read one more boring textbook?

Theory is important but looking back, I have the luxury of practical hindsight. Rather than explain how I did projects, sharing true stories shows how they were done. From ninety events, I lifted out sixty principles, from more than thirty years of experience. The principles, based on life lessons, provide takeaways from the school of hard knocks.

My purpose in writing is meant to entertain, enlighten, and inspire. But the focus of this book is not about my family or me. It's all about our amazing field partners, whose lives inspire us. I know they will inspire you.

Before you turn another page, I humbly ask you leave your cultural assumptions aside, read with an open mind, and understand all cultures have their own way of doing things. I learned this the hard way when I arrived on the Indian subcontinent decades ago. An older gentleman said, "Try hard as you want, you still won't change a billion people." Now I'm the older gentlemen and I can confirm he was right.

If you are drawn to adventure, the exotic, the dangerous, the thrill of escape, and what it's like to raise a family in a challenging environment, enjoy the ride. Embrace the hope, revel in the inspiring people I've known, and laugh at the ups and downs.

Now, my goal is to transport you into my world and take you on an unreal journey. I know no better way than to start with a few adventures. So batten down the hatches, fasten your seatbelts, and enjoy the ride.

Phil McDonald
Grand Rapids, Michigan

PART

I

Life Choices

I took the road less traveled by, and that has made all the difference.

—Robert Frost

CHAPTER 1

DIRTY LITTLE SECRET

Oh, the places you'll go.
—Dr. Seuss

IN BANGLADESH, driving a car presented a challenge and an unreal risk to the driver. Rickshaws, ox carts, trucks, buses, and people crammed narrow streets. I mean lots of people. If a pedestrian was injured or killed, the driver was always at fault. Instant vigilante justice often took the life of the driver.

Jam-packed between India and Myanmar (Burma), this small country perennially ranked as one of the world's most densely populated rural countries. Imagine half the US population packed into Wisconsin.

On a quiet spring day in 1992, I turned a corner and found myself in a strange situation. In a land where vehicles and people fought for space on any given road, my car was the only vehicle on the wide, paved street. Ahead of me I saw a lone, thin figure standing in the middle of the road.

Dressed in blue, the policeman wore a riot helmet and held a bamboo riot shield. His right arm stretched out towards me stiff as a monument. I slowed down and opened my window to the sound of his shrill whistle. My ears rang hard.

"Stop," he shouted.

"Officer, what's the problem? I need to go this way to the office."

"You cannot come this way. Very dangerous."

Not seeing anyone ahead, I looked up at him.

"Why not?"

"The boys."

"What do you mean the boys?"

"The boys are running!"

Maybe he meant the street was closed for a running race. But why the riot gear? Then it sank in. His phrase "boys are running" meant young men were rioting in the streets, burning buses and cars, basically trashing everything in sight. And coming our way.

Along the right side of the street ran a series of connected shops, each not more than ten feet wide. I heard the dreadful sound of shop owners pulling down their doors. Visualize a garage door made of narrow metal slats pulled down like a roll-top desk. The sound, eerily unmistakable, echoed as every door slammed and locked, almost in perfect succession.

Riots happened fast in this part of the world. Within seconds the air filled with tension from the deep emotion of hundreds of young men on a rampage. The wind shifted and the raw stench of burning vehicles rolled over us like a tidal wave. I now heard the distant roar of the mob. The policeman frantically grabbed my door.

"Sir, you must go now. I'm telling you, please turn around and go back. You shouldn't be here."

I slammed the gearshift in reverse, did an about-face, and raced off. A half mile later, I came to the main thoroughfare, CDA Avenue. On my left, I heard the same sound of shuttering shop doors slamming down in rapid sequence. The eruption of another mob, filled with frustration and anger at the government, engulfed this street as well.

Muslim women in veiled *burkas*, covered head to toe in black, grabbed their children and ran for safety. I locked my doors. Once the pedestrians cleared, I crossed the broad avenue, eager to get myself home.

Only one more curve to go and I would be at the foot of the hill. I squinted into the sunlight, searching the road ahead. As I rounded the turn, I came upon a lumbering ox cart in front of me and slowed down.

From both sides of the street young men rushed at me. My heart beat heavy in my chest. My eyes darted around looking for all possible escape routes. The surrounding mob and the slow ox cart left me no choice. Trapped on all sides, I slowed to a crawl.

In an effort to roll me over, my vehicle was rocked from side to side. Chants of "American go home" and "Death to America" made it clear the young men of this Islamic country knew my nationality.

Being white skinned, with blond hair and blue eyes, didn't allow me to blend in.

The rocking increased. I broke into a clammy sweat. If the mob rolled me over, I was as good as dead. One can of gasoline and a single match, I would be burned alive, turning my blue Suzuki minivan into a personal crematorium.

The ox cart finally yielded to my honking and pulled over. I stomped down on the accelerator. My vehicle lunged forward and bodies flew off. I sped up the winding road to the top of the Khulshi hill, taking turns like a Formula One race car driver.

We lived in Chittagong, a port city on the Bay of Bengal, and rented a flat up on the hill. Some friends called our subdivision "cushy." Most residents were either wealthy Bangladeshi business owners or foreigners, known as expatriates or "expats. Cushy meant your monthly house rent was three times more than anywhere else. Renters paid a premium to live on a hill in a city that flooded every year.

I honked the familiar signal for the guard to open our gate. I rolled into my garage stall and let out a sigh of relief, but only for a few seconds. I realized—those rioters knew where I lived.

In fear, I ran from the garage to the back door of our flat. While running, I shouted at the guard to lock the front gate. Once inside, I locked all the house doors. Confident our home was secure, I collapsed onto the living room sofa and waited to hear the roar of the mob.

My wife came into the living room and asked, "What's wrong?" Still panting, I gasped out a response.

"Major riots in the streets down the hill. I came around a curve, and this crazy ox cart was in front of me. Next thing I know guys on both sides were rocking my van, pounding on my windows, screaming at me. Fortunately, the ox cart pulled over, and I got away."

"Did anyone get hurt?"

"I don't think so."

Rebecca raised her eyebrows in confusion.

"So, what's the problem?"

"They know where we live."

"They won't come up here. Everything is locked and guarded. It's easier to burn vehicles on the main streets. Mobs go for the easy, low-hanging fruit. Come, it's time for lunch."

Rebecca did it again. My wife, so grounded, so logical, so calm. An American girl who grew up in Bangladesh, she knew the cultural mind-set and understood what was happening. She knew exactly the fear I felt because as a child she sat in the back of a Land Rover surrounded by an angry mob wielding machetes after her mom accidentally hit and killed a small boy.

At the table, my adrenaline decreased, although I remained unnerved. I looked over as she calmly took a bite of spaghetti. Her long brown hair draped over the green top of her *chemise salwar*. As a child, she had lived through two bloody wars before turning fifteen. I starred at her lovely almond eyes until she looked up.

"What?" she asked.

"What about our boys? How will they get home from school?"

"Oh, I'm not worried. Our school bus driver's pretty cagey. He'll know what side streets to use."

My pulse now under a hundred beats per minute and not feeling as insecure, I was ready to carry on a meaningful conversation. I wiped my mouth with a red cloth napkin, leaned back, and proceeded to pontificate with bold confidence.

"You know, this morning's paper said it's been two years since the University of Chittagong stopped classes."

"Why?"

"Apparently, the boys' dorms align themselves with political parties, and the party bosses make sure they are well armed. There are still daily gunfights between dorms, and can you believe both sides are using rocket-propelled grenades?"

My comment didn't even phase her as she reached for a piece of Italian bread.

"Doesn't surprise me. The opposition party is probably behind today's riots. I'm sure they paid guys to start it. Always trying to make the people in power look bad. Want more spaghetti?"

"Just a smidgen."

I waited while she filled my plate.

"Wow, that's more than a smidgen."

"Sorry, that's how I roll."

"The paper also said there's a nationwide strike scheduled for tomorrow."

"Well, the kids will be happy having a strike day and no school."

In our home state of cold Michigan, schools closed for snow days. In tropical Bangladesh, schools closed on days of a national strike, called a "*hartal.*" Some protest days peacefully unfolded while others turned violent and bloody. Either way, our kids enjoyed a day or two off from school.

"Did the paper say what time tomorrow the strike begins?" she asked.

"Six in the morning."

"Good, we can sleep in for once."

By midafternoon, the school bus driver brought our two older sons home safe and sound. Within minutes, their friends from our multicultural neighborhood arrived to play their daily game of imaginary "GI Joe" in our backyard. Divided up into teams, each boy used his favorite toy gun to shoot the other team.

Boys who like to play with toy guns are the same the world over, except different cultures use unique sounds to imitate a shooting gun. My American boys shouted, "bang, bang" or "pow, pow." Bangladeshi and Pakistani boys yelled, "tooch, tooch," while Filipinos rang out with "bang ow, bang ow." Russian-speaking kids hollered, "ba-bakh" or "tra-ta-ta."

By evening, our third son wasn't feeling well. Listless and lethargic, the pale three-year-old had no interest in playing with toys or watching TV. Rebecca hung up the phone and looked at me with an intentional look. I knew that look. It always meant our situation was dire.

"The nurse says we have to take Nathan down to the American hospital first thing in the morning." Located three hours south of Chittagong, a nonprofit organization operated a hospital where my wife grew up.

"What about the nationwide strike?"

"She says we just need to get out of the city before the protests start at six in the morning. Once we get over the big bridge, the countryside should be okay. I think all of us should go in case Nate's condition requires us to stay. The boys can take their homework and play with their friends on the hospital compound."

Back in Bangladesh for the second time, I was working to create educational opportunity for a persecuted minority group. By this time in my overseas career, I had discovered a dirty little secret—handouts create dependency. When locals became dependent on foreign funding, it often crippled their economy, killed personal initiative, destroyed dignity, and caused resentment.

Temporary handouts became necessary in times of natural disasters or armed conflict. However, in a country at peace, with some semblance of a working economy, a better way existed for long-term development.

Over three decades, I learned to function in other cultures, discovered how to empower others to build financially self-supporting entities, and watched as they multiplied their efforts. The antidote to dependency on foreign funds was economic sustainability. Sustainable enterprises built at the individual, family, and group levels developed financial independence, resulting in dignity, pride, and social acceptance.

My wife and children played a significant part on my journey in supporting social and economic justice. Most days in Bangladesh were quiet, predictable, and calm. Other times chaotic. Like the time we drove straight into an angry mob with our four children.

CHAPTER 2

LIFE IS A RIOT

Wherever you go, go with all your heart.
—Confucius

AT DAWN I began packing up the minivan for our trip down to the hospital. Our young son's condition worsened during the night, and my wife urged me to leave on schedule. Not just for Nate's sake, but the risk to our family if we didn't get out of town in time. I lashed the final bicycle on the luggage rack, looked at my watch, and realized it was ten minutes to six.

"Phil, we've got to go now. We can't get caught in a riot with our kids."

"Hey, this is Bangladesh. Nothing starts on time. The protests are scheduled to begin at six, but it's six rubber time, not American time."

She smiled at my knowledge of a culture that valued events and relationships over timeliness. Nevertheless, I didn't convince her.

"At least pack some tape. We're going to need it to navigate a riot."

"I always leave a roll of red electrical in the glove compartment."

Because ambulances were rare, drivers transporting the injured or sick would put a makeshift red cross on their car windshield hoping other people and vehicles would let them pass through.

As we drove down the hill, the town lay in silence as a hot tropical sun rose over the hill tracts in the distance. Residents still asleep, there wasn't any sign of life. It didn't matter. My wife began processing out loud.

"We have to make it to the Kalurghat Bridge to get out of town. Right now, even if there isn't any traffic, it will be ten after six by the time we get to the bridge. With our luck, a train will be on it, and we'll be stuck on this side with the mobs."

The rickety old bridge, built as a railroad bridge during the British colonial era, was also used by cars. Franky, we hated driving over it with our precious ones. The half-mile long monstrosity was an accident waiting to happen. My wife held her breath every time she crossed it.

The wide Karnaphuli River flowing under the bridge raged turbulent during monsoons. The rest of the year, muddy water sat dark, deep, and ominous. As a child, she had nightmares of the bridge succumbing to all the weight and crashing into the river. To her, it felt like a third-world horror movie.

"We're fine. Like I said, nothing starts on time around here," I responded.

Not one to take chances, she reached into the glove compartment, grabbed the red tape, and with straight strips created a large red cross on the inside of our windshield.

At the bottom of the hill, I turned onto the main street leading to the bridge. Within a couple of miles, I steered our little mini-van around a bend. To our horror, hundreds of chanting young men marched towards us, wielding machetes and wooden clubs the size of baseball bats. I stopped the car and froze. So much for "rubber time."

As a visible sign of modesty, Rebecca pulled up over her head an *orna,* a scarf she always wore in public. She positioned our sick son on her lap where his condition was visible.

"What do we do?" I asked.

"We play the 'dumb American card,' meaning we don't speak Bengali, only English. If that doesn't work, then I pull the 'desperate mom with a sick child' act. Bangladeshi men don't know what to do with a Western woman freaking out."

The mob approached. One of the leaders, a middle-aged man with a troubled look, left the front row and ran ahead to us. Rebecca rolled down her window as he leaned down, holding his Muslim white skull cap tight on the crown of his head. In English, he asked, "Madam, what are you doing here? We are trying to have the protest. You shouldn't be here. It's very dangerous!"

The phrase "shouldn't be here" sounded way too familiar. Rebecca used the one thing she could count on in Asian culture—their love of children. Regardless of religion or politics, Bangladeshis were protective and nurturing towards children.

Pointing to sick Nathan lying in her arms, she made her case. "Sir, we have an emergency, we must get to the American hospital in Dulahazara."

He gazed down at our sick child and then looked up at the approaching mob. After a few seconds, he stood up. "Okay, you follow me."

With his flowing white Muslim robe, he walked in front of us, raised his arms and separated the mob right down the middle as if he were Moses parting the Red Sea. On both sides of our car, angry young men motioned as if they were going to hit our car, but none of them did, lest they disobey the elder.

What seemed like a thunderous eternity with hundreds of chanting men brushing by, our crisis was over as swiftly as a passing tornado. Beyond impressed with our hero, we thanked him profusely. He smiled and waved, then trotted to catch up and disappeared into his mass of shouting humanity.

One more hurdle remained between the bridge and ourselves. A half mile behind the mob, a large group of people, sitting on woven mats, filled the street.

"Come on, who has a political rally at six in the morning?" I rhetorically asked. A politician with a raspy voice yelled into a microphone, excoriating the opposition party in power. My car inched through the crowd as they moved aside to let us through.

On an emotional roller coaster, our fear of the mob from minutes earlier now turned into complete humiliation. Windows down, both of us apologized in the local language as stunned people gazed at the crazy foreigners driving right through their rally. I'm sure they were wondering, what foreign family drives through political rallies at six in the morning?

Within two minutes the old rusted bridge, perched high above the river, was in full view with no train in sight. A *hartal* day, I had the bridge all to myself. I straddled the metal rails and slowed before the steep decline.

Once off the bridge, I looked in my rearview mirror. Our children sat motionless, eyes wide with anxiety. Except for Dani. The youngest of four and the only girl, Danielle sat in her car seat, unaware of the danger.

With big blue eyes and blonde pigtails bobbing, she played with her doll in the awkward silence of her two older brothers. Our boys witnessed the tension in me and the intentional calm in their mom. What our family just experienced was anything but normal. No one said a word. An unreal experience by Western standards, all of us knew it was a close call.

Over the wide river and through the flat countryside, the sun broke over the hills to the east, filling the sky with a soft yellow light. The landscape slipped by as emerald-colored rice paddies glowed in shades of green. Blinding flashes of a rising sun glinted off paddies filled with muddy water.

Bent over and ankle deep in mud, farmers planted bright green shards of rice seedlings. Poor sharecroppers, their earthly existence depended on a good rice harvest and had no time or interest in protesting against the government.

The system of land ownership and rate of population growth virtually guaranteed their poverty. Much of the crop went to the landlord, leaving little for a sharecropper's large extended family.

Most of Bangladesh was delta land barely higher than sea level. Traveling through the countryside required crossing a labyrinth of streams and rivers flowing down from the hill tracts to the east. All the bridges remained intact, rebuilt from the previous rainy season.

Early in the morning on a day of a national strike, driving was a breeze, with no oncoming traffic trying to muscle us off the one lane road. No game of "chicken" with oncoming buses seeing who would pull off their side of the road first. For once, the drive continued peaceful and serene.

Still recovering from our narrow escape, without a sound our older boys played on their Gameboys and read books. My heart finally stopped racing from the stress.

After a long silence, Rebecca turned to me. "Are you okay?"

"Been better. Almost got my family killed back there. Pretty sure I just won the 'Loser Dad of the Year' award."

"No, I mean your arm, you keep rubbing it."

"I have pain in my left arm radiating from my wrist up to my shoulder."

"A doctor can look at you when we get there. I bet stress is the culprit since you're gripping the steering wheel like there's no tomorrow. Your knuckles are almost white."

"There almost wasn't a tomorrow. I can't believe the protests started on time. I'm sorry I didn't trust your instincts. Another example of my out-marrying myself."

She smiled and put her hand on mine, both resting on the gear-shift between us. Her warm caress on the top of my hand helped relax the tightness seizing my body.

PRINCIPLE # 1: "Follow the rules"

In developing countries, living and working to empower others brings dignity, value, and worth. But in unsafe environments, risks to you and your family are real. Every culture has rules related to safety and danger which may be very different or even the opposite of your own culture.

After hours of driving through light green rice patties, the landscape turned into dark green jungle, which meant the hospital compound was up ahead. A few minutes later I pulled through the gate and stopped beside the hospital entrance. An American doctor dismounted his motorcycle and surprised to see us, he came over.

"Hey, what are you guys doing here? It's a national *hartal* day."

"We have a sick kid. Can you look at him?"

The doctor took one look at our delirious child with a swollen head.

"Bring him into the exam room now."

Nathan was diagnosed with a roaring infection and put on a strong course of antibiotics. Later, when Nathan improved, the doctor told us if we had waited another day, our little boy would have died.

I left Rebecca and Nathan at the hospital, drove through the large compound, and parked in front of the guest house. My two boys couldn't wait until I untied their bicycles. Off they went, roaming the fifty-acre compound just as their mom had a couple decades earlier.

The only remnant left of the original jungle, massive hardwood Gurgaon trees stood tall, spreading their large canopies over the brick lanes connecting the houses and buildings. Year by year, the increasing population resulted in more and more deforestation.

This remote jungle area, once home to tigers and elephants, changed as overpopulation drove the wildlife into the surrounding hills. By 1992, the small fifty-bed hospital provided the only quality surgical facility for thirteen million people.

The lunch bell rang. I rounded up my kids and sat at a table in the guest house dining hall. A new short-term American doctor came over and introduced himself. Tall, dark-haired, and dressed in green surgical scrubs, he wore thick glasses, yet had the look of newfound wonder in his eyes.

"Hi, I'm a third-year surgical resident out here for a three-month overseas rotation. What do you do out here? Someone called you Dr. McDonald. Are you a medical doctor?"

"No, not medical. I'm helping set up a private graduate school in Chittagong. I have a PhD in international planning."

"So, how and why did you get into this kind of work?"

After surviving our morning drive through a mob, a child with a serious medical condition, and a half-numb left arm, I wondered that myself. Despite the stress of the day, I didn't have the heart to discourage the excitement of this young surgeon. Over lunch, I told him my story.

"How did I get into this line of work? It all started one day in college when a basketball coach asked for my help."

CHAPTER 3

INTO AFRICA

He who returns from a journey is not the same as he who left.
—Chinese proverb

WHY WAS OUR college basketball coach walking towards me with such determination? After all, I had just qualified for college nationals in the 200-meter dash, and on that spring day in 1972, my mind was far away from shooting hoops. A former all-American football player, his broad shoulders created an intimidating figure bearing down on me.

"Phil, congratulations on that win!" Coach shook my hand and slapped me warmly on the shoulder.

"Kind of a fluke, since my race time isn't exactly at a national level. But coach says the competition will be a good experience."

"I guess so! They will be world-class runners. And did I hear right, the winner will probably go to the Olympics?"

"Larry from North Carolina Central hasn't lost a race all season. My goal is not to embarrass myself," I said, with more honesty than humility.

"So, what are you doing this summer?"

"I'm working at the gas station so I can earn enough to pay for fuel. My car's a gas hog. With dual quad carburetors, it only gets two miles to the gallon."

Coach knew I didn't need a summer job to pay for tuition. One of my father's perks as a professor was free tuition for his children. Plus, by living at home, my expenses were minimal.

"I want you to consider something. We put together a team of five students going to Africa this summer for six weeks. The team leader backed out, and our committee thought you would be a good replacement."

I stood stunned. For a moment I wasn't sure I'd heard right. "You want me to go where?"

"Africa."

"Exactly where in Africa?"

"Central African Republic."

Coach explained one of the team members grew up on a jungle station, and his parents asked for college kids to come out and help. Especially someone who could repair vehicles and equipment. I fit the bill.

"You'll have to come up with the funds for the trip," he said.

"How do I do that?"

"You could try to raise donations, or maybe you might just sell that muscle car of yours."

He cast a daring smile, wondering if I could part with my pride and joy.

"Can I have a few days to think about this? I should run it past my parents."

Africa. I had never heard of the Central African Republic (C.A.R.), a recent independent country the size of Texas. I also had never traveled outside the United States. The more I thought of spending six weeks on the huge continent, I came to see it could be a refreshing change of scenery.

The trip wouldn't be cheap. My folks didn't mind my going, but I would have to come up with the money. I had never asked for money before, but the choice was easy. No way could I sell my muscle car.

A dark blue Chevy Chevelle two-door coupe, with an off-white interior, the car was my baby. Sporting Crager SS wheels, Hurst T shift, and extra wide rear tires, it hosted a transplanted 327 cubic inch, 375 horsepower Corvette engine. The rhythmic, rumbling sound flowing out the dual exhaust pipes poured out nothing short of pure sweetness.

Chevys in those days resembled a lightweight tin box. My Chevelle roared on takeoff and easily popped wheelies in the first two gears. The first time I took my older sister for a ride, she cried and never rode with me again. My wife says if she had known me then she never would have dated or married me. Can't say I blame her.

Friends and family responded to my fundraising letter, and within three weeks all my funds came in. Once my new passport arrived, I counted the days until we left. At night I lay in bed imagining what it would be like in Africa. Growing up in a small town surrounded by cornfields in southern Ohio, my only frame of reference was old Tarzan movies, filmed in the thirties.

Little did I know a foreign destination never ended up the way someone imagined it in their mind. Departure day came and my parents drove me to the airport. For the first time, I stepped on a commercial aircraft and embarked on a journey that changed my life.

After long international flights over the Atlantic Ocean, Mediterranean Sea, and the Sahara Desert, our Boeing 727 touched down in Bangui, the capital city of the Central African Republic. The musty smell of rainy season hung thick in the air as we walked off the aircraft and stepped down the rolling stairway. Although midday, the dark sky hovered low with thunderclouds.

The terminal consisted of a small one-story building with a flat roof. Once white-washed, the milky gray exterior walls, complete with broken window panes and rusty thief bars, had a three-foot high band of reddish stain bordering the bottom of the walls. Tropical downpours splashed red mud up on the walls. The thief bars were rods of steel built into cement window casements.

Soldiers, dressed in camouflage fatigues and armed with machine guns, guarded each corner of the building. Like most small developing countries, the international airport also served as the nation's air force base. Security was tight as soldiers kept the peace in place of airport police. After all, soldiers launching a coup to take over a government often start by taking control of media stations and airports.

Our American hosts, Don and Marybeth, stood on top of the terminal building and met us with a hearty wave. The two came down the stairway as we approached the door. Marybeth, with short auburn hair and glasses, greeted us full of excitement. Don, a big burly guy, easily handled all our luggage.

"We'll be staying tonight at our guesthouse here in Bangui. Tomorrow we head up country to where we live in Bangassou. The trip takes two days by road," said Marybeth.

Don's pickup carted us 500 miles on dusty, red dirt roads cut through thick jungle. Four of us sat on our luggage in the truck bed, soaking up the countryside along with a layer of fine red dust, until we reached our final destination.

The Bangassou compound rose up out of dense jungle, placed on the crown of a hill. When Europeans colonized remote areas, a fortified post, compound, or station protected their personnel.

Once conquered, unfortified stations or compounds were known as places where expats lived in their own community.

In remote areas, many of those stations exist to this day. Before modern conveniences, stations were self-contained related to water, sewer, housing, and vehicle maintenance, all necessary for Western expats who expected modern living facilities.

Already dark, we pulled into the compound, unloaded, and settled into our rooms. I was itching to be the first to shower off a layer of red dirt before hitting the sack. The shower stall was simple. I looked up and found a five-gallon pail already hoisted to the ceiling, filled with warm water.

By pulling on a little string, I drenched my weary body, and once let go, it stopped the flow. Then I lathered up, shampooed my hair, and pulled again to rinse off. Done right, five gallons did the trick. Done wrong, you ended up covered in soap and insufficient rinse water.

Exhausted, yet clean, I fell into bed. I made sure all the edges of my mosquito net were tucked firmly under the mattress. My flashlight tucked under my pillow, in seconds I was sound asleep.

The jungle required no alarm clock. Our compound had something much louder. At dawn, two large drums sounded off right outside my bedroom window. The drums, hollowed out hefty tree trunks, created thundering beats that brought me up out of bed like a bat out of Hades. Once the drums stopped, an eerie silence ensued. I was truly in the jungle. This was the real deal.

I got out of bed and walked over to check out the drums through the window. So cool, I thought, until I looked up and saw the most enormous spider and spider web I had ever seen. Orange and black, sitting motionless in the center of the web, the spider and I became roommates for the next several weeks. I left him alone. With a hole in the screen, I figured he was my first line of defense against unfriendly winged creatures.

Sunday morning, the drum messages called the faithful in surrounding villages to the church located on the compound. The church sat no more than 100 meters from the house. The sanctuary, made of sun-dried bricks, had large openings for windows. Corrugated metal sheets covered the roof. The floor contained rows of narrow wooden benches.

Outside, three sides of the building were surrounded by a spacious green lawn, courtesy of daily downpours from the rainy season. The fourth side bordered thick jungle, complete with "swing worthy" vines. Later I learned this same jungle next to the church and beside our house was a haunt for black panthers, the kind with big green eyes that glowed in the dark.

The worship service with five hundred locals was a cultural delight, with singing and clapping going on for an hour. My first church service in a developing country, with all its cheerfulness and energy, soon became one I would never forget.

My college team and our hosts sat in the back row. A few minutes after the minister began his sermon, a truckload of military soldiers wearing green camouflage fatigues pulled up, all armed with AK 47s. I leaned over to Marybeth, our host, and whispered, "What's going on?"

"A few weeks ago the congregation removed the former minister from his position. He got upset and now he wants his church back."

Soldiers piled out of the truck, came into the church, and posted themselves every few yards. On cue they cocked their guns. The congregation became deadly quiet. I leaned over again.

"So he's taking it back by force? Are we in danger?"

She grinned, leaned over, and whispered, "It's okay. We aren't surprised this is happening. There were rumors. Just be quiet and don't look the soldiers in the eye. Welcome to Africa."

Copy that. All of us "newbie" college students in the back row didn't move a muscle. Last to enter the sanctuary was the colonel, a tall stately man, wearing a crisp camouflage uniform with a pistol at his side.

He stepped up on the platform, stood behind the pulpit, and waved his pistol. With a determined smile, he told everyone the service was over and to go home. Everyone went home without saying a word. The service began with excitement and singing but ended in silence, like walking out of a funeral service.

The morning's "church coup" made our lunchtime discussion quite interesting. Marybeth's father sat at the head of the table and had lived in Africa for decades. During colonial times, the area was known as French Equatorial Africa.

I mustered some courage to ask the old patriarch a question. "Sir, what was it like living here during colonial times?"

"Oh, we lived hundreds of miles north of here, now a country called Chad. It was not jungle as much as grasslands. We literally walked outside our back door and shot an antelope for supper. Did that for years. Life was a lot harder in those days. Now we have indoor plumbing, a metal roof instead of straw, and cement floors instead of dirt. Oh, and we have window screens, electric lights, and generators for electricity."

"When do you run the generator?"

"Just a few hours at night. By the way, I hear you have a pretty fancy flashlight?"

"Yes sir, I got it right before we came."

"Good. One of your duties is to turn on the generator at six in the evening and then turn it off at nine when we go to bed. This afternoon I'll show you how it's done. Fill the fuel tank during the day and remember, don't hang around out there next to the jungle at night. Start the "Jenny" and come back quickly, but whatever you do, don't run."

The wise old man neglected to tell me about the black panthers lingering near the "Jenny." Perhaps too much information for my first day in the jungle.

The next day I explored the large compound. Photography equipment hogged half my suitcase, and I roamed the area taking pictures. When the rain stopped, the sun revealed incredible subjects to photograph.

Possibly the most amazing sight to an American country boy was the size and variety of insects. Colossal butterflies, with ten to twelve-inch wingspans, landed naked in the embrace of unfiltered sunlight, exhibiting a rainbow of vibrant colors stunning to the eye.

One lime green praying mantis, over a foot in length, clung motionless to the side of a tree. Brown wasps, up to three inches long, didn't really buzz. Their sound was much louder, more of a drone.

At dusk, huge fruit bats, known as Megabats, soared with gigantic three-foot wingspans, dipping up and down through the rainforest, graceful as trapeze artists. We valued those bats, each eating up to five pounds of insects a night. Otherwise, swarms of winged creatures would have flooded our compound.

When it came to insects, nothing compared to the remarkable safari ants, also known as army ants. Nomadic, they never stopped moving, eating everything in their path. A queen produced up to four million new ants a month. Traveling together millions strong, they easily besieged a village and drove everyone out like a plague from ancient Egypt.

Sure enough, a day came when an African worker came running up to the house shouting the alarm. A new army of ants marched a beeline towards our compound. Fear and terror reigned until the old-timer calmed us down.

"We've had this happen before. Don, take a couple of these guys, go into town and buy a few barrels of kerosene. Pour the kerosene and make a moat of fire. That should be enough to change their direction."

The blazing moat worked and diverted the ant hordes off in search of someplace else to terrorize. Watching millions of ants approach us and then shift away from our fiery moat was beyond surreal. Literally, a mesmerizing, moving sea of life.

My primary job on the Bangassou hill station consisted of fixing cars, engines, and generators. I spent hours in the workshop, a small building with open-air sides covered with a rusty metal roof perched on wooden trusses supported by concrete pillars.

The floor, made of smooth sun-dried bricks, stayed dry thanks to the massive overhang of the roof. Wide enough for one vehicle and high enough for a truck, the center of the floor had a five-foot-deep pit, with stairs going down into the long, narrow working area the length of a car. The pit allowed a mechanic to stand while working on a vehicle's undercarriage.

Assigned to me were two African young men not much older than myself, whose job was to hand tools and watch out for my safety. As an American twenty-year-old with no foreign experience and naïve to the real danger surrounding me, I had no idea how much I needed them. Soon I would learn Etienne and Pierre were my human guardian angels.

Rainy season hit us full force and the compound crawled with snakes. Most, if not all, were venomous and killed on sight. Oodles of black mambas, green mambas, and Gabon vipers, the deadliest trio in the world, slithered through the compound's grass.

Their neurotoxins worked instantly and a victim could die in less than a minute. Struck in the chest, you're dead in five seconds. The grounds crew, Africans who squatted and mowed grass by hand with a sickle, killed a large snake every day. No doubt one of the most dangerous occupations in Africa.

The compound's large houses, built during French colonial days, stood together in a cul-de-sac style. The veranda on the back of our house spanned the entire backside and looked down onto a river valley, lush with thick green jungle. One afternoon, one of the other college students and I sat there reading our favorite books. Brother to Marybeth and son of the patriarch, he grew up on the compound.

"Hey, I heard about your little incident with the green mamba in the pit yesterday," he said.

"It was a close one. The little devil was hiding at the bottom of the stairs. I was about to take the last step when Pierre and Étienne each grabbed an armpit and hoisted me straight up. Pierre went down and chopped its head off. It was a little one, only a couple feet long."

"Doesn't matter, still big enough to kill you."

I chuckled until I realized he was serious. Fumbling for words, I tried to downplay it all. "I never knew changing the oil on an old French Peugeot could be so deadly."

He shifted in his chair and looked over to me with deep concentration. "Tell me, how do you deal with all the creepy crawlers down in there? As a kid, I hated getting anywhere near that pit."

The old damp pit reeked with an odor of mold and grease. An honest answer came forthwith.

"When I'm down there I'm as skittish as a long-tailed cat in a room full of rocking chairs. I'm always scanning the pit's walls and floor. You have gigantic millipedes and centipedes out here. And the black millipedes are a foot long and thick as my thumb. Sometimes I feel like I'm in a horror movie."

"Oh, millipedes get bigger than that."

"Great. Just what I wanted to hear. What gets me is how aggressive everything is out here. Animals, insects, reptiles, they're all gigantic."

"They don't call it a jungle for nothing. You'll get used to it, but you need to be alert all the time. Out here anything can happen in a moment."

Dusk descending, the African sun set majestically before us. In the distance, two rivers flowed into one, creating a confluence resembling a giant wishbone. The new river then drained into the Ubangi River, which flowed into the mother of all African rivers, the mighty Congo. A thousand miles downstream, the Congo emptied into the Atlantic Ocean.

In the distance to our northeast was dense jungle followed by savanna grasslands. All a sparsely populated area extending a thousand miles into the Sudan.

The sun disappeared in a matter of minutes. An enormous yellow sphere, the fiery ball turned orange, and then red, before slipping under the haze on the horizon. Here we were, living in a tropical paradise on the edge of a vast wilderness.

On the compound, a small clinic operated by two American nurses treated a host of tropical diseases. One of them, the owner of a VW beetle I had worked on, paid me a visit at the workshop.

"Phil, I would like to show my appreciation for all the work you've done on getting my jalopy going again. We're planning a visit to a village where one of our grateful patients has invited us for a feast. Would your college team like to join us?"

"I'm sure we would."

"It will take several hours to get there because we can only drive until the path ends. Then we walk to the river."

The walk to the river proved an understatement. After hiking for what seemed an eternity, the six of us came to a large river swollen from torrential rainfall, with a fast-moving current. With fear and apprehension, we boarded a large dugout canoe and traveled down-river a couple miles to the village.

After eating, visiting, and taking pictures, it was time to return home before nightfall. Our team piled back into the dugout canoe and pushed off. A few minutes later we had company. Perhaps the most dangerous animals in Africa, hippos didn't appreciate we'd invaded their territory. Several hippos chased our canoe.

Our two guides, sweating like boxers in the final round, paddled for their lives, yet the hippos gained on us. Even though we were their guests, one yelled for help.

"Grab a paddle guys, we're in trouble," our veteran nurse yelled.

A couple of us grabbed extra paddles and eventually escaped the hippos' territory. Safely on the other bank near our path, our team exited the canoe.

"That was close. The hippos would have capsized us and killed us all. Last week they lost someone in their village to a hippo," the nurse said.

"How did it happen?" I asked.

"He stepped on his canoe not knowing the hippo lurked under-neath. It raised up, capsized the canoe, caught him midair, and bit his leg off. He bled out and died. Fortunately, they retrieved his body before the crocs got it."

I was reeling. Every week we faced unexpected danger, a new crisis that left me emotionally ungrounded in the midst of random chaos. The unrelenting onslaught of crises upset my sense of psychological equilibrium. I lived in a continual state of "crisis shock."

___

PRINCIPLE # 2: "Be ready for crisis shock"

Unless you live in a dangerous environment, you are not emotionally prepared for "crisis shock," a psychological state that upsets your equilibrium.

___

Towards the end of our summer trip, Don invited our team for a visit to an abandoned compound owned by their NGO. The acronym "NGO" stands for "Nongovernmental Organization," referring to nonprofit organizations providing humanitarian assistance in developing countries.

A couple hours to the north of Bangassou, the abandoned Bakouma station had large colonial style houses and buildings on each side of the lane. After entering the compound, an African guard greeted us warmly. When Don asked about another worker, the guard's demeanor changed into sadness. For a few tense minutes Don and the guard carried on a conversation in Sango, the trade language.

"The guard just told me a fellow worker died from a snake bite this week here on the compound.

"Where was he on the compound?" I asked.

"Over there."

Don pointed to a large pile of rocks. "A black mamba struck him in the chest. He dropped dead within a few seconds."

Our group walked with the guard over to the rock pile, spent a few moments in silence, and then stood while the man poured out his heart. While Don consoled the employee, the rest of us walked the compound. All the large homes were vacant. After Don paid the workers, he caught up with us.

"So, Don, why are all these buildings empty?" I asked.

"Over time our American colleagues left."

"Why did they leave?"

"Could be any number of reasons. I mean, it's hard to live here. Sickness from tropical diseases can affect you the rest of your life. People get worn out living in a different culture, dealing with lions and elephants, fighting insects. Plus it really gets lonely out here, stuck on a compound with people who in another life would never be your best friend."

"I can see that. I saw the huge hole in the jungle left by the elephants crossing the road on our way here."

"What you don't see is the loneliness, especially during holiday times like Thanksgiving and Christmas. There's pressure sometimes from grandparents back home who miss your kids, or your elderly parents become ill and need your care. Or you struggle as an empty nester when your kids go off to college back in America."

After a long pause, Don returned to the empty compound issue.

"When they lived here, donations from America kept the compound going, but when they left, they took their money with them."

"What do you mean they took their money with them?'

"I mean once they returned to America and left the NGO, they took other jobs and stopped raising funds for out here."

His phrase "Took their money with them" became an eye-opener and would haunt me for years to come. It became the seed of a philosophy that later on drove my career.

"So why don't the Africans live on the compound?" I asked.

"They can't afford to keep up the place. Here in the jungle, they survive through subsistence farming. A few earn a salary on our organization's payroll, watching the place for us and keeping the grounds up."

On the long drive back to our compound, I pondered the waste of the abandoned "ghost town" compound or what I later termed a "ghost compound." Somehow, I knew it was a complicated situation I didn't fully understand.

Yet something didn't feel right about it. A legacy of the colonial past, the ghost compound served as a visual reminder of the gulf in the standards of living between Americans and the Africans.

Granted, the Americans sacrificed a great deal by living in a place so remote, with all its disease and danger. These Africans were poor, I got that. But there didn't seem to be a program to lift the local Africans from their poverty other than education. And education doesn't necessarily create jobs.

PRINCIPLE # 3: "Took their money with them"

Impoverished people entirely dependent upon outside funds are at enormous risk. If outside funds dry up, they are left destitute.

The final day before returning to America, Don and Marybeth invited our college team to a farewell dinner at their home. To my limited country boy palate, call it more of a cultural experience than a meal. I passed on the strange-smelling, fermented manioc called *gozo*, took only one bite of gamy roasted baboon, and settled for monkey meat stew, which was quite good.

Don voiced surprise I would eat live termites but pass on the baboon. Our two college girls on the team had dared me to eat termites, a local delicacy. Like an idiot I ate two, making sure I immediately crunched hard to ensure I swallowed them dead.

The meal finished, Marybeth looked right at me and presented the big question she was itching to ask. "So, what did you think of your summer out here?"

The dinner table grew quiet. As team leader, my fellow students curiously listened to what I would say.

"The other day I took a walk around the compound trying to make sense of everything I've experienced. When I stopped by the compound graveyard where a dozen Americans are buried, I became emotional."

"How so?"

"They sacrificed their lives to bring education, healthcare, and a different way of life. Then when I look at my new African friends, I feel guilty."

She glanced at her husband before looking back at me. "Why?"

"I'm a spoiled American, living in a safe place, taking my free college for granted. Back home all I care about are girls, hot cars, and playing ball. My grades are horrible because I don't study. Compared to my African friends, I take so much for granted. I feel pretty guilty."

"Guilt is a pretty strong word, isn't it?"

"They have to deal with poverty, disease, an unstable political environment, snakes, and wild animals. I'm able to go back home to my safe little college town surrounded by corn fields in the good ole USA. Back to Mountain Dew, Fritos, and playing softball under the lights on warm summer nights."

My college comrades agreed with me. A few short weeks in the African jungle opened our eyes. Then Marybeth asked the big question of the night as she directed it towards me. "So . . . do you think you could live out here?"

I put down my glass of water and cleared my throat. "I'm not sure. I shouldn't even be here except the team leader backed out. But I have to admit, this experience has given me pause about my future."

"How so?"

"In spite of all the danger, low standard of living, and hard life, I think I've been bitten by a different kind of bug. I think I'm infected with a love for overseas adventure."

Although Central Africa was amazing, what I didn't have the heart to tell her was the legacy of colonialism still remained. Her parents' generation, who spent the bulk of their career during French colonial times, had attitudes and behavior towards Africans I found appalling.

Colonialism is a mind-set, a negative attitude towards people with no ability to value the positive aspects of the host culture. Although most African nations won their political independence ten to fifteen years earlier, older foreign workers from Western countries hadn't changed their mind-set.

This played out before me that summer in a myriad of ways I couldn't help but find offensive. Africans weren't allowed to come to our front door, only the back or side door. Men old enough to be my father or grandfather addressed me, a twenty-year-old, "Monsieur," French for "Sir," while we were taught to address them by their first names. Frankly, the colonial-minded foreigners treated African adults like children who didn't know much. I found that demeaning and insulting.

PRINCIPLE # 4: "Avoid the 'white savior' complex"

Historic colonialism and neo-colonial attitudes are just forms of international racism. It manifests itself whenever Westerners think their way is best and the locals in low-income countries are incapable of helping themselves or making their own decisions.

Our summer trip came to an end. But once back home, I had changed. I no longer found satisfaction with playing in softball leagues, drinking coke, and showing off my muscle car driving around the A & W Root Beer stand.

A few weeks in Africa changed me as it shook me out of my cultural blinders. I now saw my life in a little box, centered in a small town, buried in the American heartland. Deep down I knew I wanted more.

The following summer I returned to a different part of the Central African Republic. This time I didn't go with a college team but with my best friend, Steve. A year behind me in college, he came along because his girlfriend desired an overseas career, and he wanted to see if he was cut out for it.

Also a professor's son, Steve raised funds for his travel costs, but this time I just bit the bullet and did the unthinkable—I sold my muscle car to pay for my trip.

Little did I know my second summer would be even more memorable and dangerous.

CHAPTER 4

OUT OF THE LION'S JAWS

You know you are truly alive when you're living among lions.
—Baroness Karen Christenze von Blixen-Finecke

NO QUESTION IT was panting. A slow, loud pant I had never heard before. A few seconds later I heard it again, except this time with a deep, low growl, the kind of sound only a lion can produce. By now I lay awake, motionless in my sleeping bag.

My luminous watch dial indicated it was five in the morning and barely dawn. My companions, three Americans and two African guides, slept soundly. Snoring came in languid concert, in different resonances, from all corners of our tent.

I could hear the lion circle around the tent as it uttered low groans coupled with heavy breathing. "Where are the guns?" I said to myself, then realized we had left them in the yellow four-door pickup truck parked outside. Stupid, how could we be so stupid?

My sleeping bag rested next to the tent door, and the lion stopped just inches from my head. Only canvas separated us. Terror seized me. I couldn't blink, swallow, or move a limb. Every part of me froze.

Was I dreaming? Where were we? I remembered we were north of Ndele, driving through a game reserve, staying in a village for the night. I also recalled we pitched our tent under a huge mimosa tree, and today we had planned on continuing our three-week journey into a remote northern part of the Central African Republic.

Like waking from a bad dream, I remembered our host village mourned the loss of a twelve-year-old boy. The day before he brought up the rear of a fateful line of school children walking a path to the village, when a hyena snatched him.

By the time the adults returned to the path, the boy's body had disappeared. Other than tall grass stained crimson with blood, only his ankles and feet left a trace of his tragic end. Not much meat on those bones.

My curious lion on the other side of the flimsy tent door stayed put. His putrid breath penetrated the canvas. It reminded me of the animal stench you immediately smell entering a zoo. But this was no zoo. My group dared to enter his wild territory, unarmed no less.

The panting outside suddenly stopped. My heart raced. The imagery of a gigantic paw ripping through the thin canvas wall blazed in my mind. His large mouth with sharp fangs, drooling from rotted flesh, grabbing me with bite pressure of 650 pounds per square inch.

This wasn't the way I was supposed to die. In my mind I could see the headlines of my hometown newspaper: "Local college boy killed by lion in Africa." My obituary listed my surviving parents, sister, and other relatives.

But then my imaginary obituary left me cold. It didn't state my burial site. Would I be buried right here in Africa? Would there be anything left of me or only my ankles and feet? Strange thoughts happen when your life reels past you in nanoseconds.

I waited. Nothing. The panting started again. Still paralyzed with fear, I did what any normal, desperate human being would do when they are about to die. I prayed.

More movement, but now the low growling sounded like slow motion cackling. It was on the prowl again. I could feel my heart beating bigger thumps in my chest.

I prayed harder, mainly that the guys would stay asleep and not talk, snort, snore, or do more. Then the unexpected happened. The growling stopped. I couldn't hear the lion at all. Could it be my prayers worked? Had the lion left?

A tense few minutes dragged on for what felt like an eternity as I waited to hear what the lion would do next. No farther than a hundred feet away, it bellowed out a deafening roar, as loud as dragsters racing down the strip.

A male lion's roar is heard for five miles, and with those decibels piercing the air, the other five men came off the tent floor, thrashing about, each saying in their mother tongue, "What was that, what was that?"

After fifteen seconds passed and my buddies fully awake, I informed them we had a visitor. Rubbing his eyes, Walt, our leader, said to me, "Give me my gun, he may come back."

"We left them all in the truck last night."

As disgusted as I was, Walt wrestled himself free from the cocoon of his sleeping bag, stepped over us, zipped open the tent door, unlocked the truck, and retrieved his gun. An experienced big game hunter, he knew the risks associated with lions. "He who hesitates" wouldn't be lost but eaten.

A burly guy from a steel town in Pennsylvania, he survived many years living in the bush only through his quick decisiveness. He fired off a round from his .375 magnum high powered rifle hoping to deter our intruder. It worked. The lion left on his own accord, returning to his pride at a slow trot.

Before long little wooden doors attached to mud huts opened, their occupants peeking outside. Slowly our friends from the village came to see what happened. Reassured we were all right, they made their way back to their homes to get on with their day.

Our African guide, an excellent cook, started a crackling fire. Within minutes his breakfast makings filled the air with the familiar smell of fried food mixed with the pungent scent of wood smoke.

With breakfast completed and second cups of coffee drained, we broke camp, loaded the truck, and treated some villagers' wounds with our few remaining bandages. Modern health care was nonexistent in the game park.

Shards of radiant sunlight streaked through the trees, then disappeared as the rising sun gradually climbed free of their canopy. It would be another sweltering day in the Sahel, that band of savanna sandwiched between the Sahara Desert to the north and the rainforest of the Congo Basin to our south.

After saying farewell and safe inside the truck, our two-week journey resumed on a dusty red dirt road to nowhere, under the full force of a blazing African sun. Steve, my college buddy along for the summer, broke the silence by asking a relatively simple question.

"Walt, how close were we to becoming breakfast for that lion?"

"Close. Lionesses hunt at night, and once they make a kill, their male arrives and eats first. After gorging all night, they find a shady place and sleep during the day. The fact this lion wasn't gorging somewhere means the pride was unsuccessful in hunting. He was just making rounds of his territory, which evidently included our village. But a hungry lion knew we were prey."

"Why didn't he attack us?"

"My best answer is the Lord answered ole McDonald's prayer."

"So, how do you hunt lions in the bush?"

"It's tricky. As apex predators, they're the top of the food chain, meaning they are the hunters and everything else is prey. When we hunt them it's often a situation where humans and lions are hunting each other."

"What do you mean?"

"When the male is being hunted by us, the lionesses instinctively circle to protect their protector. Plus we are an opportunity to be their next meal."

"So, how do you defend yourself?"

"One hunter with a high-powered rifle takes aim at the male while one of his team fires off buckshot from a shotgun into the male's face to keep it from charging. Two or three other people have rifles and stand behind them facing the opposite direction in case encircling lionesses decide to charge. Probably the most treacherous kind of hunting there is, especially in tall grass."

"So that explains why all the guns."

"Yes, plus you are on your own out here. No gun shops to run to. Have to be prepared for any contingency, you know, extra guns, extra ammo. Things break out here."

Still freaked out by the lion breathing down my neck, I decided to change the subject.

"Hey, can we turn on the air-conditioning? I just got bit by a Tsetse fly and those buggers hurt."

Everyone rolled up a window, and within minutes little black flies clung tenaciously to those windows, waiting for a chance to rush in. When a Tsetse fly landed on flesh, it stayed on you like a mosquito and sucked your blood with a sharp proboscis skewered deep into your skin. The bite stung like a bee.

A swat at a Tsetse fly didn't work. It had to be pinched hard and pulled out of your skin. Other than agonizing pain, the real danger proved to be sleeping sickness, an often fatal disease affecting the brain.

"The fact our windows covered so quickly with Tsetse flies means there are herds of animals close by," said Ray, Walt's colleague.

A few hours into our drive, the familiar "thump, thump, thump" of a flat tire resonated throughout the truck. Walt pulled over under a large tree.

"Well, it's about lunchtime anyway, so I'll help our guides with sandwich-making while you guys fix the flat tire," he said.

"How in the world do we pick up so many nails out in the bush?" I asked.

Everyone knew it was a rhetorical question because it disgustingly happened almost every day.

After finishing lunch, the thought of getting back in the crowded truck for several more hours weighed on me.

"Walt, do you mind if I walk ahead, and you guys pick me up once you're going? I would like to get some pictures and a little exercise."

"Be careful . . . stay on the road . . . and we'll pick you up in a few minutes," Walt answered between bites of his sandwich.

I walked briskly through a thick layer of red dust on the lonely path called our road. Occasionally, fresh human footprints were evident, even though I never saw a human. After walking at least a mile, off in the distance I saw a hartebeest grazing under a tree. This big antelope, about the size of a horse, headed towards a wooded area.

I soon learned African animals loomed much larger in person than appeared on television. Of the eight varieties found in Africa, it was a *Lelwel* hartebeest, with distinctive horns and reddish brown color. The name "hartebeest" originated from the Dutch Boers of South Africa meaning "a beast of a deer."

Why it was alone I didn't know. Maybe it was sick, or more likely it was a male that lost a battle with another male to keep control of his herd. As I approached, it wandered off into the trees. Against my better judgment, I followed. Bad idea.

Within a few hundred yards I found him and myself at a large watering hole. The beast stopped and allowed me to approach. His abnormal behavior indicated something was awry. Perhaps an illness. I clicked off a few pics, then realized the hartebeest and I were not alone. Other animals not yet in sight were coming to the watering hole.

The sound of hooves, short snorts, and breaking twigs gave away their approach. And where there were prey animals, there were sure to be predators. For the second time in one day, I felt the primal fear of being unarmed in the wild surrounded by flesh-eating big cats and large horned beasts.

Stupid, how could I be so stupid! Walt said not to leave the road, but here I was off the beaten path and would never be found, not even my ankles and feet.

I walked slowly around the muddy watering hole as quietly as I could, all the while feeling my life now flashing before me in slow motion. I needed to get out of there fast. But I couldn't run lest a fleet-footed cat be unable to resist a chase. Each step seemed like an eternity. I stopped under a tree and waited, not sure what to do.

Then I heard it. The familiar sound of our pickup sounded like sweet music to my ears. I couldn't believe it. How in the world did they find me? As the truck pulled up, Walt rolled down his window and barked at me, as only he could. I deserved it.

"Are you crazy? You shouldn't be here. What was the last thing I told you when you walked away? Don't leave the road!"

"I'm sorry, I'm sorry, I got carried away trying to get a picture of an antelope."

"Get in the truck and let's get the heck out of here."

Sheepishly I got into the vehicle while the guys looked at me as if I was nuts. I wasn't nuts, just a foolish twenty-one-year-old male with a delusional sense of invincibility. A few minutes down the road, Walt felt a need to provide commentary.

"If it wasn't for Stephen's great tracking skills, we wouldn't have found you."

"What do you mean?" I asked.

"While driving he detected your sandal prints stopped and only footprints remained. That was a red flag. Either you had been attacked by something, or you had taken off your sandals and walked barefoot. He then recognized your footprints, because wearing shoes all your life, you leave a distinct footprint with an arch. African footprints are flat because they don't wear shoes."

I thanked Stephen and he smiled warmly. Stephen gave me a new name in his language, roughly translated as "brave warrior." Walt laughed. All of us knew he laughed because I was anything but a brave warrior. I was a stupid college kid with no sense of danger.

"We're getting low on drinking water, and I know a Catholic mission compound up here. Maybe someone will be there. Last time I came a few years back it was abandoned, just like the Baptist one we stopped at a few nights ago outside Ndele," Walt said.

Walt pulled into the small compound and stopped near the front door of a house. A French missionary priest came out, and after conversing a few minutes, both he and Walt went inside the house. Walt returned a half hour later with fresh drinking water. Our truck pulled out of the compound as we waved goodbye to the priest.

"So, Walt, what's a Catholic priest doing way up here all by himself in the middle of nowhere?" Steve asked.

"It's obvious he's an alcoholic. My guess is he's stationed up here as a form of exile, having been banished from his ministry in a town. He's lonely and wanted to talk so badly I could hardly get away."

"That's sad. How long will he be up here?"

"Probably until he drinks himself to death. Fortunately, he knew the whereabouts of the village we are trying to find before nightfall."

"What's so special about this village?"

"We're entering the Sara Kaba tribal area. National Geographic featured this tribe because their women wear big wooden disks in their lips. Once the tribe found out their women were viewed as "primitive," they became embarrassed. Now they hide these women whenever foreigners come around."

"Is that why we are going? To see these ladies?"

"No, our interpreters here have friends in these villages."

"Is it safe to visit?" Steve asked.

"I'm sure it is because the French priest would have warned me otherwise. But I did find out this particular village is so remote it hasn't had a white foreigner since French colonial days, some fifteen or twenty years ago. So most of the village young people will never have seen a white foreigner. Our pink skin is going to look really strange to them."

Our truck followed a meandering road laden with the white haze of searing afternoon heat. After miles of tall elephant grass, the dirt trail led us towards a clump of tall trees. A canopy of trees protected our target village from the blistering African sun. We coasted to a stop alongside a cluster of mud huts. Folks came to greet us, but Walt proved correct. None of the ladies with lip disks were present.

The Catholic priest was also right. The young people hadn't seen white skin before. A small crowd surrounded us, examining our pale pinkish skin. Kids laughed at our appearance. Children gawked at my blond hair, blue eyes, and red beard; Steve's brown hair and hazel eyes; and Ray's black hair and height. Clearly, we were the ones being looked at as zoo animals.

Walt left us for the critical protocol of meeting with the village chief. While he was in the chief's hut asking permission to stay the night, we stretched our stiff muscles, greeted people, and stood by the truck. Out of boredom, Steve got out the soccer ball and threw it on the ground.

The teenage boys obviously had never seen a soccer ball and began throwing it up in the air instead of kicking it. The whole village laughed and chanted until something weird happened. Two testosterone-rich teenage boys got into a struggle over the ball.

Within seconds a fist fight ensued, and the whole village erupted into a polarized scene of yelling, screaming, and fighting. Half the village against the other. None of us "pink folks" knew what to do.

The old chief heard the commotion, stepped outside his hut, and raised his hand. Fighting immediately stopped, and the village instantly became quiet, demonstrating the most incredible show of respect I had ever seen. According to our interpreter, the chief told them to go to their huts until they could show more respect to their guests.

Walt then stepped out of the chief's hut, gave us a "thumbs up" sign, and we began unloading our truck to pitch camp for the night. After so many years in the bush, Walt just had a way of befriending and relating with Africans.

Dinner over, Steve looked at me with a sly grin.

"Hey, did you bring that illuminated Frisbee?" he asked.

"I sure did."

Steve and I whipped the white plastic Frisbee back and forth in a village where no one had ever seen anything flown and controlled by two people. As college kids are prone to do, we showed off flinging the Frisbee, making it curve in and out.

Kids in dusty shorts and ragged tee shirts ran all over the place, radiating with glee. None had shoes and several didn't wear shirts. Remote villages usually didn't have modern toys. Steve and I provided the evening entertainment, but the glee was about to change.

The darker it got, the harder it was to see. I turned on the truck headlamps, covered a headlight with the Frisbee, and let it soak up the light until it glowed a warm green glow. Our Frisbee performance continued but our new friends left. Soon shrieks of terror pierced the darkness each time the glowing Frisbee took flight. Ray came over.

"Walt and I think you should stop throwing the Frisbee. The villagers are terrified you are throwing evil spirits back and forth. They're all in their huts scared to death of your supernatural powers."

"Are you serious? It's just a toy," I said.

"They don't know that. They only know what they know. We're their guests so we need to be courteous. They only understand river spirits and tree spirits, not plastic Frisbees."

The fun of showing off stopped. Our entertainment turned us into possessing superpowers. As an ethnocentric American college boy, that evening I learned the value of cultural sensitivity.

PRINCIPLE # 5: "We are their guests"

Not respecting a local culture's worldview is ethnocentric and arrogant. Regardless of how remote or different a people, showing respect is being culturally sensitive.

The three of us joined Walt at the campfire. In an effort to change the conversation from our lack of respect, Ray asked me a surprising question.

"I hear you had an interesting flight coming from the States to here. Tell me about it."

"Oh, you heard about that? The Air France flight from New York to Paris was crowded. But our Air Afrique flight from Paris to Bangui was interesting. It was a full-size Boeing 727 but only had sixteen passengers: an old couple, Steve and me, and a dozen American flight attendants."

"Wait, a dozen female flight attendants?"

Steve looked over at me and we exchanged grins.

"Yep, they were on their way to the Congo to provide service for a charter flight. With so few people on board, the pilot made us all sit together in the middle of the plane."

"Let's see. Two college boys surrounded by gorgeous flight attendants. I guess you guys weren't complaining!"

"Not at all. We took turns sitting with different girls because they all were curious why two college guys were going to the heart of Africa in 1973."

"What really was interesting were our layovers," Steve said.

"What do you mean?" Walt asked.

"When we landed in Libya for a fueling stop, Phil and I were the only ones naïve enough to get off. We noticed the entire airport was pocked with recent bullet holes from a major shootout. Apparently, a military guy named Muammar Gaddafi staged a coup a couple years back and took over the country. No one got around to fixing the airport walls."

"Where did you land next?"

"That was even more interesting. From Tripoli, we flew over the Sahara and landed in Fort Lamy, Chad. Unlike at Tripoli, the purser made all of us get off and go into the terminal as transit passengers, even though we were getting back on the same plane. The terminal was huge, about the size of a large gymnasium with high ceilings. We were delayed there for at least three hours. The only place to sit was in the corner of the terminal on an elevated platform. Bored out of our minds, I pulled out my guitar and decided the place needed some music."

"So, Steve, what songs did you sing?" Ray asked.

"I started playing songs from memory. Mostly folk songs like John Denver or Bob Dylan."

Walt and Ray grinned. I couldn't wait to tell the rest of the story.

"What Steve's not telling you is the American flight attendants also joined in with us, and before long we had a concert going, with hundreds of Chadians applauding every time we completed a song. We were a hit, but the airport manager made us quit so the airport could get going again. You should have seen the look on the faces of passengers from other flights when they realized a concert was going on inside the terminal."

"Wow, that's a heck of an adventure. We should turn in though. Tomorrow we head back home, and I would like to make it all the way back to that abandoned mission compound in Ndele for the night. Tomorrow will be a long day because I don't want to run out of fuel or water. It's tough getting stranded out here and we don't want that to happen," Walt said.

"How so?" Steve asked.

"Time and sickness. We have no communication, so a lot of time will pass before our families know something is wrong and send someone to look for us. We're used to being gone weeks at a time. If you run out of water, then you end up drinking unclean water out of a stream."

Ray laughed and looked at Walt.

"Like the time you got stranded hunting Cape buffalo?" Ray said.

"What happened?" Steve asked.

"Oh, what a disaster. Vehicle problems. I sent a guy on foot back to the compound. Ray ordered the part from the capital city, waited for the part, and then sent him back with the part. Fixed my truck, but I ended up being away for over a month. Meanwhile, I ran out of clean water and drank water out of a stream. It was a miracle I didn't get sick."

"Why were you hunting Cape buffalo?"

"Fresh meat. A single buffalo provides a lot of meat. Sometimes I hunted to feed the school on our compound. Sometimes beef is expensive or in short supply. Plus, it's fun to hunt Cape buffalo."

"Fun? How so?"

"Because it's dangerous. Buffaloes are mean."

The fire dying out, we doused it with water and turned in. With ourselves and the guns tucked safely inside our blue tent, it wasn't long before we were all sawing logs, dreaming of wild beasts and super-powered Frisbees.

Our journey back to Ndele was uneventful. With an early start, the long hours in the truck took us out of the game reserve and to the abandoned station by midafternoon. Ndele was an old colonial outpost, stranded at the wild edge of Central Africa, not far from the Chad border.

Upon arrival at the abandoned mission station, Walt worked on getting the kerosene stove functional while Steve and I took turns taking a natural shower under a waterfall cascading over a rock ledge from an outcropping of rock located at the back of the compound.

While one bathed, the other stood lookout for anything looking dangerous. Life in the wilderness required not leaving anything to chance. After all, we were in an African game park. The path back to the house through the bush gave us a chance to talk alone.

"Steve, something is really bothering me."

"Oh yeah, what?"

"This is the second abandoned compound I've seen in two summers here in the C.A.R. I'm starting to wonder what these American organizations are doing to help the local people economically. Other than trading in the local market and growing their own food, there aren't any job opportunities."

"Well, they do have schools they run."

"I know, but what good is having an education if there are no jobs?"

"Good point. It's interesting to me, the only jobs out here in the bush are the ones working for the foreign organizations."

"Huh. So much for the end of colonialism," I said.

After dinner, we sat on the front veranda of the old mission house, watched the sunset, and shared stories. The compound, perched high on a hill, looked down over the town of Ndele, a small marketplace with a few thousand residents. I took the opportunity to express our appreciation.

"Walt and Ray, I want to thank you for a great summer, capped off with this trip up here to see the Bamingui-Bangoran National Park. I had a great trip last summer down south in Bangassou, but living here with your families in Kaga-Bandoro has been special."

"What were the highlights for you this summer?" Walt asked.

"Other than this extended trip, I would have to say building the basketball court in town at the community center. I mean, introducing African young people to American basketball felt great. I enjoyed making the backboards and rims from scratch in your incredible workshop. But it was more fun teaching basketball to the African guys in town. I also enjoyed playing basketball with you and your teenage boys every evening before dinner."

"What was the most exciting thing that happened to you on our compound?" Ray asked.

"Without question, getting rid of the giant black mamba that kept eating your chickens was exhilarating."

"Burning that thing out from the rock pile and getting rid of it was a real relief," Walt said.

"I've been on the college track team with McDonald these past few years, and I never saw him run so fast as when that mamba was chasing him down the hill that night," said Steve.

"I'm just glad at the bottom of the hill I could jump up on a truck because the crazy snake was gaining on me," I said.

"I'm sure both you and the snake covered that hundred yards down the hill under ten seconds!" Steve replied.

"What about the time in the shower you almost stepped on that snake that came up the drain?" I asked Steve.

"Wow, I never jumped so high in my whole life!"

"What kind of snake was it?" I asked Walt.

"We call it a 'seven-minute' snake because that's how much time you have to get anti-venom in your body if you want to live. Fortunately, I keep that stuff in our refrigerator at all times."

"So, what did you guys learn about yourselves this summer, and what are your future plans?" Ray asked.

"When I came out here I was really thinking of an international career because my fiancée wants one. But after being here, even with all the fun and excitement of Central Africa, I'm not sure I'm cut out for this. I'm glad I came to find that out," said Steve.

Steve's comment took me by surprise. As a friend, I thought he handled the stress of the summer pretty well, better than I did, but I wasn't going to argue with him. I knew he missed his fiancée, but maybe I didn't fathom his homesickness.

"What about you, Phil?" Ray asked.

"Practically, I learned lions have bad breath and to never sleep in a tent without a gun."

After a few chuckles, there was silence while they waited for me to continue. I leaned back and folded my hands in my lap.

"Well, I knew the travel bug bit me last summer. But this summer's been different. It's been like an internship learning how to live out here. In spite of the difficulties we've had, I've come to realize I am cut out for this lifestyle. It's stressful to live here, but the rewards are pretty great when you see the change in the lives of people who have such little opportunity. I've been planning on going to law school except now I'm not sure. I've learned a lot from both you and Walt this summer."

PRINCIPLE # 6: "Am I cut out for this?"

Exposure to diversity outside your realm of experience reveals a person's compatibility with a foreign culture. Better to find that out early than late.

The next day we drove the few hours to Kaga Bandoro, where Walt and Ray lived with their families. Although leaving our hosts proved difficult, both Steve and I were ready to get back home. Walt drove us to the capital city, helped us check in for our flight, and said goodbye. Steve and I climbed into the big bird for home.

The summers of 1972 and 1973 in *CentraAfrique* were pivotal in redirecting my life goals. My new vocational path shifted from law to pursuing an overseas career. But I didn't want to go it alone. That's when a wonderful person came into my life.

CHAPTER 5

FINDING A SOULMATE

A soulmate protects you from yourself. A soulmate won't let success go to your head, failure go to your heart, fear go to your confidence, nor loss go to your soul.
—Author

HIS FACE SEEMED familiar. As I looked at the picture of the guest lecturer coming to our college, he was none other than a surgeon I had heard of all my life. In our circles, he was a celebrity—giving up a lucrative career in American medicine to establish a hospital in the jungles of Bangladesh.

I had never heard of Bangladesh until the Beatles did the first major benefit concert in 1971. The concert raised funds for the genocide conducted during their war of liberation. East Pakistan gained independence from West Pakistan and a few months later became Bangladesh.

Between college and graduate school, I took a gap year and worked to save money and apply to grad schools. In the evenings I played a lot of basketball. One night I walked out of the college gym into the foyer of the athletic center, and on the announcement board hung the picture of the surgeon and his family.

I rested my basketball firmly against my hip, wiped the sweat off my face, and leaned forward to study the family picture. One family member got my attention—the guest lecturer had a daughter. What I didn't know is his daughter traveled with him on his college speaking trips to check out potential schools to attend.

When they came for a visit, I saw her from a distance at a basketball game. Then I observed her up close on Sunday morning after our church service. With brown doe-eyes and waist-length brown hair, she walked through the sanctuary with the poise and grace of a runway model. Wearing a black maxi skirt, black turtleneck, a wide gold belt and gold jewelry, she took my breath away.

"Pure class," I kept mumbling to myself.

Mike, my friend sitting next to me, elbowed me.

"Hey, what are you mumbling about? The service is over. Let's go get lunch."

"She's the one."

"What?"

"Look, Mike, that's her, the surgeon's daughter. Not only is she drop-dead gorgeous, but she looks like she just walked off Fifth Avenue. I've never seen a girl that classy. I'm going to marry her."

"Forget it. She's way out of your league."

"Oh yeah? I don't know where she's going to college, but I'll be bringing her home for Thanksgiving."

"Yeah, right."

"Want to make a bet?"

"Sure."

As destiny and some planning would have it, I got accepted to the graduate division of the same school she attended in her hometown in Michigan. With the stealth of a Navy Seal, I researched all I could about her.

I knew her class schedule, cafeteria meal schedule, and even did a "drive-by" of her parents' home. I called it strong detective work, good homework, thorough research. Later my kids would say, "Dad, you're a stalker."

My roommate served as my spy. At mealtime, he and I arrived at the cafeteria early and sat across from each other, ensuring a full 360-degree view. He sat facing the door and once he saw her come in, he would notify me in code.

"Sunshine (Rebecca), just came up in the east (east door) and is setting in the west (sitting on the west side of the cafeteria)."

This way she never caught me looking at her. For a girl who had grown up as an American on the Indian sub-continent, somehow I had the sense to be careful. After spending years at a boarding school in Pakistan with the likes of the Taliban, she would have noticed me staring at her and shunned me.

She glided through public places with an external calm that belied the wariness beneath. Always watching her surroundings, any overly interested male would have turned her off immediately.

One night at dinner my roommate convinced me to ask her out on a date. I got up my nerve, introduced myself, and walked her back to the dorm. We talked for hours. There is a whole lot more to this story, especially if she were telling it. Suffice it to say, we hit it off.

We dated for a year, virtually inseparable, meshing our class and work schedules to be together whenever we could. My father, the marriage and family professor, called it the "greenhouse effect," meaning, spending every day together allowed a couple to find out if their relationship could grow and could become soul mates.

A few months into our relationship it became profoundly evident we were soul mates. I recognized I merely wasn't falling in love. I was in complete free fall. As the British say, I was "besotted." In American English, I was thoroughly "smitten."

Mike was shocked when I brought her home at Thanksgiving to meet my parents. I not only won my bet with him, but as far as I was concerned, finding her meant I won the whole dang lottery!

By the end of the school year, it was pretty much a done deal. We promised each other not to say the word "love" unless we were serious enough to marry. Driving up through a pine tree forest we enjoyed, I pulled over and turned to her.

"I love you."

"I love you too."

We looked at diamonds and set a date the following year. On May 28, 1977, our wedding took place in a big church with a long center aisle. With 500 guests watching from the pews, I was nervous as could be.

When the minister introduced us as husband and wife, I took off down the aisle so fast, she almost tripped on her fabulous white wedding gown and cathedral-length veil.

As a wedding present, her grandmother, with help from my parents, bought us a mobile home. In a secluded mobile home park north of town, we rented a lot for our new abode. Rebecca and I furnished the place with hand-me-downs, and we settled into our honeymoon year.

I soon realized the person I married wasn't your typical American girl. By growing up in Asia with American parents, she was what anthropologists called a "Third-Culture Kid," or "TCK" for short. That meant her American culture and Bangladeshi culture blended and fused into a unique, third-culture outlook.

I recognized it one night when her nightmare woke me. While talking in her sleep, she rattled on in a foreign language. As a student of anthropology, I was intrigued. But as a typical American who only spoke one language—it just freaked me out.

That fall I finished my coursework, but to complete my masters, I needed to either write a thesis or do an overseas field project. Upon hearing that, Rebecca had a request.

"You know it's always been my desire to take you to Bangladesh and show you where I grew up. What if we spend spring semester there and you do a research project?"

My lust for foreign adventure, coupled with the opportunity to do field research, made it a no-brainer. My major professor approved, we bought tickets on Pan Am, and after final exams flew to Bangladesh via London.

Flying over the Atlantic, our flight attendant spoke to us in an American accent until halfway across the "pond," then he switched to a perfect British accent. Fascinated, I asked another flight attendant, who simply said, "Oh, he's an American who grew up in London. He doesn't even know he's switching accents. I'm sure it takes place at a subconscious level."

The flight attendant was a prime example of being a third-culture person. His American and British cultures mixed together to constitute a third-culture identity. Switching back and forth was automatic and a skill "third-culture kids" master.

When we landed in Dhaka, the capital of Bangladesh, my new bride exhibited another dose of third-culture behavior. I noticed as we walked off the plane that Rebecca instantly changed personalities, both verbally and nonverbally. She spoke fluent Bengali, yet behaved in a guarded way.

Back in a culture dominated by fundamental Islam, her demeanor changed to deal with Bangladeshi Muslim men's mind-set towards women unveiled in public. It was like someone flipped a switch in her brain. I was totally captivated.

In the arrival hall, her family was there to meet us. Patiently we waited for our luggage to show up on the belt. All our checked-on baggage never arrived. It would be two months before our luggage caught up. It meant borrowing clothes and undergarments. Yes, that's right, underwear. No Sears or Walmart in Bangladesh, so you borrowed. Considering the alternative, that's what you did.

The next day we drove the twelve hours from the capital city to the jungle hospital where my in-laws worked and where my wife grew up. After driving through rice paddies and thick jungle, the flora on the hospital compound was a pleasant surprise.

For years, my mother-in-law managed a crew who manicured lawns, groomed a variety of trees, and transplanted almost every species of orchid found in the jungle.

The lane before us unfolded an elegant jungle garden as we pulled up to the residential section. A tropical paradise, fruit trees provided an endless supply of fruit, including fresh papaya, mangos, and bananas.

Our arrival at the hospital compound came just in time to celebrate Christmas. My in-laws held a combination Christmas party/welcoming party in their home that gave their colleagues an opportunity to meet their daughter's new husband. During the party, one of the doctors came over to me.

"So, what courses did you take this past semester?"

I looked at him with a blank stare. I couldn't remember.

"Who were your professors?"

"I honestly don't remember anything."

He laughed and said, "You have short-term memory loss from jet lag."

"How could I have jet lag when I'm only twenty-five?"

"There is an eleven-hour time difference from the States, and jet lag can hit anybody of any age."

Once again, changes took place, not only the circadian rhythm of my body but another whole outlook on culture. My cultural lessons would come one after another during the few short months living there.

The hospital compound sat high on a bluff overlooking the Bay of Bengal. A fifty-acre tract of land leased by the government, the location was ideal during flood season. Formerly a World War II military camp, the property divided into two sections.

The front half faced the road and contained the hospital itself, along with staff housing. Behind the hospital rested a soccer field that doubled as a helicopter landing pad for government officials bringing their families needing medical care.

The back half was housing for the American staff, a school, a basketball/tennis court sunken in the ground called the "Hollywood Bowl," and a guest house. A red brick road joined the front and back sections.

Each section of the compound was self-contained, providing their own generator-powered electrical systems and water treatment facilities. The buildings were mostly one-story brick covered with light gray cement stucco. A screened veranda on the back of each house provided a place for drying clothes during rainy season.

My in-laws' house had a flat roof handy for drying clothes during dry season plus provided space for extra storage. In late afternoon, it served as a nice place for the family to sit and socialize in the cool of the day.

It didn't take long for me to get into playing soccer every afternoon with American and local kids. It was an excellent way to make friends. One evening after dinner, my new bride asked me an important question.

"I would like you not to play soccer tomorrow so you can meet my Bengali girlfriends. I made the mistake of showing them our wedding pictures."

"What do you mean?"

"When they saw my white dress they were horrified. Out here white is the color of death for women. It's what widows wear. Tomorrow we have to get remarried and have new pictures taken. I'll be wearing a proper red *sari*, and you'll be wearing a white Hindu *dhoti*."

Meeting my wife's childhood playmates was a blast. There wasn't an actual ceremony. Drinking tea, hearing childhood stories, and getting pictures with "proper" wedding attire was all there was to our getting "remarried."

One evening my wife's two younger brothers were keen on attending a local fair called a *Mella*. We piled into her dad's green Dodge van and drove a few miles up the road. In a remote area of a developing country, having a human-powered wooden Ferris wheel only twelve feet high was a big deal to the locals.

I studied each of the small booths selling local items until I heard my wife. In her best attempt to not sound like she was ordering me around in a male-dominated public place, she called to me. I turned around to see her ashen face hung with fear and humiliation as young Muslim men circled her. I unknowingly made a grave error by leaving "my woman, my property," unprotected in a public place.

My father-in-law heard the commotion, and he, along with his two teenage sons raced to her aid from different directions. I joined them. Together we made a circle with our arms, with Rebecca and her mom in the middle.

We elbowed and shoved our way out of the *Mella* to the van. My cultural mistake had started a "feeding frenzy," and I was very embarrassed.

PRINCIPLE # 7: "Leave your ego at the door"

Cultural blunders can whiplash your ego, but it is all part of the learning curve. Leave your ego in your home culture and prepare to make mistakes.

Back at the compound, I licked my wounds from the cultural blunder until my wife's brother took me aside and explained things.

"Out here you need to know the sexes are completely separated. If a woman goes out into public, she has to have a male escort with her at all times. She is viewed as a man's property and you have to protect her."

"Really? Property?"

"Girls are sold into marriage through a bride price."

"I'm really confused as to what happened at the *Mella*."

"The best way I can describe being in public in a Muslim culture is being in a men's locker room. Women here shouldn't be in public by themselves any more than a girl should be in a guys' locker room in the States. By walking away from my sister, you left her alone in the public 'locker room.'"

"So, what do I do?"

Marty went on to teach me a Bengali phrase to say when someone is physically getting too close to a girl or woman in your family. By saying, "Don't you have a mother and a sister?" it's a direct way of reminding the encroachers "my woman" is part of a family. Upon hearing this idiom, most Bangladeshi Muslim men back off.

After my humiliation at the *Mella,* I couldn't wait to use my new phrase. I practiced pronouncing it every day to be understandable. Then I got my chance. One day while playing basketball with my wife and teenage girls in the Hollywood Bowl, a local man stood on the road above us, watching the girls.

I marched up there, yelling my newly learned phrase only to be called back by my wife.

"What's wrong? I'm telling him to buzz off instead of staring at you girls!"

"He's a hospital employee. I've known him all my life. He's brought a message back to the single nurses' quarters telling them there is an emergency at the hospital. Bengali men are only allowed back here if they work here."

My tail firmly between my legs, I felt more humiliated and angry. In an attempt to help me cope with culture shock, the next day my wife whisked me off to a place called Cox's Bazaar. A small coastal town, Cox's had a pristine white beach that stretched ninety miles along the Indian Ocean.

The place functioned as a refuge for one straightforward reason. Bangladeshis didn't swim in those days. Totally alone, the two of us escaped the newly confusing culture. In addition to enjoying a warm tropical day on a beautiful beach, Rebecca came up with even a better idea.

If we timed it right, we could drive farther down the beach to a secluded waterfalls and return before the tide came in. The privacy, solitude, and sound of the waterfalls were exactly what I needed. With no other way out, we raced to our vehicle and crossed back over the tidal inlets right before the tide came in by late afternoon. That time alone was just what I needed.

PRINCIPLE # 8: "Lean on me"

The ability to function in a foreign culture is better if you have an experienced friend or mentor from your own culture helping you learn from your mistakes.

The next afternoon Rebecca and I sat up on the rooftop, sipping ice tea. Next to the compound, workers loaded up big wooden ships with lumber and firewood. Truck after truck arrived from the jungle and unloaded their wood. Another crew rolled the short logs down the hill to the boats.

"What did you call that place over there with all the wood?" I asked.

"It's the *lachri ghat,* the landing or dock where they ship wood. *Ghat* means dock and *lachri* means wood."

"What's the wooden ship called?"

"A *nokha.*"

A seagoing *nokha* is part of the *Dhow* family of wooden boats, used from the Arabian Sea to the Bay of Bengal. Close to eighty feet in length, twenty feet wide, and complete with oars and sails, a *Dhow* carries cargo and a crew of at least a dozen. The basic design had changed little over the centuries.

"How long does it take for the boat to get up to Chittagong?" I asked.

"I hear it's about five days, depending on the wind."

"Has any American ever taken that trip?"

She turned to me with an astonished look on her face.

"You mean on a *nokha*? No, I've never heard of anyone doing that."

"Hmm. I wonder what it would be like to ride on that ship."

CHAPTER 6

"YOU SHOULDN'T BE HERE"

Do not follow where the path may lead.
Go instead where there is no path and leave a trail.
—Ralph Waldo Emerson

STANDING AT THE door was a stocky, young Bengali man, fresh off the bus from Chittagong.

"Hello, my name is Mohammad, and I am your new interpreter."

Roughly my age, he wore Western clothes. Other than his name and neatly trimmed beard, the only other vestige of his Islamic heritage was a white skullcap. On the Indian subcontinent, Hindus and Muslims visibly distinguished themselves from each other by the color and design of their clothing.

Within minutes I knew his English-speaking ability was marginal at best. A newly minted master's degree meant he could read and write in English but not necessarily speak it very well. My hands were tied. No one else was available who could interpret for my field research project. Time was running out.

Neither Mohammad nor I had ever been in a cross-cultural working relationship. As we struggled to communicate, the only solution was a crash course in conversational English. Not wanting to lose time for his English to improve, I arranged for someone to tutor him while I journeyed up to the capital city for a visit with a professor at the University of Dhaka.

The office of the professor, Dr. Afsaruddin, was monastically bare. A wooden desk and chair, a small bookcase, and a wooden guest chair constituted the extent of furniture. The cement room boasted a single light fixture and solitary ceiling fan. A middle-aged professor with big, thick glasses, he served as chairman of the Sociology Department.

Typical of hospitality in this part of Asia, he offered a cup of tea and a biscuit, what Americans call a cookie. The look on his face showed his curiosity. After introductions and niceties, I became somewhat nervous because what I was about to ask him would be very difficult for him to answer.

My research premise questioned if a social caste system existed among Muslims similar or identical to that in Hindu communities. Islam claimed all their adherents were equal, from beggar to king. The Hindu religious caste system segregated people based on birth and occupation. In itself, it wouldn't be a big deal, except on the Indian subcontinent Muslims and Hindus despised each other.

Annual communal violence was the norm, especially when Muslims celebrated the feast of Qurban, slaughtering cows for sacrifice. Hindus believed cows were sacred, part of their chain of reincarnation. Riots were inevitable.

The key word here is "social" caste system because no two religious groups could be more different. While both groups were ethnically Bengali and spoke Bengali, Muslims and Hindus used different words in the Bengali language. The two groups practiced different customs, wore different clothes, and celebrated their own religious holidays. Even marriage between Muslims and Hindus was illegal.

With such religious hatred, asking the Muslim professor if Muslims had an occupational caste system precisely like that of Hindus was akin to an insult.

"Dr. Afsaruddin, I'm doing a research project to find out if there is a caste system among Muslim villages where they are separated or segregated by occupation, just like the Hindu villages."

He looked away, pushed his glasses up his nose, and in a thick Indian accent became very real.

"You won't find it in writing, but everyone knows all our Muslim villages are segregated by occupation just like the Hindus and Buddhists. Muslim farmers, fishermen, and even barbers all live in villages with others of the same livelihood."

To my amazement and in all intellectual honesty, he admitted Muslim communities in rural areas were segregated by occupation just like Hindus. I was relieved. Saying that out loud contradicted the Islamic belief that all Muslim men were equal, all part of a brotherhood who adhered to strict Islamic traditions.

Then he went on to say his own research revealed an important fact. When Hindus converted to Islam centuries earlier, changing their religion did not change their social structure. No one had documented that Muslim villages were segregated by vocation. In theory, he agreed with my premise, but it was my job to verify it through field research.

Back at the hospital compound, I eagerly organized my fact-finding mission. Using my father-in-law's red Suzuki trail bike, Mohammad and I set out exploring Muslim villages in the area. There were no maps. It was raw, adventurous field research.

I remember my first interview vividly. A toothless old man delighted in sharing his life story. The man listed all the children he sired, including all who died before age five. Then what he said stopped me dead in my tracks.

"Thank you for asking me these questions. No one has ever asked me anything like this. I want you to know I am grateful to Allah for allowing me to live a happy life!"

Live a happy life? Speechless, I stared at him. After explaining his saga of lifelong misery in abject poverty, living in a mud and thatched roof hut, his resilience showed through. The first of many, he declared living a happy life in rural poverty.

More often than not, those I interviewed told me their happiness came from their family and their faith in Allah. Materialism as we know it was irrelevant—there wasn't any in those days.

While walking back to our trail bike, I unknowingly dropped a piece of paper on the ground. Mohammad quickly picked it up, kissed the paper, and handed it back, grasping his wrist with his other hand as a gesture of honor.

"Why did you kiss my piece of paper when you picked it up?" I asked.

"Writing on paper represents knowledge and education. We value that dearly. Dirt is unclean, mixed with manure, and dropping knowledge on the dirt required me to restore its honor."

As I began learning the local Muslim worldview, at the same time Mohammad learned about weird Americans. One morning while he and I were gone, someone in our house discovered a cobra had taken up residence in our living room recliner.

During lunch, my father-in-law used a can of RAID insecticide to flush the serpent out. He grabbed the snake's head from behind with his hand and used his thumb to snap the snake's head forward and down, killing it instantly.

My new bride had the bright idea of playing a prank on me. She took the unmutilated dead snake out on the front step and propped it up in strike pose. Late for lunch, I walked right by the cobra without even seeing it.

A couple hours later, we heard a banging sound outside. Rebecca raced to the front door, only to discover Mohammad beating her dead snake. She stopped him, told him it was already dead, and she was playing a joke on her husband.

In total confusion and consternation, the look on his face was priceless. In his culture, marriages were arranged. Husbands and wives didn't flirt or tease each other. Rebecca's attempt to explain the practical joke was pointless. Let's face it, Westerners have weird humor at times.

Our field research revealed Muslim village after village were indeed segregated by occupation. But it was hard to find enough people to interview. Not allowed to question women, the only ones available for interviews were feeble old men. Young men just weren't around.

Late one morning, Mohammad and I left a village when a large group of young farmers approached us on a path. Holding machetes, knives, and sickles, they were not happy. About twenty yards away Mohammad turned to me and said, "Stay here, I will handle this. If they attack me, you run fast to the motorcycle."

Mohammad walked up to the mob. They instantly surrounded him. A sharp interchange ensued and soon they were shouting. I took a few steps back and was ready to bolt. After a few minutes they calmed down, turned around, and returned to their fields. Mohammad walked back to me.

"They say you shouldn't be here this time of day. The country-side is upset. We aren't allowed to come into their villages anymore."

"Why?"

"We come in the mornings to interview after the men have already left to work their fields or go to their jobs. That's when the women are supposed to take their bath in the village pond, and it makes the men very, very . . ."

"Angry."

"Yes, very angry."

I had seen fully clothed women in the village ponds but didn't know that was their daily bath. Violating a Muslim woman's privacy was one of the worst things you can do in Islamic culture.

"These men were going to hurt us until I told them you were the Doctor *Sheib's* son-in-law."

"You mean kill us."

"Probably."

It was a major cultural blunder. As a budding anthropologist, this American was clueless and the Bengali city slicker wasn't any wiser. Something as small as a schedule goof almost cost us our lives.

I assumed my Bangladeshi interpreter Mohammad knew every-thing about his culture and people. Born and raised in urban, mid-dle-class life, he didn't understand the traditions and risks of rural villages any more than I did. In every country, rich or poor, urban and rural subcultures are different.

PRINCIPLE # 9: "Different Worlds"

Urban and rural people live in different worlds, especially in a developing country. Learn to tailor your behavior to each environment.

My village research at a standstill, an interesting distraction came up when Mohammad heard a "Quran Conference" was taking place a few miles up the road. He wanted us to go. I hesitated. We rode up to the hospital to consult with Santosh Master, my go-to-guy for cultural advice.

Fascinated by the opportunity, Santosh Master offered to go along. I might have been new but wasn't dumb.

"Santosh, as a Hindu do you think you should go?" I asked.

"I will be all right. We are wearing Western clothes, and I'll use a Muslim last name if anyone asks."

I looked at Mohammad, raised my eyebrows, and with a grin he said, "Don't worry. I won't tell anyone he's a Hindu."

A hospital vehicle picked us up, and our ecumenical band of a Muslim, Hindu, and Christian drove off to attend the Islamic Quran conference. Taking the main road for some distance, we turned off and drove several miles until we came to a large open field with huge tents, called *shamianas*. The size of circus tents, these thin tarps blocked the beating rays of the noonday sun.

In the distance, a religious leader waxed eloquent over a thunderous loudspeaker system as we walked by the makeshift kitchen preparing lunch for the devotees. Large copper pots six feet in diameter wafted a tantalizing aroma of rice and curry that would feed twelve thousand people.

At the main tent, I was asked to sign the guestbook as a foreign dignitary. I watched Santosh sign his name as "S. Chowdhury," a name sometimes used by both Muslims and Hindus, which inferred he was a wealthy landowner.

A person was assigned to host us, led us in, walked us in front of the speaker, and seated us on the first row. I sat next to the Saudi Arabian ambassador. It dawned on me that Santosh and I were the only non-believing infidels foolish enough to come to such an event. After the fiery sermon, we were treated as honored guests, which put us all at ease. And the fish curry wasn't bad either.

After lunch we left the conference grounds. I noticed Hindu women standing at the entrance.

"Santosh, why would Hindu women be standing here at such a huge Islamic festival?"

"The host of this conference is an Islamic *Pir,* a mystical Sufi known for his miraculous powers, particularly healing. These ladies probably have a sick relative and are hoping the Pir will heal them."

"But they are Hindu, not Muslim."

"When your relative is sick and someone has the power to heal them, religion doesn't matter."

Santosh went on to say *Pirs* had a reputation for being quite evangelistic and through their miraculous powers converted people to Islam. Of course, he let me know in front of Mohammad that only low caste Hindus converted to Islam. He was a Brahmin, the highest caste.

I changed the subject before our conversation became too awkward.

"Santosh, do you know anyone who owns a ship at the *lakri ghat* who would let me take a trip up to Chittagong?"

"Actually, I do know a man who owns one, a new one, and he lives only a few miles from here."

Mohammad reacted quite negatively, describing all the bad things that could happen to us. People could die on the high seas for any number of reasons. Since I didn't speak the language, he knew I couldn't go on a ship voyage alone. An uneducated sailor couldn't speak English.

I offered a significant bonus to his pay and he reluctantly accepted. By the time we loaded up in the hospital van, he had calmed down a bit as we drove off in search of the man who owned the *nokha*.

Our van came to a white-washed one-story house on a large property surrounded by lush rice paddies. The driver parked outside the gate. Ushered into the ship owner's drawing room, the bearer seated us and left.

Wall hangings with Quranic inscriptions in Arabic and a large open Quran, cradled by a wooden Quran holder, gave ample evidence the shipowner was a practicing Muslim. I began to doubt if the boat trip was a good idea. Many Muslims are superstitious. Perhaps I would defile the Muslim ship, or maybe I would bring bad luck on the open seas.

CHAPTER 7

PIRATES OF THE BAY OF BENGAL

*Dreadful stories they were—about hanging, and walking
the plank, and storms at sea. . . . By his own account he must
have lived his life among some of the wickedest men
that God ever allowed upon the sea.*
—Robert Louis Stevenson

THE BEARER RETURNED with tea, biscuits, and *Chana
Chur,* a spicy snack. The shipowner came in, greeted us, and
sat down. Santosh Master made the introductions and interpreted.
The owner looked me over.

"Let me see, you are doing a school research project, and you
want to travel up to Chittagong on my boat?"

"Yes, sir. I'm here to learn all I can about Bangladesh. No
American has ever made this trip, and I would be the first on
your ship."

He thought for a minute, stroked his flowing beard, and I
thought, "Oh boy, here it comes." Then he looked straight at me
and replied, "I would be honored."

A conversation ensued regarding trip logistics, deck rules, and how Mohammad and I would fit into the ship's normal operations. After agreeing on details and a voyage date, I was anxious to know more about the boat. I already knew enough about Bangladeshi culture that it was not impolite to ask how much things cost.

"Sir, I'm curious to know how much you spent to build your new boat."

"About 6,000 dollars."

"And where was it built?"

"There is a village up the coast that builds these."

"Are only Muslim shipwrights living and working in this village?"

"Of course. This is a skill passed from father to son for centuries. Why do you ask?"

"Oh, it's just part of my research on villages here."

Before we left, a message came by runner to the owner. He read it, smiled, and looked up.

"Allah is giving us favor. There is no way he could have known, but the ship captain says they are leaving for Chittagong tonight. Can you be ready?"

"Yes, sir."

"I will let him know he will have two passengers."

We scurried back to the hospital compound. While I packed, Rebecca came in and asked what I was doing.

"Santosh knew a boat owner, and we're leaving tonight on his new boat for Chittagong."

The look on her face was a combination of admiration and horror. She came over, grabbed me by my collar, got up into my face, and said, "Don't you dare die on me. I will never forgive you if you do." Only married eight months, it became a reoccurring mantra I would hear countless times the rest of our marriage.

Rebecca and I sat on the rooftop and watched the final loading of our big boat. When the tide came in, the massive wooden beast rose out of the mud. Using long bamboo poles, sailors pushed deep into the mud with all their might, shoving the ship down the narrow inlet leading to the sea.

Admiring a gorgeous sunset, we watched the ship drift by. I wondered if they were leaving without me. After several hours my wife finally went to bed. In our living room, I sat with my green thermos ice chest, backpack, and sleeping bag. I was crushed.

Had they forgotten me or were they being polite in telling me what I wanted to hear without meaning it? Was it too dangerous and the shipowner reluctant to tell me? Did he change his mind? I pondered all the possible reasons, but the simple reality was the boat had passed me by.

Midnight came and I prepared for bed. Then a knock came at the door. Standing there were Mohammad and two sailors, ready to pick up their foreign passenger. The reason I wasn't picked up earlier? Once headed out to sea, the boat couldn't stop. The sailors all needed to get the ship moving against the rising tide in order to make it six miles out to the ocean.

Using the ship's little rowboat, the two sailors rowed to catch up. We climbed aboard up thick ropes just as they lowered anchor in the ocean. In the darkness, no introductions were made as everyone was asleep. I was led into the cabin, an open twelve-by-twenty-foot room near the rear of the boat.

The outside walls and floor of the cabin were tropical hardwood. The large windows allowed a cross breeze. A thatched roof served as the ceiling. As the guest of honor, the captain insisted I sleep in his bed, a wooden platform elevated six inches off the floor. Everyone else slept on thin straw mats spread over the floor. The gentle rocking motion of the sea put us asleep in minutes.

I awoke to a dazzling sunrise and discovered we were anchored about a mile offshore. The captain was a tall, thin man, probably in his late thirties, and his crew all young men, from teens to those in their twenties. I was the first and probably only foreigner they would ever meet.

After breakfast, I toured the boat. Deciding to fit in, I wore what they wore: a Muslim *lungi,* or tube of plaid cloth worn like a skirt tied at the waist, and a tee shirt. No one wore shoes. I didn't either.

Before long I got into the swing of things. I climbed the sixty-foot mast to take pictures and interviewed each of the sailors. Mohammad's sour mood lightened, and before long all were laughing and having a grand time. However, our ship just sat in the water for hours.

The captain had his own schedule. By midafternoon we set sail, and as we traveled north, other ships joined us from other *ghats* along the coast. At dusk, we lowered sails and dropped anchor. Together, we were a flotilla of close to thirty ships. All huddled together like a school of fish circled by predators.

With Mohammad interpreting, I had to ask the captain a question.

"Why do you travel as a group of boats?"

"It's safer that way."

With only water and boats in sight, I sat dumbfounded. What could be the danger? Even still, I didn't feel free to ask why.

Mohammad and I ate with the crew. Freshly caught shrimp off the side of the ship ended up in a tasty curry. The crew sat in a circle around a single candle. Dinner finished, we all shared what our lives were like. I was in anthropology heaven.

Overnight other boats joined our fleet. At sunrise, I was first out of the cabin, stretched, and looked over at a boat roughly thirty yards away. A sailor glanced over at me, did a double take, and stared at me with a look of deer in the headlights. Here I was, a white American guy, standing on a wooden ship in the Bay of Bengal, dressed like a Bengali sailor, waving to him.

Within seconds he called to his shipmates, and heads popped out of boats, staring at the sailor with white skin. Some probably thought I was an albino, except I had blond hair, not white hair.

While I took pictures, they cheered and posed. Nothing like a little entertainment for a hard sailor's life.

After the sailors finished their morning prayers, I joined in and helped raise anchor. With each pull of the rope, the sailors chanted about Biblical prophets:

"*Musa Nobi* (Prophet Moses) hey ya, hey ya,"

"*Dawood Nobi* (Prophet David) hey ya, hey ya."

"*Isa Nobi* (Prophet Jesus) hey ya, hey ya."

I thought they included Jesus in their chant because they knew a Christian was on board. Later I found out that Jesus, an important prophet in Islam, stood second only to the prophet Mohammad.

The Islamic law of abrogation holds that whatever comes last is best. Mohammad came after Jesus Christ, so he is better. Because the Quran came after the Bible, it is more important. Consequently, Muslims consider Jews and Christians as people of the Book. But they were still considered infidels if they didn't give Islam the pre-eminence and convert their allegiance to the final prophet.

Unwrapped canvas sails generated an enormous tug at our boat, and with a strong creaking sound we were off. Our captain was at the rear of the ship manning the huge wooden rudder and shouting out orders.

Saline sea breeze washed against my face while I helped with the rigging. I was having a blast with my newfound Muslim friends. For an unforgettable moment in time, I was part of their team, and a team needs each other. Us against the elements, or so I thought.

On our left, a series of islands came into view and our crew became eerily quiet. Like Meerkats stretching their necks, everyone looked to the islands. I noticed the other ships had all eyes on the islands. On each boat, a sailor had climbed up the main mast and hung on with one arm and peered through binoculars with the other. Across the waters, I felt tension building among the sailors.

The captain motioned Mohammad over for a serious discussion. Then Mohammad came to me with a grim, unsettled look.

"The captain says you shouldn't be here. He wants you to go into the cabin right now, close the windows, and stay inside until we say come out."

"Why?"

"The big island on our left is a known pirate's place. He is afraid if they see a white guy from a rich country they will come rob us. The sailor on the mast above us said there are three ships waiting to attack."

Surely Mohammad was mistaken, or so I thought. The captain wore a face covered with worry. He turned towards me and his piercing stare said it all. Pirates still existed. The island on our left was a real pirates' cove. And everyone knows pirates are bad people—murderers and thieves on ships.

"But what about Farouk?" I asked.

Farouk, one of the sailors, sick with malaria and locked in our cabin, acted strange.

"He won't hurt you. He's just going out of his mind from his high temperature."

Before Mohammad unlocked the cabin door, he paused.

"One more thing the captain said. If the pirates get to us, don't try to escape by jumping into the sea. The waters are full of sharks. Better to take your chances with the pirates."

Pirates or sharks. What a heck of a choice. With all the wise advice from the captain, I entered the cabin only to hear Mohammad padlock the door behind me. In his own world, Farouk didn't even notice. I lay on my borrowed captain's cot.

After a few seconds, I cracked open the captain's little foot square window. I searched the horizon until I saw the islands. Sure enough three ships in a row faced us. All at once their sails fell and filled with wind. I couldn't believe my eyes. "Holy crap," I mumbled to myself.

At that moment, a shout from a distant mast set everything in motion.

"Pirates are coming! Pirates are coming!"

A flurry of shouting, running, and grunting commenced outside my cabin. Farouk remained oblivious. I looked again through the little window to see the three pirate ships headed towards us in hot pursuit.

This was not a movie scene of Tom Hanks fleeing Somalian speedboats. With wooden sailing ships chasing our fleet, it was more like Pirates of the Caribbean. I lay stunned with disbelief. For a very long minute, the impact of real danger was just too unreal.

All the sheer, fanciful wonder I had as a child about pirates on the high seas instantly left my mind. I was stuck on a wooden sailing ship about to be attacked by real pirates.

Genuine fear quickly replaced my thrill of anthropology. For my sailor friends, this was the real world, their world, every week of their life. Chased by pirates on the open seas in the twentieth century.

Farouk, unaware of the ship's peril, sat next to me. Delirious from malarial fever, he held a covered glass jar full of giant cockroaches. He meticulously called out his names for each one. He looked over at me, pointed to one in the bottle, and laughed hilariously. Then in a soft voice continued talking to his roaches.

Soaked with sweat from his fever, he broke into convulsions, which threw the bottle to our feet. Within seconds, the bottle rolled across the cabin floor and gave the tumbling roaches the ride of their life.

I laid him down on his blanket, then tried to hold him down and comfort him. It was no use. I left him writhing and shaking so I could look out the little window.

Between keeping an eye on the approaching pirates and the other eye on mad Farouk, I didn't know what to do. Chaos reigned, inside and outside the cabin. Sailors outside were chanting, praying, and calling on Allah for deliverance.

I peeked through the little window. The pirates were gaining on us. I looked for a place to hide my Seiko watch, a birthday gift from my wife. My desperation mounted with each passing minute. And yes, I joined in with prayers of my own.

Farouk's convulsions subsided, leaving him in a semicomatose condition. No one on board had malaria medicine. I left the roach bottle at the other end of the cabin alone until its constant rolling back and forth started to drive me crazy.

I scrambled over to the roach bottle, snatched it, and stuffed it into bedding. Again I looked for a place to hide. Perhaps there was a trapdoor. Maybe I could hide in the hold. No trapdoor. The only door to the cabin was locked from the outside. The windows also locked from the outside. I was inside, trapped.

Thick floorboards were all nailed down. No tools to pry them up. Anxious as a cornered rat in a room, I ran back to the little window to see what was happening. For a while it looked like our ship was going the same speed, which meant the pirates were no longer gaining on us.

Then, out of the blue, a gust of wind came up from behind and thrust us into a faster pace. I again looked out my little window. After a few minutes I saw the pirates give up and veer off.

From dozens of ships a roar of victory resonated across the waters. We continued cruising at top speed, the boat creaking and stretching, until the pirates fell off the horizon. The captain unlocked the padlock, opened the door, and welcomed me out.

He celebrated by taking a group picture of Mohammad and me with the crew.

At sunup the next morning I was relieved to see a clear sky and no pirates. On cue, our flotilla set sail for the final leg to Chittagong. But more bad news. The lifesaving wind gust that freed us from pirates the day before suddenly returned. A tropical depression was upon us. By noon, the sky behind us turned pitch black.

Streaks of lightning sparkled across the sky. The wind grew stronger by the hour, pushing us faster towards our destination. Faster than normal. An occasional gale force wind smashed into our wooden ship. Each time it gave us pause.

All the sailors, including Mohammad and I, were again gripped with fear. This time not from criminal pirates but from an angry sea. In silence, each of us hung on to a rope. The swells in the sea soon felt like a roller coaster.

For the second day in a row our captain had a pained, worried look on his face. Fortunately, the storm brought strong wind in front of it, permitting us to stay ahead. The loud, creaking grunts, groans, and moans of the stressed vessel brought new concern.

Could our ship come apart? If it did, would I drown before a shark found me? Strange thoughts flow through your mind when imminent death confronts you.

Minutes seemed like hours. Soon audible Muslim prayers to Allah were heard. I prayed silently, even though I was screaming out to God on the inside.

The port city of Chittagong appeared over the horizon. With a steady hand, our captain steered us closer to land. What a glorious sight. But would we make it to the dock before the fury of the storm overtook us?

Before entering into Chittagong harbor, we lowered the big sail, slowing us down. Boosted by the storm surge, the ship's forward momentum coasted us into port. Crucial to the captain, the ship must get to the dock as quickly as possible.

He gave the signal to lower the rowboat. Mohammad and I said a quick goodbye, climbed overboard and timed our jump into the bobbing rowboat. A minute later, our tiny boat bobbed up and down again as we climbed onto the dock.

The storm intensified, bearing down on us with strong gusts of wind. Now onshore and rain hitting us in the face, we split up. Mohammad spent the night at his parents' house while I stayed at a guesthouse. Once the storm passed, he would return to the ship for our belongings.

Overnight the storm passed through and by morning calm settled over Chittagong. At the arranged time, Mohammad and I met up, piled our gear into the hospital van, and made our way out of the city. On the drive back to the hospital compound, I could tell Mohammad had something to say.

"Mohammad, what's on your mind?"

"Praise be to Allah we made it safely to port. The 200 ships behind us got destroyed by the storm. All were lost. I told you it could be a dangerous trip."

He looked towards me and glared. I knew what I had to do.

"You were right. I should have listened to you."

He gloated as I acknowledged his wisdom. After a long pause, I asked, "How is Farouk?"

"Farouk died last night. The doctor said nothing could be done. It was Allah's will."

In mournful solitude, we looked out the windows at storm debris. Farouk, so young, had his whole life in front of him. My sailor friends were religious but not Muslim fanatics. Just working their job, doing their prayers, and living out their happy life. Farouk's life was cut short.

Islam is fatalistic. Whether good, bad, happy or sad, whatever happens, it is Allah's will. Even still, I might have saved Farouk's life with a few strong antimalarial pills. I vowed from then on to never travel in remote areas of the developing world without antimalarial, antibiotics, and antifungal medicine.

PRINCIPLE # 10: "Be Prepared"

Never travel in remote areas of the developing world without antimalarial, antibiotics, and antifungal medicine. It could be the difference between life and death.

My ocean voyage was an incredible adventure I would never forget. Although dangerous, the time on the ship revealed more evidence for my research. The sailors were from the same village, a village of all Muslim sailors. A further confirmation of my project premise that socially, at least, Muslims did have a *de facto* caste system in the rural countryside, just like their Hindu counterparts.

Over the next few days, Muhammad and I finished summarizing our research. His last day we walked to the hostel across the road from the hospital. He checked out of his room, and we talked for a few minutes before his bus to Chittagong arrived.

While waiting, we did the Bengali thing of apologizing before saying farewell.

"Thank you for allowing me to help with your research. If I have done anything to offend you, please forgive me," said Mohammad.

"Thank you for all your help in learning your culture and doing the research. If I have done anything to offend you, please forgive me," I responded.

Brakes squealed as the bus came to a stop. We embraced and he got on the bus. Once seated, he waved a final goodbye and left for home. I never saw him again and often wondered if he ever lived a happy life.

Before returning to the States, I sat down with the two American medical doctors who supervised my research. Both had lived in Bangladesh at least fifteen years and were surprised by my findings of the segregation of villages by occupation.

The lead doctor asked a different question.

"Phil, what else did you learn while you were out here?"

"I learned how important cultural sensitivity is. That happened when we entered villages while the men were gone and the women were in the pond bathing. Because they were in the water fully-clothed, I thought they were swimming. My mistake almost got us killed."

PRINCIPLE # 11: "Ignorance is not bliss, it's dangerous"

Every culture has values, mores, and roles, especially related to gender interaction. Violating these is deeply offensive, even dangerous.

I then said, "I also learned how dangerous the ocean could be."

"When we heard 200 ships behind you were destroyed by the cyclone, we made a policy as an organization that no one would be allowed to take the trip to Chittagong on a *nokha*. Ever. It's way too dangerous," said the other doctor.

Both doctors felt I needed more education beyond my masters degree if I wanted a career in cultural research and international development. I agreed, emphasizing I desired to do more than conduct anthropological research. I wanted to make a difference in people's lives. Before I could launch my overseas career, I would need specific training in international development.

CHAPTER 8

MAKING A DIFFERENCE

Leadership and learning are indispensable to each other.
—John F. Kennedy

I RIFLED THROUGH LETTERS in our mailbox and found what I had searched for every day during the spring of 1979. I ripped open the letter, dreading a rejection. To my relief, the letter announced acceptance into a Doctor of Philosophy (PhD) program at Michigan State University.

The letter gave a date when I would meet with my advising professor. A month later I found myself overwhelmed by the university's size as I searched for a parking space. Near the center of a large campus that served 50,000 students, the Institute for International Studies was housed on the top floor of the College of Education.

Once the elevator door opened, the receptionist for the institute directed me to my advisor's office. She assured me he would show up soon. I sat outside his office and reviewed what I knew about him.

Dr. John Hanson was internationally known for his publications and consulting. After doctoral work at Harvard and the University of Illinois, he spent his career teaching and advising foreign governments on development policy. Recognized as a scholar on African development, he would forget more about Africa than I would ever know.

When Nigeria received independence from Great Britain, the African country called on Hanson. He advised the Nigerian Ministry of Planning on how to design the entire public university system for twenty-six states. His work impacted millions of Nigerian students for decades to follow.

Soon I heard the raspy voice of a middle-aged man talking to the receptionist. A huge puff of gray smoke preceded him before he and his long Cuban cigar rounded the corner to greet me. He didn't seem like the classic pipe-smoking professor. His carriage represented importance, standing straight with shoulders back.

We greeted, sat down, and for a moment an awkward silence hung in the air as thick as his cigar smoke. Dr. Hanson leaned back in his chair and exhaled a perfect smoke ring, and then got right to the point.

"Well, do you have an idea of what courses you want to take?"

Taken aback, I asked, "You mean I get to pick my courses?"

"This is a doctoral program in international planning. Most of our graduates will be government planners, consultants to foreign governments, or work for the U.S. State Department, International

Monetary Fund, or World Bank. But you need to specialize, and that means you pick courses that will make you an expert in your field."

"I'm sorry, sir, my undergraduate and masters programs were all structured with only a few electives I could choose. I didn't realize I would be building my own customized course of study."

"Our goal is for you to choose the courses that best suit your career aspirations. You tell me what you want to take, and you can pick from any graduate course offered on this campus."

Shocked by my newfound freedom in picking courses, I floated out of the institute with wild excitement. Later, I scoured the enormous catalog for courses. Over time, and with Dr. Hanson's help, I selected my own program of courses that specialized in international planning, policy analysis, and development economics. Practical courses on how to plan and set up overseas development projects, at every level in a country, would impact my entire career.

Perhaps the biggest revelation during my coursework was discovering successful development projects were those based on the local needs of the people, as determined by the local people, not the foreign expert.

One course in particular introduced me to the concept of sustainability. The norm had been for a foreigner to organize a project, fund it, and later try to turn it over to the locals. That usually didn't work.

Instead, it created dependency on the foreigner and his funds. A successful project required local buy-in, local ownership, and the means to sustain the project themselves without continual outside help.

PRINCIPLE # 12: "Skin in the game"

Success in development projects is tied to ownership because when locals own it, they have something at risk, some skin in the game.

This is the opposite of how projects were conducted during the colonial era that ended by the early nineteen sixties. When European nations owned colonies in Africa, the Middle East, and Asia, the white colonial administrators, along with white people of the missionary societies, made the decisions for the locals.

Rudyard Kipling, a renowned British poet and author, named it the "White Man's Burden." Critics claimed it was a way of justifying imperialism. Schools, hospitals, and modern infrastructure in former colonies were put in place by people of European descent. In the early eighties, now twenty years after most colonies gained their political independence, this issue still loomed real and troubling.

During one class session, the professor invited a recent graduate of our doctoral program to talk on this subject. Typical of many growing up in non-Western societies, the African man began by explaining his family background and telling his life story. When he got to the part about being educated in mission schools, he could see the scorn on some students faces.

Unlike most Asians, who prefer a more polite way of addressing confrontation, I learned West Africans could be direct. He stopped and looked directly at the students.

"You can be critical of the Christian missionaries if you want, but the fact is, they gave me an education, and I wouldn't be here without them. I'm grateful for that."

"But didn't they try to convert you?" one student asked.

"I'm not a Christian," he said bluntly. "I'm an animist. My father is a witch doctor and he can make it rain. I've seen him do it. We don't have a problem in Africa believing in the supernatural. Here you do. But where I lived, I wouldn't have been educated without mission schools. I didn't see any other organizations coming to my country and building schools in the middle of nowhere."

Point taken. The ivory towers of academia found it easy to be judgmental of the past. While a college student in Africa, I learned that colonial attitudes of superiority by Westerners continued long after political independence legally ended the era of colonialism.

In the early eighties, research revealed the importance of local acceptance of project ideas. Mistakes were made and cultural insensitivity was one of them.

One dramatic example blazed in my brain. In an attempt to educate children of nomads on the Arabian Peninsula, a Western government gave millions to build apartment buildings and schools at each oasis the nomads frequented. The foreign experts reasoned building a school at each stop, nomadic children could continue their education, and the family could live in a new apartment.

When the nomads arrived at the first oasis with new buildings, they pitched their tents and then used the apartments for barns. After all, those bathtubs made excellent watering troughs for goats. They left their livestock in the "new barns" and stayed in their tents for the night.

When asked why they didn't stay in the apartments, the nomads were flabbergasted that someone would suggest they stay in a hot cement building when they could enjoy the evening desert breezes flowing through their tents.

Millions of dollars fell wasted and useless because the Western experts assumed nomads wanted to become modern. It didn't occur to the experts they should ask the nomads what they perceived their needs to be.

Building oasis schools found some merit, so it wasn't entirely a lost cause. One night after class I asked a fellow Saudi student where his parents lived. He looked at a calendar and made some mental calculations.

"I'm not exactly sure where my parents are right now. They are nomads and between two oases. Not certain which ones this time of year."

Imagine though if the schools had not been built at Saudi oases. Instead of getting a PhD, my friend would have learned from his father to herd camels and goats. Instead, after graduation he went back to Saudi Arabia to work in the Ministry of Planning, helping other nomadic children have an opportunity to live a different life.

Perhaps the biggest mistake I've ever made was turning down an all-expenses-paid financial package from the university, one which required we move there. My wife had just finished college and started a job at a mental health hospital. I had an established job and we just built a new home. Active in our church, our friends didn't want us to leave town.

However, commuting to the university about killed me. We lived ninety miles from the campus, and for two years I drove four days a week to attend classes. Along with working fifty hours a week as a cabinetmaker for a high-end furniture manufacturer, I averaged three to four hours of sleep a night. In an effort to finish sooner, I doubled my classes each term. Some nights, driving the long, lonely highway at midnight, it seemed impossible to stay awake at the wheel.

By the third year, I was a physical and emotional wreck. In an age before personal computers, writing forty pages of term papers a week, along with reading assignments averaging 800 pages a week, I was totally swamped. I couldn't afford to hire a typist to type my papers, so my selfless wife served as my typist, confidant, and biggest cheerleader.

The emotional pressure of campus politics was daunting. Unlike many universities, Michigan State allowed their doctoral students to choose a committee of professors to oversee their degree program. How a student selected a doctoral committee, professors who read your dissertation and determined if you passed or failed, could mean graduating or not graduating.

While my father worked on a PhD at Ohio State in the 1960s, he saw some doctoral students not graduate because they picked the wrong committee members. Dad called it "getting into the club." All the professors on the committee had to agree on your induction into the doctoral "club."

I was worried. Just one committee member could ax your career. As the only American in the program and living off campus, I didn't know anyone I could ask who could help me choose the right professors for my committee.

Fortunately, a Pakistani classmate told me about Eyasu, an Ethiopian who had just defended his dissertation. Eyasu was a networker, and though he was not an American, he possessed an uncanny sense about which American professors could get along with one another. He agreed to meet with me, and after I gave him my proposed slate of professors, he smiled.

"Excellent. They are all old, about to retire. They have been working together for years, both here and abroad. There won't be any young professor trying to impress his peers at your expense. Plus, all of them really respect Dr. Hanson, your advisor."

Rebecca and I agreed to hold off starting a family until I was done with the degree. But my education became more complicated. Nearing the end of my coursework and disregarding our exhaustion, I approached her with a new challenge.

"Dr. Hanson threw out a proposal to me today."

"Oh yeah? What is it?"

"He said if I did an extra year of coursework, beefed up my dissertation committee, and expanded my dissertation, MSU would award me two PhDs."

The look on her face said it all as reality set in. I realized my ego was in the way. We were only in our twenties but knew we couldn't physically keep the crazy schedule. Earning a second degree would also require taking another set of dreaded comprehensive exams.

"Comps," as they were called, required three days of writing about everything you knew in your field. All in all, a second PhD would take much longer than one additional year. One doctorate would be enough for my career aspirations.

Content analysis was a method of investigation developed by US military intelligence to analyze German media during the Second World War. I used this research method to examine the government policies reported in 700 daily issues of each main newspaper published in both Ghana and Nigeria.

The good news was I didn't have to travel to Africa to read and analyze 1,400 newspapers. Our library had them all on microfilm, which was painstakingly read on a dimly lit screen. At the time, using microfilm was a common way for libraries to archive newspapers. The bad news was I had to sit every day for months in a library with my eyes glued to the screen of the microfilm machine. Thought I would go blind.

One thing about the content analysis methodology was fascinating. Sometimes it allowed the researcher to possibly predict events based on what was not written as much as what was covered. My eyes heavy-lidded from reading newspapers on microfilm, one day I came home from the library with a puzzled look on my face.

"What's up with you?" Rebecca asked.

"I don't know. Something's about to happen in Ghana. I mean politically. I've been buried in newspapers for months, and I can feel it by what's not being reported."

"What do you mean?"

"I get the feeling there's going to be another coup to overthrow the government."

"So mark your words. Let's watch and see what happens."

Three weeks later, on December 31, 1981, the Ghanaian government was overthrown by a military officer, J.J. Rawlings, who set Ghana on a path to democracy. Rebecca and I were stunned my prediction came true. After the news of the coup, I became a firm believer in content analysis.

The value of a seasoned professor directing my dissertation research came from his ability to steer me away from problem areas. One day I got a call from my advisor.

"Phil, we have a problem with two of the professors on your committee over research methodology. One wants you to use only quantitative statistics, and the other favors qualitative analysis as you conduct your content analysis. It's my fault because I forgot these two have their preferences. Don't worry. I'll fix it."

In Solomonic fashion, Dr. Hanson deftly negotiated a compromise before I got too far into the research. By using both quantitative and qualitative analysis in my research, both professors would be pleased.

The disagreement proved a reality check. I sent him my dissertation chapter by chapter so he could meticulously check my work and make sure of its readiness. His reputation was on the line if my research didn't pass muster.

Over fourteen months of research and writing, Dr. Hanson skillfully guided me in producing a 200-page dissertation on the comparative development policies of Ghana and Nigeria. Using a borrowed IBM Selectric II backspace erase typewriter, my very pregnant wife typed the 200-page dissertation three times before I could submit it to the committee.

Rebecca sat and typed at our kitchen table. A growing baby bump in the way, by the last draft she barely reached the keys. Dr. Hanson signed off and said, "Submit it."

When I dropped off a copy of the dissertation to each professor on my committee, one of them pulled me aside into his office.

"Phil, I have a good feeling about your upcoming dissertation defense, and before anyone else asks you, I have a job proposition for you. Have you thought of what you want to do after graduation?"

"We're looking at some overseas options. What did you have in mind?"

"Morocco is finally open to letting girls go to school, and I just received a large U.S. government grant to fund the design of an entire girls' education system for the country. How's your French? I need someone like you to help me by living on site in Morocco, working with the government ministries."

This sounded like a dream job. I could put into practice all my training in developing a country's integrated plan and policies. Most of all, such a project would rectify the social injustice against women and girls. My work could help the Moroccan people educationally, socially, and economically.

"How long is the project?"

"It will take two to three years. You'll get an annual six-figure salary, all in dollars, tax-free on both sides of the ocean. Perks include a paid month home leave each year, a car, driver, house, and household staff. The problem is, I need you over there in a couple months."

Rebecca and I discussed the advantages and disadvantages of taking the Morocco project. With our first baby due and recovering from the previous years of studies, we needed a break. A deeper concern bubbled to the surface. Our desire and commitment to work directly with local people might get forgotten. A big paying job of advising senior government officials on development policy probably could spoil us. It could trap us in a lifestyle hard to leave.

A six-figure salary in 1982, all tax-free, felt hard to turn down. However, we decided our priorities of health and family proved more important than money. I turned down the offer.

"Judgement day" came for my dissertation. Dr. Hanson invited my wife, eight months pregnant, to come along in anticipation of a celebration afterward. Upon arrival, Rebecca and I sat outside the glass conference room and held hands while the committee discussed my dissertation. Possibly the longest twenty minutes of my life. The waiting was excruciating.

Dr. Hanson called me into the conference room to defend my research and answer questions. Four years of work and tuition hung in the balance. I'll be honest, I was intimidated. What felt like my life moving in slow motion, I stood up and said to Rebecca, "Well, here goes nothing?" She smiled as she squeezed my hand.

The dissertation defense usually took two hours. But after thirty minutes answering their questions, the committee shifted gears with another set of questions totally unanticipated.

"Phil, what are you going to do after graduation?" one professor asked.

"I'm planning on working in the private sector with an NGO overseas."

"You know, I can get you a job with the United Nations or World Bank," he said.

"I know someone in USAID (United States Agency for International Development) who will hire you," another professor said.

"Have you considered being a diplomat with the State Department? I know someone," a third added.

During the next hour it became abundantly clear they wanted PhD graduates from their school to take important, prestigious overseas positions. Their job was to produce scholars who could help countries plan development policies impacting millions of people. I began to fear my career path might influence one of them to vote against me.

I held my ground and thanked them for their offers to help employ me. To the best of my ability, I explained my heart was in making change with people at the local level rather than at a national policy level. Dr. Hanson could see there was no persuading me. I was excused for their deliberations.

I sat down next to Rebecca.

"What's wrong? How did it go?"

"I think it went okay, but I don't think they're happy I'm not seeking a prestigious job."

Waiting for the news, we held hands again. Within ten minutes Dr. Hanson led the committee out of the conference room, and after a momentous pause, made his announcement.

"Congratulations Dr. McDonald!"

The committee clapped, I hugged my wife, and introduced her to the professors. Then my advisor took another committee member and us to a private country club for a nice meal. Both professors tried to talk my wife into my taking one of these high-level job offers, but she didn't budge. She was equally committed to my working at the local grassroots level.

In my educational journey, Dr. Hanson stands forever as an unusual man. For his generation, he eschewed colonialism and stressed the importance of local people making their own decisions. Between his mentorship and my studies, I felt prepared for an overseas career.

PRINCIPLE # 13: "Bring something to the table"

A long-term career requires special skills and credentials that add value to developing countries. Governments in less developed countries are rightfully sensitive to foreign workers coming to their countries and taking away jobs from their own citizens.

After graduation, we prepared to move overseas. But it would take longer than we realized because the NGO we joined required us to raise funding. Rather than the NGO paying a salary and covering expenses, by raising funds to cover ourselves, it gave us the ability to create our own donor constituency. The ability to raise funds would eventually help fund our own projects.

Our educations complete, the next stage in life began. Matthew entered our world, followed two years later by his brother Mark. I remodeled our basement and in one corner built a secure room where our furniture and other personal items would be stored while living overseas.

Foreign visa applications, renting our home, selling our cars, and packing what would stay in America and what would go overseas took longer than one could imagine.

In the days before the Chinese economic invasion of the developing world with cheap, reliable household goods, I built five wooden crates and packed twenty-two fifty-five-gallon drums. Personal goods such as laundry soap, shampoo, toilet paper, toothpaste, and pots and pans were purchased and packed.

A friend of ours owned a trucking company and volunteered to take our shipment out to the East Coast docks to be put on a ship. Fortunately, we would never ship personal goods overseas again. Once abroad, we learned to live off the land and buy what was locally available, even buying cheap Chinese toilet paper that looked like pink crepe paper but felt like sandpaper.

Our two toddlers in tow, we embarked on an overseas journey that would last decades. Ironically, our first assignment was in Bangladesh, the same place my wife grew up and where I had done field research.

With a population almost ninety percent illiterate, a tremendous need for schools and educational programs existed. Considered a "hardship post" by most embassies, living and working in Bangladesh would not be a picnic. In fact, it would test me to the core.

PART
II
Learning the Ropes

A ship is safe in harbor, but that's not what ships are for.

—G. T. Shedd

CHAPTER 9

LIVING ABROAD

Our homes are not defined by geography or one particular
location, but by memories, events, people, and places
that span the globe.
—Marilyn Gardner

OUR FIRST FEW months in Bangladesh turned out to be
a baptism by fire. Upon arrival in the capital, Dhaka, in
July, 1985, our desire was to live close to other American colleagues
employed by our NGO. At the time, no houses were available for
rent in the "NGO quarter," a suburb known as Muhammadpur.

Without want ads or real estate agents, our search required a
relentless daily effort of driving up and down streets looking on a
gate or window for a "To Let" sign, the British way of stating "For
Rent." Many such phrases reflected the fact that before the parti-
tioning of India, Bangladesh was a part of British India.

While searching for a house, we lodged in a guest house. I got
sick with an infection that laid me out flat on my back for six weeks.

After losing thirty-six pounds, my wife made an appointment with an American doctor from the *Cholera Research Institute.*

He examined me and asked, "What's your biggest problem?"

"Doc, I can't eat because I'm nauseated all the time. The only two things I can keep down are chicken noodle soup and Snickers bars."

He laughed, set his stethoscope down, leaned back, and crossed his knee.

"Based on the powerful antibiotics you've taken and now no evidence of infection, I think you are still sick because you are reacting to the strong antibiotics. Stop taking the antibiotics and see what happens."

I got better by the next day and was thankful to be whole again.

A couple months later, a two-story house became available. The landlady, a Bengali widow, lived upstairs with her two college-age sons. She offered us the ground floor if we would pay the going rate—a two-year cash advance on the rent.

That's right, all twenty-four months of rent paid up front. It just so happened the rent advance was the same amount the widow needed to pay for a wedding. What a coincidence. The only house available, she had us over a barrel. I signed the lease and forked over all the rent in cash.

As lessees of the ground floor flat, we had rights to the small front yard and adequate backyard, just the right size for our two munchkins to play outside. A six-foot cement block wall surrounded the property. To discourage potential thieves from climbing over the wall, shards of broken glass served as minisentries, all set into cement. The wall also provided privacy, essential and expected in a Muslim culture.

Inside, the drawing room, or living room, connected to a large dining room. Polished terrazzo, a solid mixture of concrete and rock flecks, covered the cement floor. All the walls sported a fresh coat of paint.

Once our flat was ready, we checked out of the guesthouse and moved into the barren unit with our suitcases. My mother-in-law sent up a truckload of bedroom furniture from the hospital. To our dismay, our crates and barrels were held up by a dock strike in the port city, Chittagong.

One room came together immediately. A veteran of international living, Rebecca opened a suitcase full of our sons' bedroom décor from Michigan. She lined the upper border of the walls with alphabet flashcards.

The same posters from their Michigan bedroom adhered to the walls with teacher's putty. Within an hour, the same bedspreads, stuffed toys, and matchbox cars made the bedroom seem like home. Brilliant.

Our boys, too young to know better, came in and said, "Oh, this is our room." They snuggled into bed the first night sure their world was intact and all was fine.

The next morning, I awoke, ready to set up our house.

"So, when do we go buy furniture?" I asked Rebecca.

"What do you mean, buy furniture? We have to order it."

"From where?"

"I know a street that has woodworking shops."

"But I saw a store with furniture in the front window."

"Those were samples, but I want to order my own designs I like."

She sifted through her designs and set a few aside.

"How long will it take for them to be made?" I asked.

"This is Bangladesh. They will say it will be ready in a month, but it will take two."

That day we hopped a rickshaw and took along a bunch of catalogs she'd brought from the States. My wife showed the shop owner catalog pictures of furniture. He scribbled dimensions on a notepad, and then they negotiated a price and agreed on a delivery date.

This furniture shopping experience was only the beginning. Every day we spent a great deal of time going from shop to shop to buy basic household articles. Rebecca made purchase decisions and I paid for them the only way possible—in cash.

My strength back from the infection, I was anxious to resume my early morning workout. Except I noticed a pain in my leg.

"So, why are you limping?" Rebecca asked.

"It's a deep pain in my lower thigh. I keep rubbing it but it's getting worse."

Two weeks later I discovered a fast-growing tumor in my left thigh, and by week four it had grown to the size of a golf ball. A trip down to the American hospital removed the tumor, and thankfully it was benign. Although in pain, I enjoyed recuperating in the quiet jungle setting.

Back in busy, crowded Dhaka, I recovered for a few more days, moving around on crutches. Rebecca came home with good news.

"The dock strike is over. Our crates and barrels will arrive tomorrow on a truck."

"Great, love it. Can't wait to unpack with this big hole in my leg."

Determined to move in, I spent painful days bending over 55-gallon drums helping my wife empty our precious food and personal items from the USA. Most of our food items ended up stored off the kitchen in a room called the "godown," a term used on the Indian subcontinent for a large pantry or storeroom.

I hung curtains fabricated by a tailor on thin pipe serving as curtain rods. I then installed new ceiling fans in each room. Delivery day came, and our new appliances arrived on a caravan of flatbed rickshaws. Four months after arriving in the country, it all came together and we felt settled in. Well, almost settled in.

I didn't realize moving to a foreign country involved many changes that happened all at once. Relocation not only meant setting up a household but required other tasks. Red tape, such as government registrations (residence visa, work permit, driver's license), was time-consuming.

At the same time, I learned local banking procedures, how foreign currency exchange worked, and figured out locations and transportation. A lot of change happened in the first few months.

PRINCIPLE # 14: "Relocation is a juggling act"

When moving to a new country, many changes happen all at once and require a flexible attitude.

In 1985, few Bangladeshis spoke English. Our main task the first year was learning the official language, Bengali. A modicum of Bengali ability was essential, since ninety percent of the population couldn't read or write.

The best way to learn a culture is to learn its language. Embedded in language is what a culture holds dear—its values. One learns those values through stories, jokes, idioms, and what should be said and what shouldn't. Our NGO enrolled us in a private language school that specialized in teaching the Bengali language to foreigners.

For me, holding the highest academic degree possible, an earned PhD, my ego cringed learning to say in Bengali, "My name is Phil." The four-year-old street kids spoke better Bengali than I.

How I practically learned to speak the language happened after class, particularly in resolving conflicts between household employees. Most expats, along with middle-class and upper-class Bangladeshis, employed household help and we were expected to do so as well. Culturally, if you had a household and could afford to hire help, you were supposed to employ household staff.

Furthermore, the strict Islamic culture didn't approve of a woman to shop for food in the bazaar by herself. A male cook shopped for food. Before grocery stores, our cook made all our food from scratch. If you wanted hamburgers, the cook bought a hunk of beef, used a hand meat grinder to turn it into ground beef, prepared dough and baked the buns, cut the potatoes for potato chips, deep-fried the chips, and made ketchup from scratch. That was just lunch.

With babies, cloth diapers, dirt and smog, our household needed what the British called a "bearer." A bearer cleaned the house, washed and ironed clothes, set the table, cleared the table, answered the door, and performed other sundry duties.

The *darwan,* also referred to as a *chokidar,* was the employee responsible for outside security, especially opening and closing the front gate. If we weren't around, the cook was in charge of the other two. I hired a cook, bearer, and *darwan.* All three were indispensable, and a dollar a day for each was an excellent wage at the time.

Bangladesh society was not only stratified by social class but also by religion. No one trusted anyone from a different religion, which led to constant bickering and fights between our help. With a Buddhist cook, a Christian bearer, and a Muslim *darwan,* there was no shortage of drama. In the male-dominant culture, I settled the fights, not my wife.

As a rookie employer, I took the fighting employees out to the front veranda and settled their disputes. Meanwhile, my wife listened from behind the front door. I heard both sides, called a timeout, and went inside the door.

"What's the word for difficult?" I whispered.

"*Koteen,*" she whispered back.

I hurried back to the door, rounded the corner, and walked with all the dignity I could collect. I used my new word as if I'd known it my whole life. She was my full-time language consultant. Another indication I totally out-married myself!

PRINCIPLE # 15: "When in Rome, do as the Romans do"

The best way to learn a culture is to learn its language. Embedded in language is what a culture holds dear—its values. One learns those values through stories, jokes, idioms, and what should be said and what shouldn't.

Our *darwan,* Nurul, watched the premises at night, and once the sun came up, he tended to the lawn and flowers. Once the cook and bearer came in at sunrise, Nurul went home, slept during the day, and reported for duty in the evening.

Nurul's four kids couldn't afford to go to school so he didn't get much sleep during the day. A few nights a week, his father worked on his behalf. "Grandpa" loved our baby boy, and when Mark woke up, he took him from me so little Markie's parents could sleep longer.

Grandpa always wore the same worn-out gray clothes and the same slightly dirty Muslim skull cap. Exhibiting great joy, Grandpa pushed Markie's stroller all around the neighborhood early in the morning. If he wasn't using the stroller, he carried him, all the while singing and talking to him. He was the consummate grandpa, except he had a problem.

Grandpa's bad cough passed on tuberculosis to our baby. I informed Nurul about his dad's disease and paid for his medication. His cough didn't go away. I then told Nurul I needed to talk to his father.

"Uncle, I need to discuss something with you. It breaks my heart to say this but until your lungs are healed, I can't let you watch my baby. Your cough is making him sick like you."

The old man was crushed. He understood, whimpered out a goodbye "*Salam*" and left. I learned that day how much people from the Indian subcontinent truly loved children. No doubt Grandpa loved children, especially my baby boy.

Nurul got into fights with the two other servants because he was not only a Muslim but also an ethnic minority. A Bihari, from the Bihar state in India, he lived a mile away in a refugee camp maintained by the International Red Cross.

During the 1971 East Pakistan war of independence, the Biharis sided with West Pakistan. After West Pakistan's genocide of three million Bengalis, all in the manner of nine months, India came to the rescue and helped East Pakistan, now Bangladesh, gain their independence.

The war over, West Pakistan sympathizers living in Bangladesh were herded into refugee camps. Needless to say, with millions slaughtered by Pakistan, including a whole generation of the educated class, Bangladeshis hated West Pakistan sympathizers, especially the Biharis.

Their hatred manifested itself once a year when "someone" would torch the Bihari refugee camp, burning it to the ground. The fire trucks would arrive but wouldn't put out the fire until the refugee leaders had rounded up enough money to pay them. In the meantime, it was open season with Bihari women and girls raped and Bihari men beaten up.

One morning I heard people shouting out in the street. I ran to the front door and saw flames and smoke coming up from the direction of the refugee camp. Nurul came running up to me with eyes wide as silver dollars.

"*Sheib* (sir), I need to go find my family. They are burning our camp again!"

"Don't run, Nurul, here, take a rickshaw."

I thrust money into his hand, he jumped into a rickshaw and raced to his family. He didn't return for a few days. With much of the camp burned to the ground, I thought he probably had to rebuild his shack. Then one night he showed up for work.

"Nurul, what happened to your family?"

"Praise be to Allah, they are all right and our *basha* (house) received little damage. The fire didn't reach our corner of the camp. For once the fire department put out the fire."

"I'm glad you are back. I need your help with something."

During the months while waiting for our furniture order, we needed a bed. My mother-in-law sent up my wife's childhood bed on the hospital truck, including its coconut fiber mattress. The mattress was in bad shape, and I needed Nurul to help me dispose of it.

"*Sheib*, if you are going to throw out the mattress, could I have it?"

"Sure, Nurul, but how will you get it to the camp?"

"No problem, I'll take it in a rickshaw."

"Um, pretty sure it's too big for a rickshaw, but I will help you."

I signed out the NGO car and strapped the mattress on the roof. When I drove to his refugee camp for the first time, the squalor left me dumbstruck. Fifty thousand Biharis lived in the one-square-mile camp, an endless maze of shacks standing shoulder to shoulder. Overpopulated, the stench was unbearable.

Four large public restrooms serviced the whole camp. Residents woke up at two A.M. and stood in line to use the closest bathroom. One learned to sleep standing up. When the line moved, the person in front of you woke you up, and then you, in turn, woke up the person behind you. Everyone took a few paces forward, all night. No wonder Nurul was testy. He had been living in that system of squalor for fifteen years.

In any country, moving a floppy mattress is usually a clumsy maneuver. By bending and folding, somehow we managed to get the queen-sized mattress down the narrow muddy path and inside his tiny shack.

Once situated inside on the dirt floor, only a foot was left around the bed for the rest of the entire living area. His family was ecstatic. I was in shock, a form of culture shock I would later call poverty shock.

PRINCIPLE # 16: "Unjust living conditions"

Culture shock comes in many forms, including poverty shock and privilege guilt.

Nurul, his wife, and four kids would live, sleep, and play on the mattress. The bed was now their home. After all, it was better than sleeping on hard ground. Serving me hot *cha,* a sweet tea similar to Indian *chai,* the family showered their gratitude upon my guilty soul. I returned home speechless.

For such a poor family, a worn-out, tattered mattress filled with old shredded coconut fiber was a luxurious gift. Later, when I bought a nice new foam mattress for our bed, my guilt made it difficult to shell out the money. Who was I? Why wasn't I living in that refugee camp instead of Nurul?

For millions of Bangladeshis, survival was a desperate day-to-day existence. I found my new environment changed me. And not necessarily for the good. In such challenging conditions, with tons of angst and desperation, I wasn't a nice good ole boy from the American farm belt anymore.

I became hard, harsh, and uncaring. Any little thing caused my temper to flare. All a direct result of the oppressive environment. My wife's whole life abroad accustomed her to these realities, but I was going through an initial stage of culture shock. Over time I realized my harsh behavior was a psychological coping mechanism.

What I didn't know? Everything was about to get worse.

CHAPTER 10

A DOZEN BRICKS

*As long as poverty, injustice, and gross inequality persist
in our world, none of us can truly rest.*
—Nelson Mandela

THE SHRILL SOUND of a whistle pierced the night silence, ruining a perfect night's sleep. Our neighborhood *chokidar* blew his whistle every two hours as he walked up and down streets. Over time our ears and minds learned to ignore it.

At dawn, in an eerily but predictable fashion, a more startling sound broke the night's stillness. In traditional Islamic culture, it was time for morning prayers.

When it was light enough to distinguish between a white hair and black hair, the *muezzin* from each mosque did a microphone check by blowing into his microphone. Check completed, he began his amplified cry that implored the faithful to roll out of bed for the first prayer of the day. Depending on the time of year, it could be as early as 4:30 in the morning.

Most days, the melodious chanting sounded off key. The more prominent mosques had the best singers. In downtown Dhaka, the *muezzin* at the national mosque had an incredible voice, a sound so clear he could have sung in any opera house in the world.

The *adhan* (call to prayer) finished, I fell back to sleep within minutes. One morning I couldn't get back to sleep. Markie, our baby boy, didn't go back to sleep either. With daylight slipping through the curtains, I saw him standing up in his crib, staring at the mural painted on the wall.

His grandmother, an artist, had painted the characters from *Jungle Book*. Well, all the characters except Mowgli, because Markie was to be Mowgli once he was old enough to understand the story. The little guy cooed as I changed his diaper. Then I took him outside and handed him to Nurul for a morning ride in his stroller.

Not able to go back to sleep, I ventured out for a jog. The early morning air lingered cool, crisp and refreshing. I took a big breath before I headed out to the main street. Thousands of homeless people slept along both sides of the thoroughfare. I tried my best not to disturb their slumber. At times, the odor of wood smoke and unwashed humanity became overwhelming.

My jog over, I cooled down and grabbed a quick shower before breakfast. Seated at the table and playing with my food, my wife noticed something amiss.

"So what's up? You've hardly touched your pancakes. Something bothering you?"

Our bearer also sensed my abnormal behavior. Like a flash, he took our kids out of their high chairs and whisked them outside to play.

"I was out jogging, lost my balance, and had to jump over a homeless person."

"Did you wake him?"

"No, he was dead."

"How do you know?"

"When I jumped over him I looked down and his eyes were wide open. Flies were buzzing all around, plus he had a vacant, hollow. . ."

"What?"

"A still look in his eyes. Like nothing was there. On my way back I saw two men throw his body into a big dump truck with other bodies."

"He could have died from either starvation or illness. Probably shouldn't go jogging until the truck is done picking up the dead bodies. Life is fragile and people die easily out here."

"Sure . . . he probably died of starvation," I muttered, cutting through an enormous pile of pancakes. It was too late. I had already lost my appetite. People all around me were starving to death, and I'd never missed a meal in my life. Just when I thought I was adjusting to culture shock, pangs of guilt and confusion rolled over me.

"By the way, we are invited to Tim's house for dinner tonight," she said.

That night going to Tim's, we walked by the neighborhood garbage dump at the corner of the street. A mound of paper and trash, cooks capped it with a fresh load of discarded food. On top of the garbage heap, a toddler cried after losing a fight with a mangy, stray dog for some choice piece of garbage.

The dirty toddler, with no mother in sight, looked close in age to my little boy Matt, whom I held in my arms. The sound of the tiny boy crying on top of a garbage heap pierced my soul. As much as I wanted to bring that little child to a sumptuous dinner, I couldn't. Throughout the country at that very moment, millions of little boys and girls were rummaging through garbage. Poverty was real. For some reason, we were favored, they were not. Life wasn't fair.

In a land of desperate poverty, one bright spot came from a warm climate. From October through the following June, the weather was perfect. Cloudless blue skies, warm tropical breezes, and bright sunny days made days consistently beautiful.

One afternoon after nap time, Matt and Mark played outside in their new sandbox. A *cot mistri* (carpenter) built it from leftover crate wood, including a top, critical for keeping out stray cats. Nurul painted the box a deep navy blue.

Around the square box, Nurul kept the grass short lest any creepy crawlers headed unnoticed towards my children. I took a break from my work and walked out into our backyard, into a small world of toys and sand.

The jackfruit trees leaned against the boundary walls and hung heavy with huge, ripening jackfruit. A member of the mulberry tree family and national fruit of Bangladesh, the trees produced the largest fruit known to man. Each piece of light green fruit could grow up to thirty inches long and weigh up to eighty pounds.

Along the base of the boundary walls, gorgeous flowers displayed a kaleidoscope of color. Diligently weeding, Nurul was tending a hoe. He stood up and said, "*Sheib*, look at the sky."

I turned around and saw a foreboding black sky coming up on the southern horizon. Massive columns of white billowy clouds advanced against a backdrop black as coal. Lightning strikes danced across the darkness, followed by booming peals of distant thunder. The sky put us on notice. The ugly monsoon storm season had rolled in from the Bay of Bengal.

Monsoons ushered in the rainy season. Over the three months of June through August, the heavens opened up and poured down 120 inches of rain—roughly ten feet of rainwater. That first week thirty-six inches of rain fell in five days. Imagine, our home state of Michigan receiving all its annual precipitation in just one week.

Bangladeshi rivers already swollen from Himalayan snow melts, and now torrential monsoon rain, created annual flooding of enormous proportions. Add tons of rain, measure in flat delta land, and it became a recipe for disastrous suffering. At worst, eighty percent of the country could be under water, with soggy humans, reptiles, and wildlife fighting one another for high ground.

All those factors together made each rainy season begin with the perfect storm. Streets turned into rivers where cars inched along. Rowboats navigated the deeper areas. Along the streets were open storm sewers with all manner of garbage, refuse, and dead vermin. Now overflowed, those putrid sewers turned our neighborhood into a floating cesspool.

Because the Islamic calendar is shorter than a twelve-month year, Allah forbid if the annual Muslim festival of *Qurban* coincided with the monsoons. Then sewage-filled inundated streets turned red from the blood of thousands of cows, slaughtered to atone for the sins of the year. Creepy, reeking, rivers of blood in the streets.

Further complicating things, a combination of heat, humidity, and raw sewage became a spawning ground for all kinds of known and unknown diseases. Epidemics spread like wildfire. Outbreaks of cholera and typhoid fever, especially hard on the elderly and children, happened every year. During monsoon season, I felt as though we were living on a different planet.

Not owning a car and riding in a rickshaw holding two toddlers on our laps was sheer misery. Two American adults would hardly fit on the tiny rickshaw seat. We held umbrellas in front of us to shield the driving rain from our toddlers on our lap, bracing our feet against a little floorboard to keep from falling out.

Often rickshaws hit a hidden pothole, sending riders flying. If not, it still meant arriving drenched from sheets of rainwater. The clay mud was slippery as ice. Walking where a street was supposed to be, knee-high in sewage water, was downright treacherous. It didn't take much to sprain an ankle or bruise your shins.

The last thing you wanted to do was scrape or cut yourself in that water. If that happened, you exposed your body to the most concentrated forms of bacteria known to man. Safe to say, during monsoons, the country became one gigantic petri dish. If a different culture wasn't enough to annoy you as a foreigner, the physical environment did all but guarantee it.

During that first week of monsoons, I received a reality check on how tough life could really be during rainy season. Especially for poor people. Nurul, my often cantankerous but faithful night watchman, came to me and asked for an advance on his weekly *betone* (wages). For his sake and mine, I didn't want to start a precedent of giving advances on wages.

"How much of an advance do you need?" I asked him.

"Eighty *taka* (two dollars)."

"What do you need it for and why now? Can't you wait until payday?"

Payday was only a couple days later.

"The flood waters are rising and starting to come into our house in the refugee camp. My wife cooks in the little place off the side of our room. She wants me to buy bricks to elevate our cooking fire so she can keep cooking food. She also wants a few bricks to squat on so her feet aren't in the water with all the worms."

"How many do you need?"

"New bricks run about six taka each (fifteen cents), and ideally it would be nice if I could buy a dozen."

Nurul waited in eager anticipation for my response to his colossal request for a whole two dollars, enough to buy a dozen new bricks. Here I was, having a conversation with a grown man, father of four, about sun-dried bricks, which for him was a matter of life and death.

My hard heart started to melt. I looked away, choking up. Somehow I reached inside myself and regained my composure. "Nurul, I'm not going to give you an advance. This is an unusual request, and instead of loaning it against your pay, I want to give you the money as a gift."

Not expecting a gift, he beamed as I shelled out two dollars in local currency. His happiness cut through me like a knife. The deluge of thirty-six inches of rain that week paled into insignificance. I stood in my dry veranda and watched him cheerfully ride away in a rickshaw to buy bricks.

Embarrassed at myself, I went inside and crumpled down into my new upholstered chair. Our living room was clean and dry. Nurul's was wet and wormy. I sat alone and gazed at a blurring, polished tile floor as I wiped away tears.

His gratitude and happiness overwhelmed me. I wallowed in coping with culture stress, poverty shock, and privilege guilt. I complained every day of living in a chaotic, broken, and now flooded country. But I didn't live in the filth of a refugee camp. All suffering is relative.

Although daily life was miserable, Nurul taught me that one can still be happy. Living so close to death, he was just thankful to live another day, in a tiny one-room shack with his four kids playing on a worn-out queen size coconut fiber mattress.

Now his wife would be relieved she could stand worm-free on a few bricks while cooking their daily meal of rice. They couldn't afford meat. In the developing world, most poor families ate meat only once a week, if they could afford it. It was astonishing how two dollars' worth of bricks could make a desperately poor family so joyful.

As a Westerner, I found it ironic that achieving a certain affluent lifestyle often brought negative thinking, misery, and unhappiness? In the West, we never seemed to have enough to be happy.

To be truly effective in an impoverished country, I learned a foreign development worker must understand the reality of poverty. In my case, Nurul personally taught me how difficult daily life was for a family living in a hopeless place. If I were to survive and become successful, I had to adjust my expectations.

PRINCIPLE # 17: "Don't worry, be happy"
Happiness all comes down to managing your expectations.

Day after day, monsoon rains poured down tons of water. In the Northern hemisphere, a person could feel cooped up and come down with "cabin fever" during the long snowy winter. In the tropics, rainy season gave me cabin fever, a desire to get out of the house and go somewhere.

My cabin fever became tolerable each time I remembered we didn't have a car, and I didn't feel like wading through sewage water. I especially didn't like being drenched from frequent showers. When the walls felt as if they were closing in, I wandered out to the screened veranda outside our front door. During the rains, Nurul sat in there and shouted at beggar kids to get away from our front gate.

Ordinarily a *Sheib* didn't sit and talk with his house help. I was supposed to make decisions and give orders, not have conversations with uneducated men. I did it anyway, building my Bengali vocabulary, word by word, phrase by phrase. Between Nurul's broken English and my more broken Bengali, we communicated.

Late one afternoon out on the front veranda, Nurul and I sat on *moras,* or short, thatched stools. A gentle rain fell. The call to prayer filled the air, and Nurul dutifully rolled out his green jute prayer rug onto the smooth veranda floor.

His prayer was rote, with several positions on the rug displaying submission to Allah. Upon completing his *namaz,* he rolled up the rug and sat back down on his *mora.* From his tin lunch container, he took out a warm *chapatti* from a wrapped newspaper packet and washed it down with sugary *cha.*

The smell of fresh chapattis, those deep fried, crepe-like thin pieces of bread, infused the moist air in the veranda. Always hospitable with food, he offered me one, but knowing he had four hungry kids at home, I graciously declined.

His prayers and afternoon tea finished, for several minutes we sat in silence. He looked over at me and asked, "*Sheib,* why are there so many religions in Bangladesh?"

"Bangladesh was once a part of India, and some of the oldest religions in the world started in India. Religions try to answer the question—is there life after death."

"What do they all believe?"

I paused before answering, thinking how I would explain metaphysical concepts to a man with only a fourth-grade education. I wasn't worried about the topic because in such an Eastern religious culture, I knew people loved to talk about religion and politics.

From my American, Western culture, with roots from Europe, bringing up those topics would be considered impolite or inconsiderate. Not so in the East, especially Islamic societies.

PRINCIPLE # 18: "Safe conversations"

Every culture has wildly different safe and unsafe topics of discussion. To be inoffensive and fit in, learning these is critical.

"Well, Hindus believe in appeasing their choice of gods, working to a better next life."

I began counting off religions on my fingers.

"Buddhists are similar but try to deny suffering to achieve a better next life. Both religions believe in reincarnation. Animists, like the tribal groups in the hill tracts, believe in pleasing the spirits of their ancestors who live in places like trees, wind, and water. Muslims believe keeping the law and obeying the Quran will get them into paradise."

"What about Christians? Aren't all Americans Christians?"

"Just because a person is born in America and has a Christian name doesn't mean he is a true Christian. In my country I would call them 'cultural Christians,' because if they were true believers they would practice their faith."

"I understand. We have people who are not true believers in Islam."

"Here there are people born with Muslim names who don't go to the Mosque, don't pray, and don't make sacrifices. I would say such people are 'cultural Muslims,' not true Muslims because they also don't practice their faith," I said.

"So, what are unbelievers called?"

"One group, called agnostics, don't really know for sure if there is life after death. The other group is called atheists, who don't believe there is any God or life after death."

With a look of fascination, he turned his *mora* to face me. Pouring another cup of *cha,* he took a sip and looked right at me. Unlike those of Western cultures, cultures of the East usually have no problem discussing politics and religion, especially religion.

"Tell me what devout Christians believe about their religion."

"Christians base their beliefs on the Bible just as Muslims base theirs on the Quran. The Bible says all people do things that disappoint a holy God, and because of that, they can't go to heaven."

"Muslims believe that too," he said.

"Christians believe in Jesus Christ, who Muslims call the prophet *Isa.* Jesus was a special person who lived a sinless life and died to become a human sacrifice to pay for all of mankind's shortcomings."

"So, do Christians sacrifice cows as we do during *Qurban*?"

"No, the Bible says only a human can die a sacrificial death for another human, and *Isa* (Jesus) was the only person qualified to pay our debt."

"So, what does a Christian have to do to get into paradise?"

"All one has to do to become a Christian is recognize he can't be good enough to save himself and make a decision."

"Decision about what?"

"A decision to believe the value of *Isa's* (Jesus') sacrificial death can be applied to his account. When that happens, God forgives all his bad thoughts and deeds. Believing in Jesus means you transfer your faith from off your good works and onto what Jesus did on your behalf when he died on the cross."

"But, *Sheib,* what does a Christian have to do in his religion other than believe in *Isa?*"

"By trusting in *Isa,* he doesn't have to do anything. He just lives a grateful life for being forgiven and follows the teachings of the Bible. We can't be good enough to earn our salvation."

A big smile broke on Nurul's face, and he began shaking his head from side to side.

"No, *Sheib,* I'm sorry, your religion is too easy, way too easy."

Surprised, I asked Nurul what he meant by "too easy."

"In my religion, I have to do things. I have to say out loud there is only one God, Allah, and the Prophet Muhammed is his messenger; pray five times a day; give alms to the poor; fast for a month each year; and hope someday to make a pilgrimage to Mecca. It's a lot of work to be a good Muslim."

"Wouldn't it be nice if you didn't have to do good works, all your wrongs were forgiven, and when you died you went straight to heaven?"

He started to laugh.

"*Sheib*, I hear what you are saying, but this religion is too simple, too easy, it's not a real religion."

Too easy? Not a real religion? I hadn't thought of the Christian faith that way. Apparently, I had not communicated what true Christianity entailed, particularly a person can be forgiven because of God's love and forgiveness.

The front door made a creaking sound and opened. Rebecca leaned out.

"Phil, I need you, can you come?"

Inside the house, Markie, our nineteen-month-old, was spinning around on the terrazzo floor, his ear to the floor, crying in pain.

"I can't take it anymore," Rebecca said, her voice shaking with fear. "We've got to talk to an ear, nose, and throat specialist. I'm going over and use our friend's telephone to call the States."

Hours later she returned.

"The ENT specialist in Michigan says I need to get Markie back there immediately. We probably overtreated his ear infections with antibiotics and now there is a danger of fungus eating away inside his head."

"What do you mean?"

"The doctor said we overtreated him with antibiotics."

"What?"

"We killed off his friendly bacteria, leaving a vacuum for the fungus to take over. We upset the equilibrium of the bacteria/fungus battle that goes on in our body all the time."

Because Marky's condition was a medical emergency, the airline put them on the next international flight out. My wife knew she had to act because in a place with inadequate health care, delaying could be catastrophic.

PRINCIPLE # 19: "Own your health care"

In areas with insufficient healthcare, don't wait or leave anything to chance. You have to own your health care.

Matt and I stayed in Dhaka. A few days later I got a call from America. Rebecca blurted out phrases between sobs.

"Mark has to have surgery right away. The tests show the fungus is eating through his mastoid bone, and if it penetrates to his brain, he could die in days. Please come home. I can't go through this surgery by myself, especially if it's too late."

CHAPTER 11

MOVING TO MANILA

*Passion is energy. Feel the power that comes
from focusing on what excites you.*

—Oprah Winfrey

SUMMER IN MICHIGAN was a welcome relief from the oppressive heat and humidity of monsoon season. I looked forward to being back in the States for the first time since moving to Bangladesh. Because Mark's condition was life or death, I was able to buy plane tickets, arriving home two days later.

At the airport, Rebecca flew into our arms for a three-way hug. While waiting at the baggage carousel, she said, "Mark's surgery is tomorrow morning. The surgeon agreed to wait until you got home."

Early the next morning we arrived at the hospital, checked in, and soon little Mark was being prepped for surgery. Two pastors from a church came to pray over our baby boy because of the delicate operation being performed on a nineteen-month-old.

"You better pray like hell," said our surgeon as he walked into our area filled with clergy suits. A grin on his face, he couldn't resist getting under their skin and then got serious. "We should have your boy back to you in a couple of hours if all goes well."

Waiting. Difficult for any family member, especially parents of a toddler. Conversation made the time go faster. After several cups of coffee regaling ministers with stories of Bangladesh, before we knew it, the surgery was complete.

Down the hall we heard the squeaky wheels of a pediatric gurney. Not just any wheeled bed, but one fashioned with a cage to keep our toddler from falling out once the anesthesia wore off. A few minutes later the surgeon appeared.

A family friend, back in the day he and my father-in-law did their surgical residency together, right in our hometown. He sat for a moment and exhaled a big sigh.

"It was difficult but surgery went well. I had to grind out most of the mastoid bone to get all the fungus. It's like a sponge of bone, so I took it all out and then polished the inside cavity, so if there is any fungus left, it will be hard for it to attach itself. The bad news is there isn't much bone left between his mastoid and his brain. The good news is I'm pretty sure I got all the fungus. And we got it just in time."

Rebecca and I sat rattled, comprehending the seriousness of the news.

"Now you can honestly say your son has a hole in his head. He'll be fine."

At that precise moment, comic relief was what we needed.

"How long will it be before we can go back to Bangladesh?" I asked.

"It will be several months, probably by this fall sometime. But you need to think about working in another country that has good ENT care."

Mark's surgeon served in Pakistan with the Peace Corp, so he understood our desire to return overseas. Our homework was cut out for us, and we researched countries where our NGO worked that had good medical specialists in ear, nose, and throat (ENT). The best option was in the Philippines.

Metro-Manila had good Filipino ENT doctors, plus our organization recently joined a consortium to start a private graduate school. I could teach classes in a master's degree program. The position required moving our household from Bangladesh to our new post in Manila.

The ENT doctor granted medical clearance to leave, and we returned to Dhaka to close up our house. Days turned into weeks as we packed, gave away some things, and sold off stuff we didn't want to take to the Philippines. I called it "international downtime," a necessary expenditure of time and energy to move from one country to another.

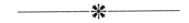

Our move to the Philippines was a welcome relief from our difficult time in Bangladesh. After 400 years of Spanish colonial rule, arriving at Christmastime in this Catholic country was more than festive, with familiar sights and sounds of the nativity.

Manila was a robust modern city with five-star hotels and public buildings decorated to the hilt. Christmas-themed ballets, operas, and concerts were in full tilt. On top of everything else, Filipinos were excellent English speakers.

Our NGO maintained a guest house with a swimming pool. Once the holidays were over, we began the arduous task of searching for a place to live. Before the Internet and online rental listings, we relied on newspapers and word of mouth. But nothing met our needs. Weeks went by and we became discouraged. Finally, a friend of a friend insisted we talk to Mildred.

Mildred, a national TV personality, was classy and gorgeous. Even more amazing, she was more beautiful on the inside. Within minutes of meeting each other, my classy wife and Mildred hit it off, talking decorating, raising boys, and living in Manila. For Rebecca, Mildred made our move to the Philippines a delight.

The fully furnished and decorated three-bedroom home was perfect. Located in a guarded subdivision, it was in close proximity to my office at the new school. Like our house in Dhaka, a walled backyard was the right size for our kids to play.

Inside, the main living and dining area sported an arboretum under a glass roof. All the main floors and stairway were marble, due to its low price. Best of all, the house was ready to move into, with rooms nicely decorated with heavy Spanish-style furniture.

"Mildred, why did you move from here, and why is it still furnished?" I asked.

"My husband is a Lieutenant Colonel in the Constabulary, and his boss, General Ramos, made us move into the military cantonment up the hill. My husband is a target of the communists, so it's for our own safety. But we hated to move out."

In Manila alone, communist rebels of the National People's Party (NPA) assassinated a policeman a day and a Lieutenant Colonel a week. Known as sparrow units, two insurgents on a motorcycle would pull up to a policeman, and the one on the back would pull out a revolver and kill the cop at point blank range. In retaliation, right-wing death squads killed communists. The country was on the verge of civil war.

Mildred broke the awkward silence.

"We weren't sure we were going to rent out the house because it's our home. Having met you, I really want you to rent it and take care of it for me."

Mildred offered a ridiculously low amount of rent, and we agreed to rent her villa. She drew up the papers and to my surprise the lease agreement was between Rebecca and Mildred. Unlike other Asian countries where men made the decisions and signed the documents, the Catholic Philippines was a matriarchal culture.

A gardener and duck came with the house. We excused the gardener but kept the duck. Our friends called it "McDonald's Duck," which morphed into "Donald Duck," and finally became known simply as "McDuck." Matt and Mark were in heaven chasing around the waddling, quacking brown duck.

PRINCIPLE # 20: "A grand adventure"

International living as a family is a grand adventure and worth the effort, as it presents opportunities like no other.

Responsible for lawn care, I hired a college student to mow our grass once a week. His pay covered his tuition in full. Mildred's rusty old reel hand mower still worked. It didn't occur to me I should show him how to mow because I thought every guy knew how to mow a lawn.

A half hour later I looked out in the backyard. To me, the way he mowed seemed unorthodox. He stood and mowed by pushing the reel mower forward as far as he could reach. Then he pulled it back to himself and mowed one reel width again to the left.

Once he mowed a full circle by standing in the middle, he moved to another part of the lawn and did the same thing. When all the circles were finished, his machine cut what grass was left between circles.

Those of us from the West think linearly, meaning we mow in straight lines because we think in squares. Asians think in circles. I never "corrected" his method because all that mattered was the lawn got mowed.

What irritated my mower was the duck that lived in our yard. He hated that duck. One day he caught McDuck, tied its leg to a bush, and left him there with food and water. The next day our boys discovered McDuck had died, probably from a broken heart. Our first family pet was dead, and we grieved over that annoying, adorable duck.

PRINCIPLE # 21: "Lighten up"

Learn to accept a foreign culture's way of doing things, especially if it isn't critical. If you do, it will lower your stress. All that matters is it gets done.

Settled into my new office at the school, I split my time between course preparation, teaching, and administration. Extension graduate education was a new idea, and our goal was to create teaching sites in major Asian cities.

In an attempt to stem the "brain drain," the concept was to bring American professors to the students instead of bringing foreign students to America to study. The track record was ninety percent of students from poor developing countries never went back home after studying in the States or Europe. After what I already lived through in the third world, I couldn't say I blamed them.

Inherent was the fact that if our plan worked, we would be providing an educational opportunity for thousands of students to obtain an accredited master's degree. Not just any master's degree.

One from an American institution of higher learning they would never get otherwise.

This paradigm, a new method of delivering education, required a massive amount of planning and paperwork. Our office was an extension of a graduate school in America, and as administrators, we had to please and convince the US accrediting agency that our educational programs met their academic standards.

Otherwise, our overseas program could cause our stateside parent institution to lose their accreditation. Consequently, a lot was at stake, so we worked extremely hard to prove our educational delivery in a foreign land was just as good as in America.

A son of a professor, I had no illusions of what was required of a professor. Status and prestige aside, the job entailed a great deal of repetitive work. Teaching the same material year after year becomes monotonous. I saw my dad get bored to the point he took early retirement.

Dad used to say adding a new course to a college curriculum was like pulling hen's teeth. Academia could be rigid. Although I enjoyed teaching, I learned I needed more of a challenge. Other than teaching, as administrative staff, our primary task in Manila was setting up new programs and new teaching sites around Asia.

That turned my buttons. I found I enjoyed starting something new from scratch. Call it an entrepreneurial spirit, a creative outlet, but it was a significant discovery on what motivated me. I learned planning and setting up new things energized me.

PRINCIPLE # 22: "Follow your passion"

Early in your career, learn what you are good at and what you are passionate about. Then saddle up your horse; you have a trail to blaze.

My colleagues, two other American professors, were equally excited, making our faculty meetings productive. My PhD in educational planning came in handy as we organized teaching sites in the major cities of South and Southeast Asia: Hong Kong, Rangoon, Bangkok, Singapore, Bangalore, to name a few. It was ambitious but we were all young, passionate about the cause, and loved to travel.

One day I needed a specific book and ventured out to a bookstore. I pulled into the parking lot, got out of my newly purchased car, and heard rapid-fire gunshots coming from across the street. A Filipina pulled in beside me.

"Sir, get down," she shouted.

I hit the deck as bullets flew everywhere. Across the street a bank robbery was in process. The bank's armed guards fired back. With concrete buildings lining both sides of the street, bullets ricocheted in all directions. I hugged the ground.

The firefight lasted at least a minute, followed by silence. I'm here to tell you, humans shooting at each other constitutes a very, very long minute.

CHAPTER 12

RANGOON

> Within a system which denies the existence of basic human rights,
> fear tends to be the order of the day. Fear of imprisonment,
> fear of torture, fear of death, fear of losing friends, family,
> property or means of livelihood, fear of poverty,
> fear of isolation, fear of failure.
>
> —Daw Aung San Suu Kyi

LIKE PRAIRIE DOGS peering out their holes, a few of us peeked over our car hoods wondering when it was safe to get up. I stood up and started for the bookstore door when the robbers returned, guns blazing. All of us bystanders hit the deck a second time.

The bank guards held them off and the robbers gave up the fight. I kept thinking those security guards sure didn't get paid enough.

I bought my book but found it difficult to just walk out the door of the store. I scrutinized the street through the glass door, looked both ways, and sprinted to my car. Late for our afternoon faculty meeting, I told my two colleagues about the gun battle.

"Since you weren't in the military like us, I guess you aren't used to bullets whizzing by," said Joe, a former U.S. marine.

Ron, the director of our graduate program, had served in the US military and was in a jovial mood.

"Welcome to Manila. We average six bank robberies a day, and with the communist rebellion, its part war zone and part Wild West. You'll get used to it."

Ron wasn't kidding about the Wild West. Every time we took our kids to McDonald's for a hamburger or "McSpaghetti," a Filipino specialty, we waited in line to enter the restaurant. Customers in front of us checked their guns in at the door to two uniformed, heavily armed security guards.

The communists kidnapped wealthy kids for ransom. Wealthy families drove up to the restaurant in their luxury cars, accompanied by a vehicle in front and behind, full of armed bodyguards. Walkie-talkies in hand, all communicated continuously with one another. In addition to their bodyguards, the wealthy hired right-wing death squads to exact revenge on communists.

Mildred also warned us about the sound of gunfire. Down the hill from our subdivision was a military gun range. Every afternoon the irritating noise of automatic weapons echoed across the valley. Our toddlers eventually learned to nap through it. Even still, the constant sound was aggravating, especially the "thud, thud, thud" sound of a fifty-caliber machine gun.

Rebecca, who survived two wars before the age of fifteen, knew firsthand how important it was to lead our children. As a parent, whatever emotion you show, whether fear, anger, disgust, delight or acceptance, your children will mimic.

PRINCIPLE # 23: "Take a chill pill"

As Western foreigners living in a politically unstable country, the rule is parents need to remain calm and go with the flow, because as the parents go, so go the children.

Ron returned to the States for fundraising and reporting. I was left in charge. Several weeks went by. About to leave the office one day, the secretary came around the corner.

"You have an international call on line one."

I picked up the phone and heard Ron's voice.

"Phil, I got good news. After more than twenty years, Burma has agreed to grant Americans visas. I know a guy who can get us into Rangoon and help us set up a teaching site. I need you to meet him there and teach the first class."

"Who is he?" I asked.

"He's an American. Everyone calls him Uncle Jim because he lived in India for forty years. He went to Burma many times back when it was still a British colony. He's retired now but he wants to go back to Rangoon, maybe for the last time. He's in his late seventies."

Between 1964 and 1987, Burma, later known as Myanmar, was off limits to Americans. During the cold war, the Soviet Union and Burma had a close relationship. For all intents and purposes, it was a Soviet satellite, and Soviet advisors helped the Burmese military dictatorship stay in power and keep control.

When Burma got its independence from Great Britain in 1948, it had the second strongest economy in Southeast Asia. After the military coup in 1962, the dictatorship adopted socialist policies that destroyed the economy. Now Ron wanted me to go there.

Burma. That closed-off country I lived next to in Bangladesh. In 1971, during the Bangladesh war of independence, the Pakistan army's genocide was advancing towards the hospital compound. The Americans, including Rebecca, were forced to evacuate the compound and escaped through Burma.

Now it was my turn to visit the mysterious country. There were restrictions. I could only travel to Rangoon by air and couldn't go outside of Rangoon without special permission. A totalitarian state kept control by restricting movement of its citizens. A visa was required to visit another city.

Rebecca drove me to the Manila airport for my flight to Bangkok, Thailand. I kissed her goodbye, and then she looked up into my face with that intentional look.

"I'm not sure I have a good feeling about this trip. Please call me once you get to Rangoon."

"I'll try. We're staying at the only hotel in Rangoon that allows foreigners. I assume they have phones that make international calls."

The only air service to Burma from Manila was through Bangkok, Thailand. The plan was I would meet Uncle Jim at the gate in the Bangkok airport and fly together to Rangoon. When I got to the gate, there wasn't anyone who looked like Uncle Jim. I thought I might have to go this alone.

After the fantastic experience on board the Thai Airways flight from Manila, I was in for a shock. The Burma Airways aircraft, an old and dirty turboprop, shook on takeoff.

Our in-flight meal consisted of two pieces of bread separated with a thin slice of cheese, all wrapped in waxed paper. I opened my sandwich and realized we had company.

The smell of cheese became a dinner bell to resident cockroaches. Tentacles appeared from everywhere, starting from the empty pouch on the seat in front of me and crawling over my headrest onto my shoulder. The plane was infested.

Hungry, I ate the sandwich as fast as possible but passed on the glass of water, not knowing if it was filtered. No way was I sharing my food with the bugs. Later, I learned from an American pilot that roaches eat wires. Normal airlines close up and fumigate a plane for at least a day if even one bug is discovered. But Burma Airways was not a normal airline.

In Rangoon, we deplaned and walked across the tarmac to the back side of the terminal. A rickety wagon pulled by men delivered our luggage. Now dark, I stumbled over broken cement searching for my suitcase. Before long, my bag was the only one left. I grabbed it and ventured inside for my next stop—immigration and customs.

An old facility built during colonial days, it felt worn out. The building had a high ceiling with an occasional lightbulb hanging from a wire. Walls were dirty and cobwebs dangled over broken window panes. The atmosphere was quiet, controlled, and intimidating.

My immigration officer and customs officer were one and the same. He led me to my table. In broken English, he asked for my passport. I handed it to him with my right hand while touching my right elbow with my left hand, a sign of respect in that part of the world.

Surprised a Western foreigner knew of such a gesture, he stepped back in wonder. His stern demeanor instantly changed and he visibly relaxed. That caused me to relax.

PRINCIPLE # 24: "Show some respect"

All cultures require respect. Knowing how to express respect in the proper way, even if it may seem silly or odd to you, may endear you to your host culture and drive your success.

He studied my passport intensely before giving me instructions.

"You take all items out of suitcase. Line them up on table. List them on paper. When you come back to leave airport, all items on list must be with you or else you not leaving Burma."

Got it. Clearly he wasn't joking. I listed everything. A former Boy Scout, I packed my suitcase prepared for anything and everything. Friends called my bag a portable pharmacy. To this day I use an elaborate checklist when I travel.

Forty-five minutes later he returned and meticulously checked my belongings against my list. I thought my list was complete until he reminded me to record my suitcase, briefcase, and all the clothes I was wearing. Of course, I forgot to log my watch, eyeglasses, and wedding ring.

But I wasn't done. I had to show him all my credit cards and cash in each currency, which he dutifully counted out in front of me to make sure my amounts were accurate. When I came back to the airport, I needed to return with receipts and leftover currencies to prove my expenditures were legitimate. My expenses and receipts would have to match, or I would be accused of smuggling in money. I guess I got off easy because he didn't make me count out my pills in each bottle.

The officer stamped the list and tucked it in my passport. My first introduction to a totalitarian, communist police state clearly taught me that a person was owned by the government. Totalitarian meant that the government totally controlled your life.

He frisked me for a second time and then led me to the arrival hall. I muscled my way through a crowd to get through the exit door. Outside, I looked for an old American. Still no sign of Uncle Jim.

The empty airport parking lot was a surprise. Absent were taxis or vehicles of any kind, and the city was too far for any rickshaws. I didn't know what to do. An older Burmese gentleman moseyed over.

"You Dr. McDonald?"

"Yes."

"Uncle Jim coming. Getting vehicle. I know him many years."

"What's your name?"

"Not here. I tell you later."

He wouldn't shake hands. In silence we stood staring out into a vacant parking lot until a pickup driven by a Burmese driver careened around the corner. The vehicle pulled up. Uncle Jim stepped out from the passenger seat onto the curbside and walked up to me.

"You must be Phil."

"Yes, sir, and am I glad to see you."

No time to shake hands, I sensed he was in a hurry. He nervously put his hands on his hips and leaned forward past my face and spoke softly into my ear.

"We need to get out of here fast so I can tell you something important. Government agents have been assigned to us, so I can't tell you here with all these people listening."

Before Uncle Jim hopped back into the pickup, the old man who found me slid over in the middle of the bench seat. I climbed into the back bed of the pickup, and with the bumps in the road, I held on to my bags for dear life. Once in town, our truck pulled off the main road, went down a side street, and came to a stop.

The three men in the front seat waited until reassured we weren't followed. Uncle Jim got out.

"The airport was in disarray, so I wanted to get out of there before I told you the bad news. A few hours ago another Burma Airways flight crashed north of here. I heard Americans were on that plane. The airline started the year with a fleet of six planes and now they have crashed two."

That fateful day, Sunday, October 11, 1987, Burma suffered its worst air disaster ever. The pilot accidentally flew the Folker 27 into a mountain, killing forty-nine, including thirty-nine foreigners, fourteen of them Americans. In June of the same year, another Burma Airways plane also crashed into a mountain, killing all forty-five people.

"Why are they crashing planes?" I asked.

"Poor training and poor maintenance. The bad news is we get to fly out of here on one of the remaining aircraft. There are no other airlines allowed to fly in here other than Aeroflot."

Aeroflot was the international carrier for the Soviet Union, and during the cold war the airline was off limits to Americans.

"When we get to the hotel and check you in, don't be surprised when they take your passport and keep it. The government holds them responsible for us. By the way, the hotel is overbooked, so we are sharing a room."

Checked in and up in our hotel room, I unpacked and called the hotel receptionist to book an international call. Each time I rang the front desk, I got a busy signal. I dialed over and over for an hour. Jim sensed my frustration.

"I'm going down to the lobby to see if I can find out what's going on."

A half hour later Jim came back.

"Well, the fourteen dead Americans were all staying here. They had flown up country to visit a tourist site when it crashed. Right now the hotel staff and diplomats are cleaning out all the dead foreigners' rooms. Also found out there are only three international phone lines out of the country, and they expect them to be jammed for the next few days."

I got ready for bed and sat down dejected. Jim saw my forlorn look and in a soft, raspy voice said something that would haunt me for several days.

"Hate to mention this, but once our families hear several Americans died in a plane crash in Burma, and don't hear from us, they're going to think we're dead too."

CHAPTER 13

"PHIL IS MISSING"

No one seems to know where he is. All our sources could confirm
is that Phil flew into Burma the same day as the plane crash.
Phil is missing.

—Mildred Templo, Filipina media personality,
and wife of General Templo

UNCLE JIM NUDGED me awake at dawn. Up for hours,
the elderly man had trouble sleeping.

"Get ready," he whispered in my ear. "We're having breakfast at
a student's house around the corner. Believe me, his wife is a great
cook, and her food is better than anything we would get here."

His demeanor was creepy and I must have shown my reaction.
He leaned into my ear again.

"I have to whisper because our room is bugged. Don't say anything out loud that is important to why we are here, where we are
going, or who we are with."

The old man was so used to operating in a police state, the night
before he forgot to warn me about what to say out loud. With the

authorities listening to us, it felt as though I was part of an undercover operation. And that was a very strange feeling.

My hotel bath towel was more a rag than anything else. Though once white, it was now a grayish, thin piece of cloth. I noticed Jim washed out his pair of pants, shirt, and underwear, all drying on his towel rack.

"Yep, I travel light. Carry an extra set of clothes. Every night I wash what I wore that day and let them dry while I wear the other set the next day," Jim said in a normal tone of voice.

I noticed his little bag of laundry detergent in the bathroom and got the feeling he had traveled like that for years, many years.

Before leaving, I attempted another call to my wife but no luck. I hung up the phone with a sick feeling. Every day not getting through would increase her anxiety and my stress.

According to Uncle Jim, the student's apartment was nice for Rangoon standards. A modest-sized great room contained a living area, dining area, and kitchen. Soft rays of an early morning sun glowed on the teak floor. The room's curtains were drawn for privacy, but the front door remained open to see when our ride arrived.

My student, a tall but overweight Burmese, wore thick glasses. Middle-aged, he only went by Dr. Z. The whole society lived in secrecy and paranoia. In a communist police state, where everyone told on their neighbors, people were afraid to say their own name out loud.

Dr. Z's wife, tall and elegant, glided around the kitchen in a majestic green sarong. Breakfast was enjoyable—a piece of buttered toast and a bowl of dove egg soup. Miniature hard-boiled eggs floated in a clear broth flavored by pungent cilantro. The soup was amazing. Typical of Asian hospitality, she hovered. Graceful and humble, she didn't say much.

"What's your story, Dr. Z?" I asked.

"I was fortunate to be the first Burmese student to earn a doctorate from the Sorbonne University in Paris. After I completed my degree, I came back to a good government job in the procurement department. Unfortunately, my boss got our whole department into a lot of trouble."

"What happened?"

"He bought an old ship from North Korea but charged our government for a new one and personally pocketed the difference. The police came and arrested our whole department. I spent two years in jail for something I didn't do or even know about."

"So, what did you do when you got out?"

"With a prison record, my reputation was shattered. Our education system is quite lacking, so I make a living by tutoring students."

I felt weird as Dr. Z's professor. A brilliant electrical engineer, the formula in his dissertation became a template for electrical grids throughout Europe. A true scholar sidelined in a country run by a corrupt, brutal regime.

In essence, a world-class education from a prestigious European university didn't mean much in a communist state with limited employment opportunities.

The old pickup that brought us from the airport pulled up outside Dr. Z's apartment. I turned around and gazed out the open front door at the vehicle waiting for us.

"Not too many vehicles on the road. How did you find this vehicle?" I asked.

Uncle Jim wiped his chin before responding.

"Friend of a friend. The government doesn't allow any imported cars and doesn't make them. Used cars and trucks are quite expensive."

"How expensive?"

Uncle Jim didn't know the answer. Dr. Z quickly did some calculations in his mind.

"In our currency, that pickup out there cost 60,000 US dollars, and fuel costs forty dollars a gallon," said Dr. Z.

With a spoonful of soup almost to my mouth, I sat stunned, wondering if I heard him wrong.

"Did you . . . did you say 6,000 or 60,000?" I asked.

"60,000."

"How does your friend afford it?" I asked Uncle Jim.

Jim slowly raised another spoonful of soup to his mouth.

"He owns a gold mine."

I burst out laughing. At this point I put my soup spoon down for good. My eyebrows raised, I just had to explore this.

"He owns a gold mine?

"Yep, every country needs gold, especially one that's cut off from the world economic system."

"Wait a minute. I thought this was a communist country where the government owns everything."

Uncle Jim continued to sip soup and looked over at Dr. Z to explain.

"Technically, the government does own all the land and all enterprises. But practically, government officials don't make much money. I should know, I was one. There is an underground economy. Under the table, private enterprise does exist as long as you pay off a government official to look the other way."

Breakfast finished, we thanked Mrs. Z and headed for the door. Dr. Z's wife reminded him to carry his government identification documentation. No one left home without it. Well, everyone except Uncle Jim and me.

Hopefully our passports were in safe keeping at the hotel. Feeling naked without some form of identification, I vowed from then on, whenever I traveled, to carry a photocopy of my passport, especially in a totalitarian state.

Uncle Jim got in with the gold miner's driver, along with the older man who met me at the airport. Dr. Z and I climbed into the pickup bed and sat on dirty burlap bags. Why were the two of us with earned doctorates seated in the truck bed? Our youth took a backseat to the older passengers seated in the front.

Like much of Asia, the Burmese venerated age and the elderly were given priority. Credentials certainly didn't put us in the back bed of the pickup; being younger did. Asians have a thing about pecking order when it comes to age.

The clunker of a pickup dodged potholes as we snaked through Rangoon's backstreets. The driver stopped and parked in front of a large house where students waited in an upstairs room. Huge open rafters served as the ceiling. A teak table and wooden chair served as my desk. On the corner of my table sat a little brass bell.

The floors, walls, rafters, and roof built out of dark tropical hardwood accompanied wide open windows without screens. A chilly morning breeze flowed through the room. Our makeshift classroom, with no decorations or chalkboard, worked for us.

Once seated, my fourteen students would face me from behind similar wooden tables and chairs. As I unpacked my briefcase of new, thick books from America, student chatter stopped. All stood mesmerized, staring at my books. No book publishing industry existed in their country. The students regarded my reference textbooks more precious than gold.

Uncle Jim stood in the back corner and motioned me over to introduce a couple of students who traveled the farthest.

"These guys came from way up north near the Chinese border, about a thousand miles from here. It took them over a week to get here traveling by foot, horseback, ferry, and the train."

Their long journey, just to hear me lecture, humbled me.

Time for class to start, I rang the little brass bell. In Asia, typically the professor, the master, only spoke. At the opening of any new class though, I deliberately broke the Asian custom. I did the American custom by asking the students to introduce themselves.

Although this made them uncomfortable, I had a method to my madness. It allowed me to gauge their spoken English. Most could say their name, where they were from, but not much more. By midmorning, the younger students struggled to understand my spoken English. During the break I motioned Dr. Z over and asked his opinion.

"Those of us who went to school during British colonial days learned good English. But after independence, our schools changed the teaching medium from English to Burmese. That's why these younger students don't know much English," he said.

"I'm not quite sure what to do."

"It might help if you could lecture with a British accent because that's all the students have ever heard, mostly by listening to the BBC."

"Um, I'm not comfortable with that."

This first class was a test, an assessment of the Burmese students' academic ability to learn at a master's degree level. All of them were vetted for credentials, meaning all were university graduates with high marks.

No question they were smart, but not understanding spoken English well was a problem. Dr. Z agreed to interpret for me. That presented a new challenge because it cut in half what material I could teach. When I said something, I had to wait the same amount of time or longer while he repeated it in Burmese.

Out of nervousness on the first day, I caught myself using American idioms as I spoke. Dr. Z would stop me with a confused look on his face, unable to interpret my expression. My mistake of using colloquial words or phrases delayed us even further as I searched my brain to speak more simply.

PRINCIPLE # 25: "Know your audience"

Don't use idioms when speaking to persons where English isn't their first language. American idioms like "Wait, what?" or "Shut up, get out" are cultural expressions that don't literally mean what is being said. If you are not "in the know," then idioms are confusing.

Back home in the Philippines, my wife waited for some word about her husband's fate. One morning, a persistent knock on her bedroom door demanded her attention. Her wet hair up in a towel, Rebecca opened it a crack to see our housekeeper, Ging-Ging.

"You have an important phone call from sir's office."

"Tell them I'm coming," Rebecca said as she hurried to get dressed. She picked up the phone.

"Sorry for the delay," Rebecca said.

"It's okay. Have you heard from Phil?" the secretary asked.

"No, he said he would call me once he got to Rangoon."

A long pause came on the end of the line.

"Did you hear about the plane crash in Burma?"

"No."

"All we know is a plane crashed Sunday, and everyone on board was killed, including fourteen Americans. I thought you should know."

"Do we know who they were?"

"No one is releasing the names until next of kin are notified."

Another long pause followed until Rebecca said, "Okay. I'll see what I can find out. Let me know if you hear anything."

Rebecca hung up the phone and slowly sat down. Thoughts raced through her mind as to what to do. After calls to the American embassy, other embassies, and Thai Airways, she got nowhere. Burma didn't have an embassy in Manila. Part of the Soviet orbit, it was cut off from the free world and liked it that way.

Days went by without anyone contacting her as "next of kin." No answers from anyone, she called Mildred. A few hours later, Mildred called back.

"I had my husband's office make some contacts and finally reached someone who had the passenger manifest. They said Phil's name isn't on the list."

"But he hasn't called."

"Maybe he is still alive."

"No, he would have called by now."

Mildred paused, knowing she had no other answers.

"No one seems to know where he is. All our sources could confirm is that Phil flew into Burma the same day as the plane crash. Phil is missing."

---————————❋————————---

Every morning before class and evening after class, I tried to book an international call home. In an age before mobile phones, satellite phones, and the Internet, it was downright frustrating. Uncle Jim grew frustrated listening to me.

After more failed attempts, he stormed downstairs and yelled at the locals, colonial style. I'm glad I wasn't down there because I'd seen how he treated the Burmese. He talked down to them as if they were children. Although I didn't approve of his condescending behavior, nevertheless it got results A few minutes later he returned, having leveraged his "superior position" as the white foreigner with the Burmese hotel manager.

"I told the manager he'd better book you an international telephone line, or I would report him to the authorities. He said to wait by the phone."

Moments later the phone rang. I picked up, gave the operator our house phone number in Manila, and hung up. Within a few minutes my phone rang again.

"Sir, I'm connecting you to your number."

The phone at our Manila house rang several times. I wondered if it was a wrong number. In the developing world, it wasn't unusual on a feeble landline to dial the right phone number and get someone else. Rebecca answered the phone.

"Hey, it's me, in Rangoon."

Momentary silence followed with deep sobs. I waited until she could talk.

"I thought you were dead. No one could find out where you were. All we knew was the plane crashed and everyone on board was dead. Even Mildred said you were missing."

"It did crash but it wasn't my plane. A domestic flight up country crashed right before I landed from Bangkok."

"Why didn't you call?"

"I've been trying for days, but there are only three international lines servicing the whole country. Uncle Jim finally got someone to get through to you."

"When are you coming home?"

"I'm on schedule, so in a couple days."

I didn't tell her about the horrific track record of Burma Airways crashing planes that year. Frankly, I didn't even want to think about getting on one of their remaining planes. But the only way home, I was ready to leave.

On my last day of class Uncle Jim pulled me aside and said, "The students are grateful for us, so we are invited to a feast after class."

Students met us at another large house on the outskirts of Rangoon. As their teacher, I sat on an elevated platform. As an American raised to treat everyone equally, it was awkward to be literally seated higher than all the others.

Gifts were given and speeches made. I kept thinking of the week-long trek home for many of them. I felt so unworthy when I thought of their sacrifice for more education. Their trip to Rangoon for classroom hours of instruction would be the first of many trips towards their master's degree. Once back home, over the following three months, the students would have readings and term papers to complete to fulfill the requirements for each course.

The next morning the gold miner's driver drove Uncle Jim and me to the airport. Our boarding passes in hand, the same customs official came and escorted us to our tables. I emptied my suitcase and pulled out my official list of personal goods. He checked each item off, handed it back, and I was free to go. Operative word "free" to go. I was eager to leave his totalitarian state.

Our rickety Burma Airways plane touched down on the Bangkok runway. I let out a sigh of relief. Inside the terminal I said goodbye to Uncle Jim, he nodded, shook my hand, turned around, and walked to his gate. I never saw Uncle Jim again.

Back home in Manila felt good. A taxi dropped me off at our house, and two little munchkins ran out and hugged my legs.

"Daddy, we were worried about you. Mommy didn't know where you were!" said Matt.

I gave a bear hug to the love of my life. Then I whispered into her ear, "Even though you thought I was dead, I kept my promise. I didn't die on you."

The owner of a vacant lot next to our house decided it was time to build his new home. Filipinos were friendly and outgoing, but his construction crew was surly and unfriendly. Even seemed shifty at times. I soon discovered why.

Our water pressure only fluctuated when the construction crew worked at the site. Desperate for water and unbeknown to us, they had tapped into our water line.

Outside in the backyard with my boys, I heard a shriek come from the upstairs bathroom attached to our master bedroom. Off our bedroom was a small balcony. A few moments later Rebecca appeared in a robe with shampoo still in her hair.

"Would you please stop what you are doing so I can finish washing my hair. At least steal our water when I'm done," she shouted.

The disinterested workers laughed and I hit a breaking point. Incensed, I marched over and commanded the foreman to unhook from our water line. He defiantly refused.

My only recourse, I called my landlord, the busy Lieutenant Colonel fighting a war against communist rebels. He promised to help. One of his captains showed up and we strolled the backyard. I showed him where and how they tapped into our water line.

He thought for a moment and then walked over to the wall separating our yard from their construction site.

"You guys need to unhook from this water line," the captain said.

"We can't."

"Why?"

"Because we have to make cement and the water company is too slow in hooking us up."

A heated exchange between the captain and the workers only made the workers more defiant, something an army officer rarely experiences. The officer stayed calm but bristled underneath. He pulled me back inside my house so the workers couldn't hear our conversation.

"Wow, your landlord is not going to be happy when I tell him how they treat you and how they just treated me. I'll talk to him and we will make this problem go away. I suppose we could go through the courts but that will take too long. I have another idea."

Days went by as our water crisis worsened. Our daily need to wash clothes and dishes, take baths, and have drinking water in a hot climate created daily tension in our household. More seriously, I worried about our two house girls' safety in our absence.

By the day, the workers grew bolder in their comments to the housekeepers. I couldn't wait any longer. I called the captain. He assured me the problem would be taken care of by the next afternoon.

The next day during lunch, I heard the distinctive roar of a heavy equipment engine followed by periodic clinking of the links on an excavator's tracks. Ging-Ging looked out our front door and ran back to the dining room, her eyes filled with astonishment and fear.

"Sir, I think you need to come see this."

I approached the open front door and stood in disbelief. An army tank, followed by a truckload of soldiers, came clunking down the hill into our subdivision. I stood confused. Why was a tank pulling into our neighborhood?

My eyes widened when the tank turned onto our street and headed right towards our house.

CHAPTER 14

A MILLION DOLLARS

Life has more imagination than we carry in our dreams.
—Christopher Columbus

CAMP AGUINALDO, the main military base in the Philippines, was less than a mile from our house. During World War II, the Japanese built a landing strip behind the military camp, and after the war, Filipinos turned it into a major street. Our subdivision connected to this thoroughfare.

To our astonishment, the military captain decided to take our water line problem into his own hands. He commandeered a tank and truckload of soldiers. They left the fortified base and drove down the beautiful boulevard for a little "training exercise" in our neighborhood.

I stood at my open front door as the tank passed our house and stopped at the house construction site next door. I ran back to the table, told my wife what was happening, and bounded upstairs to our bedroom balcony to get an elevated view. A minute later, Rebecca joined me on the balcony.

Soon the lid on the tank's turret flipped open. The captain appeared from the bowels of the tank and yelled at the workers to line up in front of the half-built house. The arrogant workers stood paralyzed. Unbelievably, the workers didn't obey.

Later it dawned on me the workers were probably frozen in fear. I could identify with that. I froze in fear with the friendly lion outside my tent in the C.A.R. When you are in a "fear-frozen" state, you simply are incapable of moving anything connected to your body.

The annoyed captain leaned down into the tank and gave an order. A moment later the tank turned its drab green turret ninety degrees and aimed the huge gun barrel directly at the new house. Soldiers piled out of the truck, lined up on both sides of the tank, and pointed their weapons. For a moment, it felt like an execution squad. This time, the workers obeyed and lined up, some shaking with fear. The captain barked an explicit order to the workers.

"I'm going to say this once and only once. Disconnect the water line right now!"

Two workers scrambled to the back corner of the lot, turned the valve off, and disconnected the pipe. Pipe wrenches in hand, they returned to the worker lineup.

"Is it disconnected?" the captain asked.

"Yes, sir," the foreman replied.

"Good. Don't make me come back here, or I'll blast all your hard work away. Do you understand?"

"Yes, sir."

The captain looked up at us, smiled and waved. We grinned and politely waved back. Then he gave one more scowling look towards the workers, shook his finger back and forth before disappearing into the bowels of the tank. His little visit to our subdivision created a marked transformation in the workers' attitude. Our household never had an issue with water pressure again.

Rebecca and I resumed lunch, only to be interrupted by Ging-Ging a few minutes later with a new problem.

"Sir, the clothes dryer makes a loud scratching noise every time I turn it on."

Mildred's clothes dryer was located in the back of the carport attached to the end of our house. I went out, turned the dryer on, and within a few seconds heard a horrible scratching sound.

"Hmm, that's strange," I said.

"It happens every time," said Ging-Ging.

Turned it off and the sound went away. Turned it on again, and this time not only did I hear scratching, but I saw little kitten paws shooting out from the bottom of the dryer. I instantly knew why the dryer had a problem.

I had vented the dryer to dissipate heat away from our hot carport by installing a white plastic six-inch PVC drain pipe that ran fifteen feet down the inside of the carport on the concrete floor. Never occurred to me anything would crawl up inside the tube into the dryer. A stray mother cat had the bright idea of giving birth to her kittens inside the safe, warm dryer cavity.

Every time the dryer turned on, the tumbler scared the kittens. They went crazy scratching at the dryer metal walls. The rest of the afternoon I dismantled the dryer, rescued the kittens, and reassembled the dryer. Then I put wire screen on the end of the PVC pipe to keep critters out.

"Did you get the dryer fixed?" asked Rebecca.

"Yep. All in a day of running a household in the Philippines. Got our water pressure problem solved as well. Have to love how military men solve problems."

"Do you remember you leave for India tomorrow?"

"Yep, my lecture notes are ready. I'm ready for a break from all this house drama."

My trip to India was no less dramatic. I met up with another American professor in the Calcutta airport before boarding a domestic flight to Bangalore. An airline bus drove us out to an Indian Airlines Boeing 737 sitting on the tarmac.

By this time in my overseas career, I learned always to book a window seat and look out the window to see if my luggage was actually being put on the aircraft. Before computers, it wasn't unusual to lose your checked-in bags half the time. On this plane, strangely no luggage cart ever arrived.

All passengers seated and the aircraft door closed, the cabin waited for the safety announcement. It never happened. For fifteen minutes everyone sat in odd quietness. I looked across at my professor friend. He shrugged his shoulders, indicating he didn't know what was happening either. The pilot came on the loudspeaker.

"All passengers, listen carefully to my instructions. In thirty seconds another plane will pull up beside us, and we have only three minutes to get off this plane and get onto the other. Sit in the same seat you are sitting in now. Move quickly and start now."

Before the pilot finished speaking, an identical Boeing 737 pulled up immediately to our left, so close I thought it would clip our plane. In a panic, we all grabbed our overhead bags and hustled out and down the plane and up into the other one.

As soon as the last passenger was on board and seated, the plane raced off across the tarmac. I turned to an Indian businessman sitting next to me.

"Sir, why did we change planes so quickly?" I asked.

"Safety precautions."

"Why?"

"Haven't you heard? Today the government executed the two people who assassinated Prime Minister Indira Gandhi. It now seems our first plane was a decoy in case someone planted a bomb in retaliation for the executions. I'm very sure that is why we switched planes so quickly."

In 1986, Prime Minister Gandhi was assassinated by two of her Sikh bodyguards in retaliation for the army's attack on a Sikh temple. On that same day, one assassin was killed by other bodyguards, but after a lengthy trial, the other bodyguard and his conspiring uncle were found guilty and executed on January 6, 1989, the very day of our Calcutta-Bangalore flight.

Our lectures took place in Bangalore, a city perched at a higher elevation where it was cool during the summers. During the British Raj era, colonial officials working in South India came up to their summer homes to escape the heat.

Long before Bangalore became India's "Silicon Valley," the city was known for its granite. Everywhere I looked I saw granite. Granite boundary walls surrounded homes, including granite mailboxes. Open storm sewers made of long granite slabs lined both sides of a street.

Our American host, who set up the school, graciously took us for a tour around the city.

"So, what's the deal with all this granite?" I asked.

"It's plentiful and cheap. I once had a visiting American businessman who asked me to source granite for his monument company. He said if I just set up the relationship with an Indian supplier and ship him a container a month, he would pay me a million a year."

My head snapped back. I couldn't believe what I just heard.

"A million rupees or a million dollars?"

"A million dollars."

"So, why didn't you do it?"

"We run a nonprofit school. We don't do business."

Wow. I was shocked at his cavalier attitude towards such a tremendous opportunity.

"Just think what you could do for education here in India with a million bucks a year."

"It's not what we do."

While his attitude bothered me, something clicked inside my brain that allowed me to see things differently.

For the first time, I clearly realized that funds could be generated overseas in developing countries to fund our nonprofit programs. The mentality of international nonprofits at the time was all developing countries were poor and needed funds from rich Western countries. Even though nonprofit organizations were allowed to earn money, they raised it through donations.

Eureka. Everything would be different. This "light bulb" moment changed my life. It changed my mission. And it would change the lives and fortunes of thousands of people over the rest of my career. Learning how to do it successfully would be another stage in my journey.

PRINCIPLE # 26: "The power of sustainability"

When foreign or local NGOs can fund their programs from locally earned income, it reduces their need for continual donations from foreign sources.

My ticket back to Manila routed me from Bangalore to Madras, on to Singapore, and finally to Manila. The Bangalore airport was crowded as I forced my way to the ticket counter. The flight to Madras was canceled. Fortunately, I arrived in time to catch an earlier flight delayed but already boarded.

The signboard said my new flight already departed; however, the agent assured me he could get me on. The airliner was already taxiing towards the runway, so I was highly skeptical. He called upstairs, and they agreed to hold the plane. Outside the terminal, I felt silly running with my luggage.

The only time I ever ran after a moving plane on a wide-open tarmac, a flight attendant opened the door, and after the aircraft stopped, came down the steps. He opened the cargo hold, threw in my suitcase, and we climbed up into the airplane to a group of glaring, impatient travelers.

In the Madras airport, I checked in early for my flight to Singapore on Singapore Airlines, one of the finest airlines in the world. Although I didn't leave until the evening, I made the mistake of going through immigration and customs early.

Not allowed to leave, I sat in a hot departure lounge with no food, water, or air conditioning. By the time my flight was called eleven hours later, I was one sweaty, ornery mess.

A Boeing 747 held hundreds of passengers, and on this night, half of them were children. Indian mothers and children were returning to Australia after enjoying the Christmas holiday visiting relatives. A departure time of midnight meant kids and babies were more tired than me.

On takeoff, our aircraft slowly rolled down the runway, gathering speed in what always seems forever when a 747 lifts off. With the front of his plane already in the air, the pilot suddenly slammed the nose down and came to a screeching halt at the end of the runway.

Children no longer cried but screamed. Adults looked at one another in fear and astonishment. The plane sat motionless at the end of the dark runway as we smelled the tires' burnt rubber. The pilot came on the speaker.

"Ladies and gentlemen, this is your captain speaking. Sorry about that aborted takeoff. We have a mechanical problem, and we have to go back and check it out."

The plane made an about-face on the runway, taxied back towards the terminal, and parked on a side runway. I looked out my window and saw two mechanics on a ladder under the wing. A half hour later, the pilot came back on.

"Well, I'm sorry to say we have to replace a part so our wheels can go up after takeoff. They tell me it will take an hour to remove the rivets in the wing, an hour to replace the part, and another hour to replace the rivets. Here's what we're going to do. I'm turning all the lights off in the plane, and all of you are going to go to sleep. I'll wake you up when we are ready to go."

All the lights turned off and within five minutes everyone was asleep. Not even a whimper or a sound of any kind was heard. Before long I also fell asleep. Exactly three hours later the lights came on and the engines fired up.

"Awe right, mates, we're ready to go, so buckle up. I'll make up some time in the air."

Once airborne, the captain pulled a hard left bank I didn't know was possible with a 747. Now I was sure he'd been a fighter pilot. The rest of the trip was uneventful, and I safely arrived back in Manila.

Rebecca met me at our front door with a kiss and a question.

"So, how were your flights?"

"Mm, they were unusual."

I explained the decoy plane in Calcutta, stopping an airliner on the Bangalore tarmac to get on, and the Aussie pilot's behavior in Madras. Growing up in Asia, she had her own wild airplane stories, but now I generated a few more of my own. My two young boys gave me their welcome hug around each leg, and it was good to be home.

"You have a look of wonder on your face. What's up with that?" Rebecca asked.

"I had an epiphany on this trip," I said.

"About what?"

Struggling to put my big idea into words, I paused, bit my lip, and smiled.

"There is a better way than just giving handouts to everyone in poor countries. What if we could fund NGO programs from money generated right in the foreign country?"

She stared at me with giant eyes. I already knew what was going on in her head.

"You know our NGO has a policy against doing business or making money in foreign countries," she said.

"Yes, I know. We help people, but we don't help people help themselves. I'm not saying we should make money for our own personal benefit. I'm saying it would help fund local programs. Think about it. All the NGO programs where we loan money or give money, it causes resentment among the locals who are dependent upon us. There has to be a better way."

"You have two problems. First, I need to remind you again our NGO won't allow you to earn money, even for nonprofit programs. And second, you have to have an excellent opportunity like granite to make it worth the risk and time," she said.

I winked at her and said, "It doesn't hurt to dream, does it?"

CHAPTER 15

"COUP D'ÉTAT"

My biggest disappointment was, of course, the coup attempts.
—Corazon Aquino

A HAZY MORNING and my turn to drive, I picked up Ron from his home in our subdivision and headed to our school office. The best route took us along the back of Camp Aguinaldo on Katipunan Avenue.

At the back corner of the military cantonment, I turned onto White Plains Avenue and drove along the side of the base. A mile later, the avenue ended at an intersection with EDSA, a major eight-lane traffic artery running in front of the military facility.

The military establishment occupied a square mile. High white walls surrounded the entire base, and at each corner loomed a lookout tower, called a bird's nest. For months no sentries manned the nests—until this particular morning.

As I approached the traffic signal at EDSA, I slowed down. Ron looked up and saw two soldiers in the bird's nest.

"This isn't good. Why are guys up in that bird's nest?" he asked.

The answer to his question became clear as we drew closer to the intersection. The stoplight turned red and I braked to a stop. Across the street an armored personnel carrier (APC) was stopped in the middle of EDSA. Soldiers stood ready with automatic weapons.

A former military officer, Ron looked up to see a machine gun aimed down at the soldiers behind their APC.

"Go, go, run the red light!" he yelled. "Or we're going to be caught in the middle of a firefight!"

I gunned the accelerator. Once through the intersection, I glanced into a rearview mirror. Guns on both sides blazed. I gripped the steering wheel tight. Ron remained quiet until I turned onto a side street.

"Phil, that was close. But it's no use going to the office."

"I know, the last coup stranded us at the office until midnight. I say we work our way back home through side streets."

At each intersection, both of us scanned the street for soldiers. Eventually we looped around and made it into our subdivision. I dropped Ron off at his house, came around the block, and parked in our carport.

"What are you doing home?" Rebecca asked.

"Another coup is taking place so we came back. It's not safe to be outside our subdivision when soldiers are on the streets and I have to get some new lecture notes prepared. Can you protect me?"

I found it difficult working at home because small boys didn't understand why Daddy couldn't come out to play—that is, play all day.

"Sure, I'll protect you. It's a nice day, so they can play out in the backyard."

At first, I tried studying in my home office located on the ground floor. That didn't work. The constant sound of automatic gunfire, explosions from rocket-propelled grenades, and the periodic "thud, thud, thud" of large machine guns distracted me.

I retreated upstairs to our bedroom and turned the air conditioner on high to drown out some of the noise. I spread textbooks all over the bed, sat in a chair, and made notes on my lap.

By midafternoon the battle for Camp Aguinaldo continued with no letup. I took a break, came down our marble stairs, and sipped a cold lemonade on the veranda.

"Wonder how Colonel Mitch is doing up there inside the cantonment?" I asked.

"I'm sure he's directing the troops. I wonder if Mildred is all right. I hope she isn't up there, but someplace else safe," Rebecca replied.

A total of six coup attempts occurred during the three years we lived in Manila. Mitch, our landlord, was the right-hand man for General Ramos, who five years later would become President Ramos. Colonel Gringo Honasan, a classmate of Mitch at the Philippine Military Academy, led a group of colonels that morning to overthrow then-President Cory Aquino.

Gringo and his men took over part of Camp Aguinaldo while Mitch and his troops controlled the other part. The fighting remained loud and intense as the two classmates directed his side of the battle.

I guzzled the last of my lemonade and said to Rebecca, "Did you see what Matt and Mark are doing in the backyard?"

"They're playing G.I. Joe in the sandbox," she replied and then paused at the irony. "What else do you think they would be playing?"

"I know, feels like we are living in some movie. Don't you think that it is weird all the sound effects of real battle accompany our kids battling in the sandbox? Kind of bizarre, isn't it?"

"Yep, it's unreal. We live an unusual life."

As parents, we knew the importance of keeping our cool. If parents act scared with gunfire all around, then their kids will more than freak out. Used to the sound of machine gun practice at the range down the hill, my young children were not alarmed at the loud sound of gunfire.

I went back up to the bedroom to finish writing a lecture. The strong smell of gunpowder dominated the air. Smoke billowed up from Camp Aguinaldo as the afternoon battle intensified. I wondered how long the struggle would continue.

A rapid set of knocks on the bedroom door came from little hands. I opened the bedroom door to Marky's excited shouts.

"Daddy, Daddy, come, come. The planes are coming! The planes are coming!"

My four-year-old son demonstrated with a toy plane, swishing it back and forth. Marky and I hustled down to the backyard. The sight of real fighter jets made the whole scene surreal.

On the horizon a fighter jet with a net full of bombs came into view. Ten seconds later it dipped towards the military cantonment. The four of us gazed up at the plane. We were close enough to see a puff of smoke under the fuselage.

I wondered if the plane was hit from fire from below. Actually, the puff of smoke came from a small explosive that opened the net and released bombs into the cantonment. The explosions were deafening.

Columns of thick black smoke instantly rose into the air. All gunfire ceased. The coup was over.

"Daddy, Daddy, did you see that?" Matt asked.

"Yes, yes I did," I said with sadness in my voice.

Our innocent little boys didn't understand that seconds before human beings died from those bombs. This coup attempt turned out to be the bloodiest of all, with fifty-three dead and 200 wounded in a single day of battle. Forces loyal to President Aquino, the first woman president in Asia, rebuffed a serious attempt to take over her government.

Rebel soldiers had attacked the presidential palace, took over an airbase, three television stations, two military bases, a provincial airport, and almost conquered the central command and control center, Camp Aguinaldo. By the next day, all facilities were retaken by pro-government forces.

Much to our relief, our landlord and good friend, Colonel Mitch Templo, survived the battle inside Camp Aguinaldo. Fortunately, his wife and two children escaped harm's way. Within a day, the city of Manila returned to normal.

A predominantly Roman Catholic country, Filipinos didn't work on Sunday. A Protestant church close by held services in English, attended by both Filipino and American parishioners. On Sunday mornings, the McDonalds' routine included a stop at Dunkin Donuts before church and eating lunch at an authentic Mongolian barbeque after the service.

On one particular Sunday evening, our kids weren't feeling well, and so I went to the evening church service alone. Afterward, I ventured out to the dark parking lot and sat down in my car. In the dark I fumbled around and searched for the key opening to turn on the ignition.

As soon as I turned the key, I saw the green backlight of the instrument panel come on. But even before I started the engine, something unusual blocked part of my gauges.

Then it moved. A skinny snake was coiled up a few inches from my hands on the steering wheel. In one movement, I opened the door, jumped out, and slammed the door shut.

Through the window I saw the silhouette of the snake against the freakish green light. I mumbled to myself the same thing Dr.

Indiana Jones muttered in the movie *Raiders of the Lost Ark:* "Snakes, why did it have to be snakes."

An American friend came out of the building. I motioned him over.

"Hey, Ed, come here a second. I have a snake in my car."

Of course, by now the wily snake left the dashboard. Never mind, Ed had a solution.

"Let me get some RAID, and I'll be right back," Ed said.

In a few minutes he returned with a large can of insect repellent. I cracked the door open while he emptied the entire can into the car. Then he slammed the door hard.

"This usually works because it irritates them. Let's give it a few minutes," Ed said.

"Do you think the snake is poisonous?" I asked.

"All snakes in Manila are poisonous."

"But it's so skinny and small."

"Doesn't matter. It's not the size of the snake, but the potency of the venom."

His comment reminded me of my green mamba incident in a slimy mechanic's pit in Africa, exactly fifteen years earlier.

Others in the parking area came over to observe our attempt to dislodge the snake. Ed gave me a stick while he held a baseball bat. He didn't seem alarmed or nervous. Ed grew up on a ranch in Colorado, where he regularly confronted venomous snakes of all kinds.

The moment of truth arrived. I opened the driver's side door while Ed stood poised. In seconds, an avalanche of small critters poured out over the door sill. Gigantic cockroaches, small lizards, even a mouse made their escape. But no snake. A Filipino young man started to laugh.

"Sir, it's a jungle in there. You should clean your car more often," he said.

Bugs revealed why the snake was in my car. The confined space was a smorgasbord of edible delights, similar to a chicken coop for a hungry fox except with more variety. Ed saw I wasn't amused.

"Listen. Tomorrow when it's daylight I'll look for the snake. If I don't find it, I'll hire a couple of college kids from the province who will dismantle your interior until they find it. We did it all the time in the province. They know how to find snakes in a car. It won't cost much."

Perhaps the only thing worse than snakes on a plane is one living in your car. Manila, a metropolitan area of eleven million people, shouldn't have poisonous snakes. If I learned anything from living in the tropics, I knew snakes liked moisture. Whether the location was a concrete jungle like Metro Manila, or out in remote jungle, either way, snakes were on the move during rainy season.

I answered the phone the next day, but Ed's news wasn't good.

"I had two college guys completely remove everything from inside your car. Seats, dash, carpets, door panels, all were taken out and checked. Sorry to say, there's no sign of a snake. There was a hole under the dash big enough for the snake to come in from the engine compartment. Maybe it went back out the hole during the night."

I picked up the car. When I opened the door to get in, I instantly felt a creepy feeling. What if somehow the snake was still in the car or had crawled back in? How was Rebecca going to feel safe driving in Manila traffic wondering if the snake would slither over the head-rest and down on her?

When Rebecca heard the news, she said, "Nope, there is no way. I'm not driving that car until you're sure the snake is gone."

She may have grown up hunting with her brothers in the tropical jungles of Bangladesh, but she had an ingrained hatred of all things creepy and crawly.

Day after day I drove the car, always aware of a potential unwanted riding companion. At every stop light, I looked over my shoulder. If a fly landed on me, I jumped. I had graduated from creepy bugs and a green Mamba in an African mechanic's pit to the possibility of a personal serpent in my car. What a promotion.

Weeks went by with no snake. But I was never sure it wouldn't turn up. Weeks turned into months, and finally, Rebecca came to believe our car was safe, or at least she pretended. Given a choice, she would take a cab over our family car.

Manila was notorious for traffic jams and long delays. Many times I sat motionless for three hours. I bored easily, so to pass the time, I kept a stash of books and magazines in the car. All the while, trusting my car's air conditioner wouldn't overheat the engine as my black car baked in the heat. Note to self, don't ever own another black car in the hot tropics.

One particular day during a long traffic jam, I read a book on stress. In the appendix I found a written personal stress test. The scale was from one to 300 with a score of 300 indicating maximum human stress. For fun I took the test and scored a perfect 300.

The results said, *"You are a candidate for sudden death from heart attack or stroke."* Great. Having the possibility of a poisonous snake as a traveling companion only ratcheted up my anxiety. That wasn't one of the questions, meaning I probably scored higher than 300.

My stress score off the charts, fortunately the Christmas holidays came, and a group of us traveled on a bus up to Baguio, a resort town in the mountains. The new surroundings gave us a much needed and refreshing vacation. I was worn out from surly construction workers, kittens scratching metal, tanks and armed soldiers. And a snake in my car. Oh, and the senseless coups, there's that.

Our NGO owned a compound in Baguio. Each family had their own cottage. Although each cottage had a kitchen, we often ate out, because who wants to cook on vacation. The large compound had fun things for kids to do, and with the crisp mountain air, it didn't take much for adults to fall asleep while reading a favorite book.

In all the years we lived overseas as a family, perhaps the biggest mistake we made was not taking enough vacation time. Time to decompress from all the cross-cultural stress. Stress accumulates and sneaks up on you until you're at a breaking point.

Our trip to Baguio over, the Christmas holidays turned out to be more than refreshing. A couple months later, Rebecca announced she was pregnant. That Christmas in 1988 turned into a memory.

PRINCIPLE # 27: "Use it or lose it"

Make sure you take your allotted vacation time. It takes time to decompress from cross-cultural stress. Stress accumulates and sneaks up on you until you're at a breaking point.

Our time in Manila finally came to an end. My three years of service to the graduate school complete, we made plans to return to America. Sorry to see us leave, Mitch and Mildred grandly showed their friendship.

In true Filipino fashion, where personal relationships are everything, they honored us with a farewell party at a luxury hotel. When Mitch and Mildred found out I sold our car, the couple insisted on taking us to the airport on the day of our departure.

"Mildred, you need to understand Americans don't travel light. We'll have eight suitcases plus carry-on bags," I said.

"That won't be a problem at all," she said.

On the day of our departure, a police motorcade showed up at our door. Our colonel friend was about to be promoted to general, and with the war against communist rebels still raging, he now had his own security detail. Lights flashing and sirens blaring, we enjoyed the ride of our lives, traveling an hour to the international airport in total luxury. Felt like we were V.I.P.s.

PRINCIPLE # 28: "Find a human 'roof' to protect you"

If possible, make friends in high places. Whether in peacetime or war, the core of international work is personal relationships, especially with government officials who can come to your aid.

Our experience in the Philippines taught me the importance of proper coping methods, especially the lessons that came with living in a country at war with communist insurgents.

Such methods include being flexible yet vigilant, learning to be calm under enormous stress, and taking time for rest. How you manage stress can make or break a family in a cross-cultural environment. Friends in high places help reduce stress, especially when you have a missing husband, need a military tank, or a personal motorcade to the airport.

Our return to the States removed the stress of cross-cultural living, but it wasn't worry-free. We didn't know what in the world we were going to do next. Or where in the world for that matter.

PART
III
Road to Empowerment

You cannot build character and courage by taking away a man's
initiative and independence.
—William J. H. Boetcker

CHAPTER 16

FREEDOM

True individual freedom cannot exist without
economic security and independence.
—Franklin D. Roosevelt

ABRAHAM LINCOLN, a great American president, ended legal slavery and freed millions. Born in poverty, he was no stranger to adversity. Before he could marry his first love, she died of typhoid fever. Later he married into a southern family who owned and traded slaves. His wife's family served and died for the Confederacy.

Mary, his wife, suffered her whole life from migraines, depression, and possibly bipolar disorder. Their first son died at age four from tuberculosis, another at age twelve from typhoid. After losing two U.S. Senate bids, he won the U.S. presidential election of 1860, as an antislave candidate.

Between his election win and the inauguration, Lincoln evaded several assassination attempts. Seven southern states rejected his leadership and left the Union. Six weeks after becoming president, war broke out between Northern and Southern states. Two years into the war, Lincoln almost declared war against Britain. Through persistence, resolve, and steadfastness, President Lincoln eventually led the Northern states to victory, ending slavery.

Just as the legal termination of slavery did not end American racism in 1860, the legal end of colonialism didn't change racist, colonial attitudes around the world. A whole century later, colonialism, or international racism, was still legal.

The years I worked overseas I learned of the subtle and insidious nature of colonialism. Those of a colonial mind-set thought local employees of foreign NGOs never seemed skilled enough, trusted enough, or experienced enough to assume real leadership. Before we took another overseas assignment, I thought long and hard about this issue.

What I didn't know was my next assignment would allow me to work with a Lincoln-like man of quiet dignity, a man of character and faith. His resolve would change many in his country, giving them confidence, dignity, and self-worth.

Our return from the Philippines in May of 1989 provided needed rest. Our little house on a quiet cul-de-sac in Michigan served as a perfect refuge to ease back into American culture. After living years in slow-paced cultures, returning to American caused "reentry shock," making me feel as though I had stepped on a moving sidewalk.

The variety and selection of food and goods in a supermarket practically paralyzed me. I stood gaping at rows and rows of multiple brands that competed for my money.

Rebecca's whole life had consisted of moving back and forth between fast and slow-paced cultures. Home for her wasn't a geographical place but merely being with family. Her ability to adapt came automatically. For me, I felt left behind.

In September, Rebecca gave birth to our third son, Nathan. Our cozy 900-square-foot home with brown shutters was a cocoon of enjoyment. Matt and Mark had their own bedroom, we had ours, and the baby room was decorated with bright colors and hanging mobiles.

However, I knew our time in America was only temporary. Then a letter came from Bangladesh in early 1990. I walked into the dining room and handed Rebecca the letter.

"Remember Bipul from Bangladesh?" I asked.

"How could anyone forget Bipul? One of the tallest Bengali men I know. He worked in the office in Chittagong."

In those days the average height of a Bengali man was about five feet, two inches. Over six feet tall, Bipul towered above his peers. With less than one percent of the Bangladesh population Christian, there weren't many tall Christians.

"Well, he completed his education here in America and returned to Bangladesh. He just wrote saying all his education didn't prepare him to fulfill his dream of starting a graduate school. He wants me to come back to Bangladesh and help him. What do you think?"

She studied the letter before looking up.

"No question you're the person with the credentials and experience to help him set up a school. It's going to take a lot of money they don't have out there."

"I don't have a problem helping him set up a school. In fact, I don't really have a problem helping him raise funds from here. Bangladesh is the second poorest country in the world. My issue is, who's going to control it?"

Rebecca knew precisely what I meant. Since a child, she witnessed the ongoing control of local nationals by foreigners from Western nations. Foreigner expats provided most, if not all, of the funds, made the decisions, and dictated the operations in developing countries.

"Dr. Bipul has been a faithful employee of the NGO for twenty years, but you know he'll still be under the thumb of Americans if he remains part of the NGO. Look how much the organization controls us and we are Americans. This is our chance to change things and actually help empower a Bangladeshi for once," I said.

"So, what are you saying?"

"After thirty years, all the NGO programs in Bangladesh are still controlled and financed by Americans. Older colleagues are always saying 'someday' there will be trained Bangladeshis who can 'take over' and run things. 'Someday' never comes and I'm tired of the colonialism. If anyone should be free of colonialism, it's Bipul. He has more education than most of the Americans out there."

I wrote back to Dr. Bipul saying I would consider helping him, but on one condition—the new school project had to be independent of the NGO. Short on American personnel, our NGO American colleagues in Bangladesh surprisingly agreed to let us come back and allowed me the freedom to help start the school independent of the NGO. Once our transfer was approved by headquarters, we had a new overseas assignment.

Bipul desired to have no part of the diaspora known as the brain drain. He was the one in ten who chose to go back and use his education to train his countrymen. I knew if American donors could meet this polished and capable man in person, we had a good chance of raising funds for the school.

I invited him to come back to America for a fundraising visit. Over several months the two of us traversed the country and met with potential donors until enough funds were raised to set up our school project. Dr. Bipul returned to Bangladesh. My family made preparations to return once our boys' school year was complete.

In the meantime, another little addition to our family arrived. In April, 1991, Rebecca gave birth to a baby girl, Danielle. I can't begin to explain the joy of having a girl in a mostly boy house.

That same month a major cyclone crashed into Bangladesh. Due to incredible devastation, the storm received wide attention in the American media. Equivalent to a category 5 hurricane, the cyclone packed winds up to 160 miles an hour and killed close to 139,000 people.

The cover of *Time* magazine showed an aerial view of a beach covered with thousands of human and animal corpses. Reporters from a local TV news station showed up at my door and taped an interview of what life was like in Bangladesh.

To our surprise, a few donors met with us and lodged their concerns about taking a newborn back into such a poor country. One elderly man drove to our house and pleaded with us to leave our children with his wife instead of taking them overseas to what he called "some God-forsaken country."

My wife grew up in that "God-forsaken country" and firmly believed her children would be better for it. If my wife could handle it, so could I. To this day, we are convinced that raising children in a diverse, multicultural setting is the richest life ever.

Despite pleas from well-meaning friends to reconsider our return to Bangladesh, we moved ahead with our travel plans. Our house packed and ready again for rental, three months later we loaded up our three boys, a baby girl we nicknamed Dani, a mountain of luggage, and headed to the airport. Friends showed up to say goodbye.

Upon our return to Chittagong, the stench of death from the cyclone still hung in the air. In spite of the fact the city was recovering from a major catastrophe, we once again engaged in the "set-up" process of living in a foreign country. Step one, situate ourselves in our NGO guesthouse so Matt and Mark could begin school.

Step two, search for a place to live. No individual houses were for rent in areas close to our colleagues. After a month of searching, we found a large ground floor flat. But there was a problem. Located up the hill in Khulshi, a haven for foreign expatriates and wealthy Bangladeshis, it certainly would be out of our price range. Desperate, we arranged to see the house anyway.

The landlord, Mr. Khan, spoke excellent English, and during our first conversation, we discovered he had rented a house in Chittagong to my wife's family, some thirty years prior. Thrilled to see her grown up and with her own brood of kids, he gave us a phenomenally low price on the rent. Bengali people are quite sentimental about relationships, especially long-term ones.

Step three, move from the guesthouse and settle into the rented house. By custom, the tenant of the ground floor got sole use of the front carport and walled backyard. But after moving in, Rebecca was not happy.

"Phil, you need to call Mr. Khan and tell him the cow in the backyard has to go. It keeps wiping its poopy butt against our clean sheets on the line. Our wringer washer is running day and night."

I informed Mr. Khan, and the next day the *darwan* moved the uncompliant cow to a vacant lot down the street. With four flats of renters, Mr. Khan hired his own *darwans,* one to guard his property by day and another by night. The day guard, a convicted murderer who somehow got his freedom, was a scary guy but we had no choice in the matter.

One afternoon I drove into our housing compound to see Mr. Khan beating up the convicted murderer with a vengeance. He punched and kicked with such vigor, it surprised me how the old landlord in his sixties had that much strength and energy to do such a number on a husky young man.

I parked my car in our assigned garage stall. Then I walked over to find out what happened.

"He's a *chore* (thief), and I'm finding out where he took my cow. *Qurban* is tomorrow, and I need to sacrifice that cow for my family," said Mr. Khan.

The moaning *darwan* laid motionless at our feet. Mr. Khan gave him another hard kick, screamed at him, and turned his attention back to me.

"That should do it. He'll tell me where the cow is in a few minutes. So, how is your day?"

"Um, good, I guess. Is he . . . is he going to be all right?" I asked.

"Who, him? He won't be unless he tells me where my cow's hidden."

Mr. Khan threatened to kick one more time when the *darwan* caved and confessed he stole the cow. The battered *darwan* achingly got up and hobbled off. A few minutes later he returned with the cow in tow. Needless to say, he was fired on the spot and told never to return.

My wife never liked the convicted murderer. The feeling was mutual, probably because he got upset with her one afternoon when she came to the rescue of a woman caught stealing a toaster from our next-door neighbor.

Tied to a telephone pole across the street, the neighborhood guards beat her, kicked her, and cut off most of her hair. Rebecca heard the commotion, went out, and threw off the *darwans* beating the lady thief's frail body.

Then she ripped the *darwans* up and down in Bengali. I mean choice Bengali words, some I didn't understand but still recognized their import. My wife has always had a thing about sticking up for the underdog.

Oh, and my wife wasn't particularly happy with me either. Sound asleep, I awoke from a nap in a daze and heard my wife yelling at the *darwans* outside. In retrospect, I probably should have hustled out a tad faster to help her out.

After Mr. Khan fired him, the ex-convict and now ex-*darwan* stayed away from our property, at least for a little while. The Muslim practice of *Purdah* means a home is a private, safe place for women, where they don't have to cover their heads or faces, where they can be at ease.

Rebecca came into my study with hands on her hips and a look of disgust on her face as she reported the privacy of our home had been violated.

"The fired *darwan* is standing in our living room and startled me when I came out of our bedroom," she sputtered. "He's a Muslim. He knows better. Get rid of him! He knows he shouldn't be in here!"

In Islamic culture, it was totally inappropriate for any man to step into my home space unannounced. The convict stood smug. No question he was up to no good. She didn't need to ask me twice because I didn't like the guy myself.

Not that I approved of the beating he received from Mr. Khan. But I did understand why my landlord did what was acceptable in his culture to get the result he needed.

I politely asked the convicted murderer to leave our house, but he defiantly refused. I retrieved a gun from my bedroom, came back, and ordered him out. The weapon, a Chinese knockoff of an AK 47 assault rifle, was actually a pellet gun, but the *darwan* wasn't the wiser.

As a culture, most Bangladeshis are afraid of guns, but not this guy. He got up, moseyed outside, and sat on the curb without leaving our property. I stuck the rifle in his chest and told him to leave, or I would pull the trigger. He smirked, turned, and walked out the gate, never to return again. His total lack of fear unnerved me.

A few months later I saw him during my morning jog. He stopped me on the street, greeted me warmly, and acted as if I was his long-lost friend. By now, I began to wonder about his state of mind. Mental health facilities were few, leaving most to be taken care of by family or society.

In public, mentally ill people were ignored. In fact, Islam was tolerant of those with physical and mental disabled disabilities. Often whole towns fed, clothed, and generally looked after people who were mentally ill.

For example, in Chittagong, all of us ignored a naked, mentally disabled person in the center of town who stood all day in the street directing traffic. Even in the cool months, all he wore was a scarf around his neck.

My primary goal in helping Dr. Bipul set up an educational institution in Bangladesh was complete independence from any foreign organization. He and I met regularly and planned out all the necessities of setting up a graduate school. Even though I spent years helping set up a grad school in the Philippines, it still required a great deal of work. Every culture has its own view of education.

Decisions about educational philosophy, vision, strategy, board governance, administration, professors, staff, facilities, student qualifications, curriculum, degrees, graduation requirements, enrollment procedures, and legal registration totally consumed us for months.

Dr. Bipul, trained as an accountant, had a mind for details and working together was easy. His personal experience studying in the American education system expedited our work tremendously. Even still, when our planning phases came to a conclusion and the closer we came to pulling the trigger to start, I noticed we weren't on the same page.

"Bipul, is everything all right?" I asked.

"Phil, I think you should be the president of the graduate school, not me."

"Why do you think that? I thought we agreed to make this a truly Bangladeshi school?"

"But you have the PhD in international planning, and you've been an administrator in a graduate school. I haven't."

Dr. Bipul leaned back into his chair, his arms crossed over his chest. The bearer delivered tea but sensed the tension in the room and promptly took his leave.

"Bipul, you have a doctorate as well, you are from here, and I'm temporary. I guess I don't understand."

"Maybe we should make the school be under the NGO. You be president, and I'll just be one of your professor colleagues."

I was shocked at the about-face. At an impasse, I suggested we sleep on it and resume the conversation the next day. I drove home and parked my little minivan in the garage at the back of our property. I ate supper in confused quietness.

Dinner finished, the kids were excused to play or do homework. I sat in silence. Rebecca knew something was bothering me.

"Okay, what's going on? You haven't said a word since you got home."

"Bipul thinks our school shouldn't be independent but belong under the NGO. He's quite adamant about it. I feel like he's getting cold feet about breaking off from our organization. And he said I should be president, not him."

I could see the wheels turning in her head. Asian friends called her the "white woman with a brown heart" because she understood the Asian mind-set so well and loved them so much. Desperate for a solution to my problem, I needed a dose of her Asian perspective. It didn't take her long to diagnose my problem.

"Don't you see what's going on?" she said gently. "Look at it through Bipul's eyes. He has all these degrees but would be stepping out starting something new yet unproven. Plus, he'd be leaving the security of his job for the last twenty years. The risks to him are high."

"What do you mean?"

"This is an Asian shame culture that won't accept failure if anything goes wrong. He will lose face and his reputation."

Our overhead fan humming, we sat in muggy stillness and contemplated how to resolve Bipul's legitimate concerns. In my eagerness to start a new school, I realized I hadn't done an adequate job of analyzing risks, especially social risk.

If the school failed, I could get on a plane and leave, while Dr. Bipul would live with the consequences for the rest of his life. I didn't have much "skin in the game." My colleague had all his skin in the game. Rebecca pursed her lips and then summarized her analysis.

"Here's what I think is happening. With all his degrees, Bipul assumes that if he stays in the NGO, he will be treated as an equal among Americans. But he doesn't realize some of our American colleagues may be threatened by his degrees. So either out of simple habit, defensiveness, or racist colonialism, they won't ever treat him as an equal. They'll try to control and micromanage him. They do that to their own, for sure they will do it to him. Look how we were micromanaged."

I leaned back in my chair and sadly nodded in agreement. She then said something I didn't fully fathom at first, but then it struck a real chord. In fact, it was an epiphany.

"Bipul also doesn't understand that compared to American colleagues, he isn't equal to them. He is superior to them in so many ways. His knowledge of the culture and language, plus his leadership ability and integrity, all set him up for success. Only he knows best his land, his people, and the need to be free. He's like a Bangladeshi Abe Lincoln in disguise. This kind of person doesn't grow on trees. You're working with a man who has the skill, passion, and drive to become a hero leader, who will stand up for his people."

Her statement "he will stand up for his people" totally described Bipul. During the Bangladesh war of independence, he protected a disadvantaged minority group by literally standing in a doorway, barring a Pakistani soldier from entering. The soldier pressed a bayonet so hard into Bipul's chest, blood stained his white shirt.

"So, what do I do?" I asked.

"All he needs is to be set up and resourced. Then he will be free of American control so he can shine. You must convince him to leave the security of our NGO. You have to assure him he is doing the right thing for his future. Not just for him, but for all his people."

PRINCIPLE # 29: "Can't lose face"

In cultures of the East, honor and shame are strong values, and those from Western cultures ignore them at their peril.

I tossed and turned all night. Everything my dear wife said resonated as common sense, which for most people isn't very common. What she asked me to do was a tall order. The longer I thought about it, the responsibility weighed on me to persuade him to take a leap of faith. For Bipul and me, it would be a defining moment in our relationship.

At dawn, I bolted upright in bed, hands gripping the sheets, knowing my words could change a man's life. I had to convince him. I could hardly wait for Bipul to arrive for our morning meeting at my house.

I greeted Bipul, and we sat in awkward silence while the bearer served us tea and biscuits.

"Bipul, I've been thinking about our conversation yesterday. As far as staying in under the American organization, I think you and I would live to regret it. You know foreign NGOs get kicked out of the country all the time. If that happens, your school would go down with the ship. If you are separate and independent, you could continue."

I paused and looked away for a second.

"Go on," he said.

"I hate to say this, but after you've worked twenty years for our organization, you know which Americans will accept you as an equal and who won't. I'm sorry to say, colonialism still exists, especially by those older ones in leadership. They will try to control you as they do us."

I set my teacup down. He stared at me with a distressed look.

"Bipul, I feel you need the freedom to think like a Bangladeshi and do what's best for Bangladeshis, not what's best for some foreign NGO."

My Bangladeshi friend began nodding his head in agreement. He knew this to be true. But I wasn't done.

"I know you well enough that if the school fails, your integrity won't allow you to blame others. But I want you to know, if you are president and it fails, blame me. Tell everyone it was my idea to set it up independent from the NGO and make me the bad guy. You really do need to be president and be independent. Would you please reconsider?"

He searched my face, processing the fact that I told him I would be willing to take the blame. He sat stoically for a few moments, and then a serene calmness came over him. The societal risks were out in the open. Bottom line, he was not willing to put all his eggs in a foreign NGO basket.

With that, his outlook shifted and buoyant hope reappeared. He was finally ready to be president and our project was back on track. I knew once he was truly independent of foreign NGO control, he would be free from a good deal of colonial baggage. And free to soar as a leader.

PRINCIPLE # 30: "Where do I fit?"

A primary motivator in Eastern cultures is how an individual is viewed by the group. Unlike the West, where individuality is valued, in the East, it's all about the group, not the person.

I learned two valuable lessons from this experience. First, Easterners find their identity as members of a group, not solely as an individual. It starts with obligations to the immediate family, then extended family, the neighborhood, their faith community, ethnic community, and on and on. Eastern relationships are complicated.

As a Westerner, with roots in Euro-American individualism, I didn't understand the depth of family or group obligations in Eastern social relationships. I was stunned when a Nepali friend later told me, "When I enter a room at a social gathering, I quickly look to see who my family is obligated to and who is obligated to us."

Second, Westerners don't understand honor and shame cultures. Consequently, those from the West are sometimes too direct and can easily offend or dishonor an Easterner while not even knowing it. In the East, it's all about saving face. Intermediaries are called in to handle misunderstandings, disagreements and preserve relationships.

Poet Rudyard Kipling's opening lines of "The Ballad of East and West," first published in 1889, reflects our deep cultural differences and is still relevant today: "Oh, East is East, and West is West, and never the twain shall meet."

CHAPTER 17

"YOUR HOUSE HAS BEEN STOLEN"

Credible leaders raise self-esteem. Leaders who make a difference
to others cause people to feel that they too can make a difference.
They set people's spirits free and enable them to become more
than they might have thought possible.
—James Kouzes and Barry Posner

IN BANGLADESH, all the Americans in the NGO were
required to meet four times a year at the hospital compound,
and each set of meetings lasted two to five days. That's right, two
to five long days of meetings, held in the morning, afternoon,
and evening.

Meetings. The bane of my career in nonprofit organizations was
always meetings. Unlike the for-profit world, where market forces
demand constant decisions and focus, the not-for-profit world loves
to talk and talk and talk about issues.

Endless meetings, task forces, and subcommittees, were followed by endless reporting on those meetings. The lack of urgency
was frustrating. The boredom became downright mind-bending.

Much of our time was spent serving on committees about projects—health care, literacy, agriculture, education, and the list went on and on. I kid you not, our NGO had nineteen standing committees in all. Our children loved it because they were off school and got to play with their friends. Myself? I was bored senseless. Did I say I hated meetings?

During a general session of all the adults, a note was passed over to me that arrived with the mail sent down by the runner from our office in Chittagong. In a time where communications were unreliable or nonexistent, companies and organizations in developing countries hired runners to hand deliver time-sensitive messages.

A "runner" for our NGO was full-time employee whose job entailed being a courier of correspondence, spare parts, supplies, what have you, between the city and the jungle hospital compound.

I opened the note:

"Sir, I regret to inform you that your house has been stolen."

I showed the note to my wife. After reading it her eyes locked mine in horror. The Bangladeshi person working in our city office, whose first language wasn't English, confused the word "stolen" with "robbed." It didn't matter—we definitely got the idea. Excusing myself from the meetings, I drove the long three hours to see what happened at our home.

All I could think of while driving was how much did we lose. I heard the story about the vacant house next to us. The last tenant was a Scandinavian family, who upon returning from home leave in

Europe, discovered the house had been robbed. Everything of value was gone. I mean everything.

Not only their personal goods, furniture, and appliances were missing but also all the wiring, light fixtures, cupboards, windows, toilets, anything that could be removed. Reportedly, they got back in their vehicle, drove to the airport, and returned to Scandinavia for good.

My wife mentally prepared herself for the worst. She made a checklist of how we would replace all our kids' clothes, diapers, toys, and all our household belongings.

When I found the only things missing were a few dining room things, wall hangings, and pictures, I called Mr. Khan and asked him if I should even call the police.

"No, no, don't call the police, you can't trust them. My son once had a Rolex watch stolen from his house and reported it. The police came and beat his servants until they gave up the watch. To this day the chief of police is wearing my son's watch," he said.

"So, what should I do?"

"Ninety percent of the time, a robbery is an inside job, meaning between your servant and an outside thief. Fire your bearer right now before more stuff goes missing."

I fired the bearer. A core duty of household staff was to watch our house whenever we were gone. In a poor country, a home left alone was a candidate for robbery. Of course, the degree of security was entirely dependent upon the employee's integrity.

My family returned, and the search was on for a bearer replacement. Our timing was horrible. No other trained bearers in our town were available for hire. Out of desperation, Rebecca sent word down to the hospital.

One of our colleagues wrote back and said none were for hire there as well. The colleague did recommend we hire an untrained teenage boy from a Hindu village. His family was extremely poor, all on the brink of starvation.

His mother a widow, and her eldest son struggling with a developmental disability, this younger brother was desperate for work. My wife and I were suckers for helping widows, and neither of us wanted a family to starve to death, especially if we could hire the teenager.

We agreed to hire him yet he never came. A month went by until our colleague arranged for someone to bring him. The village boy was afraid of the city and had never ridden a public bus. Upon arrival, I showed Babul the room where he would stay.

Fresh from the village, I taught him how to turn on a light switch, flush the toilet, turn the faucets on the sink and shower, make his bed, open and close windows, and lock his door. The next day Rebecca pulled me aside.

"Phil, Babul's arms and legs are covered in scabies. Because he's eighteen he's a man, and I can't talk to him about his body."

The task fell to me. Like most impoverished people, Babul's family couldn't afford soap. I demonstrated how to wash using a bar of soap. He was an eager learner in everything I taught him, yet remained frightened of the city. He didn't leave our housing compound for weeks.

Dr. Bipul and I intensely executed our plan in setting up the school. A beautiful new building came up for rent, we signed a lease, and arranged for remodeling. Our next task was to furnish the rooms on three floors, and because it would board students, our shopping list was long.

Our problem was in procurement. No ready-made items were available. Large items such as desks, chairs, tables, beds, and mattresses had to be custom ordered, all handmade.

There also was no concept of a fixed price. Everything was negotiable. Once a shop was selected, negotiations took place. The procurement process took weeks to order everything, months to make, and then we staged delivery. Most items came on a specialty vehicle—a bicycle rickshaw. The back of the rickshaw had a small, flat platform.

When it came to curtains for dozens of windows and bedspreads for many beds, my wife went into overdrive. She hired a Muslim tailor from down at the hospital. The tailor lived at our house for weeks and turned our back veranda into his temporary workshop.

Rebecca was in heaven decorating the building. We lived tired those days, but the sweet feeling of accomplishment drove us on.

With a long week of shopping for the school setup finally over, I drove home to discover a message from our hospital administrator. A young American medical doctor and his wife needed to be picked up at the airport and escorted down to the hospital. We usually didn't do this but in an emergency, as team members we helped out.

In Islamic culture, the work week starts on Sunday and ends on Thursday. Friday is the holy day and Saturday is a rest day. Friday morning the hospital van picked us up from our home. We retrieved the young doctor and his wife from the airport, crossed the big bridge, and drove south towards the hospital.

By noon, the two-lane country road was lined with people walking to the mosque for Friday prayers. In one large town, traffic moved mercilessly slow until we saw a dreadful sight. A bus up ahead had the misfortune of hitting and killing a small child, right outside a mosque and connected to a madrasa, an Islamic school.

The timing couldn't have been worse for the bus driver, as the child was killed just as prayers ended. Young students from the madrasa wanted instant justice. Passengers were let off the bus. The driver stayed trapped inside. Rocked from side to side, the driver went berserk with fear, running back and forth like a caged mouse.

In our van, I was sitting up front beside the driver. Rebecca and the young couple sat in the seat behind. As we passed the mob rocking the bus, traffic came to a complete stop.

"What do we do, what should I do?" asked the doctor's wife.

"Don't make eye contact with the rioters and look down. Here, put this scarf over your head," Rebecca calmly said.

"But are we going to be all right?" asked the wife.

"Look, I grew up here and I've been in too many riots to count. As a woman in public, you need to become invisible or unapproachable. A scarf does the trick in a Muslim land."

Nervous enough, our Muslim driver broke out in a sweat.

"What's wrong?" I asked him in Bengali.

"I just heard someone say they were going after fuel to burn the bus."

I knew better than interpret what he said into English. Our guests would have freaked out. I was freaked out. Our van was only five feet from the side of the bus. For the next two minutes we waited, blood pounded loud in my ears, adrenalin raced through my body. Sure enough, someone came with a canister of fuel and doused the bus.

Fortunately for us, traffic began to move just when the fuel ignited. Flames leaped up the side of the bus. As our van slowly left the scene, I turned around and saw the bus driver burned to death. Categorically, the most horrific event I ever witnessed.

In a riot environment, no one could have stopped the frenzied mob, especially me as a foreigner. If I had tried to intervene and pull the "*Sheib* card," all of us could have been killed as well.

Back home after an exhausting day on the road, I longed for a hot meal, my nightly bowl of popcorn, and a soft bed. But our day wasn't over. My wife came into our house and saw our baby girl crawling across the gray terrazzo floor towards her mother with something dangling out of her mouth.

"Who gave Dani a piece of spaghetti? She's not allowed to have solid food yet."

No one answered. My wife gasped when the tip of the piece of "spaghetti" wiggled. A worm. Our baby daughter had intestinal worms in her tummy. And one was hungry enough that it took the liberty to venture up her esophagus scrounging for food.

Emotionally shaken, Rebecca lost it. Frantic, she called her medical doctor father in the States.

"I can handle wars, coups, cyclones, and burning buses, but I can't handle my baby girl with worms," she wept into the phone.

Doctor dad calmed her down and prescribed the right medicine. The battle against Dani's worms took two whole days before the drug worked its magic, resulting in a pile of dead worms coming out into her diaper. The calamity was over.

The end of dry season was beastly hot. Not steamy hot like during wet monsoons, I mean hot as in dry heat. We had already experienced forty straight days over 100 degrees Fahrenheit. The grass in our yard was brown, and the only reason the roses growing up our cement stucco wall were still brilliant in bloom was our gardener's prudence in watering them every day.

Kids have amazing hearing. In America, kids hear the ice cream truck coming down their street and run inside and ask their parents for money. In Bangladesh we didn't have ice cream trucks. We had something better—snake charmers.

Before I even heard the lilting sound of the snake charmer's flute outside, my sons, ages nine and seven, came asking for money. Babul was equally excited and showed up in my room along with Matt and Mark.

"Dad, Dad, can we have some money?"

I looked at Babul.

"It is ok, *Sheib*, I already talked to the charmer. He only wants forty taka."

"Only wants forty taka? That's a lot of money, almost a day's wage."

"Please, Dad, please?"

My heart turned to butter, and even though it was a lot of money in local currency, it wasn't much in American money. From a village with no snake charmers, Babul was as eager for me to fork over money just as much as my kids.

I told Babul to lower the price and he went out to negotiate. Negotiations failed and the rate remained at forty taka, about one U.S. dollar. With kids pleading, I caved and agreed to the price.

Almost all snake charmers in Bangladesh were of the Bede, a nomadic ethnic group who traditionally lived, traveled, and earned a living on the river. Some called them "Water Gypsies" or "River Gypsies," and usually they stayed in one place for only a couple of months. Like most Bangladeshis, these nomads spoke Bengali, were Muslim, except they didn't live in villages.

Typical of Bangladesh, one learned his trade from his father, who learned it from his father, with the occupational lineage going back thousands of years. Most villages in Bangladesh were segregated by occupation, not just the Hindu ones but as my research demonstrated, Muslim villages as well.

The Bede made their living along the rivers working in the snake sector—snake catching, snake selling, and snake charming. The chap at my door was at the top of the supply chain, interfacing with the retail public as a performer.

Not able to afford a turban, colorful beads, or nicely woven baskets for his snakes, his appearance indicated he was quite poor. He wore a Muslim-colored *lungi,* the skirt worn by working-class men, with a tee shirt. The charmer couldn't afford shoes.

With searing heat, I insisted the performance take place in the shade of my carport. I moved the car, grabbed my video camera, and like any responsible parent instructed my kids to stay back from the snakes.

The snake charmer opened his jute bags. Nothing happened. What an odd occurrence, as cobras usually stick out their diabolical little heads, sniff the air, gradually slither out, and then open their hoods ready for battle.

The noncooperating snakes embarrassed the charmer, which can't happen in Asia. Desperate to not lose face, he took drastic action and dumped the long, wiggling, devilish creatures out of their bags.

At this point my kids all went "ooh" and "ah" because even innocent children have some primal reaction to real danger. But this wasn't a typical day. The snakes were not acting their usual, cunning selves.

Out of more frustration, the charmer decided to hit them with his *latti,* a wooden rod. After all, if he ever wanted back in our gate his livelihood depended on a good performance. He played his flute, a *punji,* while his knee swayed back and forth. The swaying knee enticed the snakes to swing back and forth, but this day they just weren't cooperating. The skinny creatures acted dazed or drunk.

Sluggishly, the two sick snakes slightly opened their hoods but listed to one side. I thought they were about to fall over and pass out. After another hard swat with the *latti,* one snake had enough, slithered around, squared up, and faced the charmer, which means his "butt" faced us.

What happened next was unforeseen. In an instant, the sick cobra let loose and sprayed the grossest, bile-green colored diarrhea one can imagine. We all jumped back from the green slime.

"Oh cool," my sons shouted.

Matt raced into the house screaming at the top of his lungs.

"Mom, cobras have diarrhea, cobras have diarrea! It's so cool. You missed it but we have it on video."

Mark looked up at me with a look of sheer astonishment.

"Hey, Dad, did you know cobras get sick and have diarrhea?"

"No, son. I honestly didn't know snakes got sick."

The performance ended. No doubt his snakes were going on the disabled list. I felt for the charmer and instructed Babul to hand him the negotiated money. After all, he needed to feed his family too.

The Bede snake handlers were the poorest of the poor, with ninety-eight percent of the Bede living below the poverty line. Ninety-five percent of Bede children never attended school. Totally embarrassed, the charmer took the money, packed up his sick snakes, and in a flash scurried out the gate.

What could be worse than having my carport painted in green slime on one of the hottest days of the year? Babul saw my reaction and came over with a forlorn look.

"Don't worry, *Sheib*. Once he leaves I will clean up the mess."

Babul was the best. The last thing I wanted to do was wash my carport. Actually, I wasn't allowed to clean. The one time I picked up a broom, a Bengali man quickly snatched it out of my hand and commanded me never to pick up a broom again.

I was a *Sheib*, an educated man, and my job in their caste-influenced culture was to give orders. Someone else carried out the work. For me to do menial tasks done by "servants," as they were called, I would dishonor and shame myself. Also, the employee would think that I thought he wasn't capable of doing his job, causing him to lose face. All over a broom. When in Rome, do as the Romans.

———————— ❈ ————————

Progress on the school project was deliberate and methodical. The startup checklist required a great deal of discussion, but Bipul and I were a good match. More a visionary and a planner, I struggled with all the details. Dr. Bipul, trained as an accountant, thrived on details and executing plans came easy.

I knew what needed to be done and he made it happen. Many Bangladeshis could be moody, or as one of them told me, impulsive and whimsical. Dr. Bipul was reliable, steady, and predictable as they come, so when something was on his mind, I noticed.

"Bipul, you doing okay?"

"Since I've returned to Bangladesh, I've received the job offers from big foreign organizations based in Dhaka."

Large nonprofit organizations with huge budgets hired away the best, most trained people from smaller NGO organizations. My heart sank when I heard the offers and wondered if all our hard work on the school would be for naught.

My strategy for the school to be wholly controlled and operated by a Bangladeshi trustee board needed a champion to be the founder. Dr. Bipul was the only person with the passion, credentials, and life experience to bring our plan to fruition.

"So, what are going to do?" I asked.

"You know my dream was to start this school, but I realized something. I could have a small job with the big money from a Dhaka NGO or I could have a big job with the small money starting this school."

"Interesting. What's it going to be?"

In anticipation, I chewed my lips and listened to the beat of my frantic heart, blood pounding through it at a rapid rate. Deep down I knew Bipul wasn't motivated by money. His late father, a Presbyterian minister, raised Bipul in a comfortable upper-middle-class family.

"I've decided to do the big job with the small money."

My heart collapsed with relief. Another personal decision by our champion solidified our resolve. No question taking a big paying job with a large NGO was the safer bet for Bipul. But in the long run, we both knew he wouldn't be satisfied. He had a dream and he was the only one capable of achieving it.

PRINCIPLE # 31: "Trust your champion"

Empowering someone requires trust in the person you are working with because as the facilitator, you are dependent upon his or her integrity, values, and capability.

Bipul resigned from his NGO position. We recruited a board of all Bangladeshi members who voted themselves in as trustees and elected Dr. Bipul as their first president. After twenty years, his being under the thumb of the foreign organization was finally over.

So opened the great liberating project of Dr. Bipul's life. My role changed from educational planner to consultant and part-time professor. I was privileged to use my skills and influence to help empower a worthy, capable, and courageous man. A man who knew his people, his nation, and his culture better than any foreigner ever would.

In a twist of fate, Rebecca and I were about to embark on another journey of international living in Bangladesh. This time, not with Bangladeshis, but with other foreign expats.

CHAPTER 18

DÉTENTE

If you seek peace, if you seek prosperity for the Soviet Union and
Eastern Europe, if you seek liberalization, come here to this gate. . . .
Mr. Gorbachev, tear down this wall!
—Ronald Reagan

FROM EARLIEST CHILDHOOD, I grew up fearing the communists of the Soviet Union. The Cold War between the USSR and the USA unnerved Americans, with the ever-present threat of nuclear annihilation. I vividly remember the nuclear bomb drills in primary school.

Yet life is full of surprises. Never in my wildest dreams could I imagine raising my family in Bangladesh surrounded by Soviet communists. On the very top of our hill in Khulshi, a large compound housed a smaller version of an embassy, the Soviet Consulate.

Tall communication towers placed strategically on tops of gray buildings were only a stone's throw from my front door. Soviet diplomats lived all around us, their kids playing with our kids. My wife and I tried befriending the adults but no one ever talked to us.

Later on we found out Soviet policy forbade their diplomats from talking to any American. As their enemy, they would be in deep trouble for any contact with a U.S. citizen. One couple we saw all the time because the top floor of our building was perpetually rented by the Soviet government. The couple left, and the apartment remained empty for several months.

Breakfast over and kids off to school, I walked to the back veranda and looked out on the four-stall garage where each tenant parked their car. Each stall had a metal gate instead of an actual garage door. Drinking a cup of hot, sweet *Cha,* Babul looked intently through the veranda screen towards the garage.

"What are you looking at?" I asked.

"The new Soviet diplomat who moved in upstairs can't seem to back out his car."

The two of us sipped *cha* and watched as the young man attempted multiple times to back out. When the car finally made it out, I noticed that in his nervousness, the driver left his notebook on top of his vehicle. I ran out to warn him.

"Stop, stop," I shouted.

Startled seeing an American running towards him, he stopped the car, got out, and stood up. I pointed to the notebook still on the roof. Anxiety left his face as he retrieved it. Chagrined, in broken English he softly admitted he was learning to drive. Over the next several days, Alex, the twenty-six-year-old junior diplomat, became more and more friendly.

A few weeks later, his new Russian bride, Lena, a computer specialist, appeared from Moscow. Rebecca invited them to dinner. They asked permission from their boss, were denied, but came to dinner anyway. The dissolution of the Soviet empire was already happening on a personal level, even ignoring a direct order to not eat with us.

In a fundamentalist Muslim culture with no city nightlife, the newlyweds were starved for friendship. In the evening after our kids went to bed, we played cards, during which they practiced their English.

Other times, Rebecca and Lena would go into the kitchen and teach each other Russian and American recipes while Alex and I listened to the BBC on my little Sony shortwave radio.

Unbeknownst to us, they had an agenda—they wanted to start a family. Our secret weapon was three-year-old Nathan, whom they adored. Lena wanted to know how to be a good mother, and Alex desired to be a good father.

One time in the afternoon, they wanted to see Nathan. Even though Natie was already down for a nap, the four of us silently stood over Nate's bed. For an extensive amount of time, Alex and Lena starred at our toddler sleeping on his tummy with his diapered butt up in the air.

It never occurred to Rebecca and me we were indirectly mentoring a young couple in how to raise a family. How to raise children became a theme that drove our friendship.

The Soviet Union was falling apart and it was difficult to avoid politics. One day Alex saw Rebecca in the driveway and sarcastically asked her why she hadn't congratulated him on their holiday celebrating the communist revolution. He compared it to America's July fourth independence day.

"Congratulations, Alex. I don't care about politics. You are our friend and we care about you."

Later that night she took up a fresh batch of cookies and congratulated them.

The historic day arrived when each Soviet government installation around the world was ordered to lower the red communist flag and hoist up the Russian flag. Alex asked us if we would attend. It was the only time we ever entered the consulate compound.

Surprised we were the only foreign guests invited, and Americans no less, the consulate staff watched the flag ceremony in awkward silence. The head of the consulate, an old guard communist, refused to come out of his office and participate. Within a few minutes it was over. Everyone quietly went back to their offices while Rebecca and I walked home.

A note arrived at our door that afternoon. The invitation asked us to attend a party that night upstairs in Alex and Lena's apartment. Again, we were the only foreign guests at the party. Most guests appeared as Sadness wearing a smile.

Some didn't mind at all we were invited. Others did. A burly diplomat wearing thick glasses came over and in seething anger yelled at me in Russian. I mean he was up in my Kool-Aid and short on sugar. I was sure he was going to punch me. I stepped back. Alex quickly intervened and interpreted.

"So you Americans finally won. Are you proud of yourselves?"

I turned to the burly diplomat and, in my calmest, most sincere voice possible, responded, "I'm sorry. As Americans we don't feel like we won anything. We are relieved the Cold War is finally over. Now we can be friends instead of enemies. As far as I know, Americans are not gloating at your political change. I know my wife and I have come to enjoy our friendship with the host of this home. My children call them Uncle Alex and Aunt Lena."

The diplomat, festering with bitterness and loss of national pride, stood perfectly still until his chin quivered, his eyes welled up, and he began to weep. He excused himself from the room. We didn't stay long.

For some, our presence represented a beacon of freedom. For others, we were salt in their wounds. Alex enlightened us later by explaining how communism was their god, and now their god was dead. He told how he personally felt an empty void in his heart.

While my days were consumed with setting up the school, my wife was responsible for three guest houses our NGO operated in three parts of the country. A busy mom, she had her hands full.

However, three young Muslim sisters from the wealthiest family in the city, if not the entire country, pleaded with her to teach them English. Meeting weekly, the four ladies got along great. Rebecca could explain things in Bengali most American English speakers wouldn't even think was important.

Several months into their training they came to their tutoring session giggly and happy. Blurting out the news, Rebecca and I were invited to one of the girl's engagement party that evening.

A young man from a wealthy family was home for Christmas break from a university in England. The respective parents reached an agreement on the marriage of their children. Now it was time to declare their engagement formally.

The two had never met and didn't have any say in the matter. Marriage in Asian Bangladesh is more about the family than the bride and groom. As far as their parents were concerned, they were still kids. In parts of Asia, one isn't considered a real adult until you pass thirty years of age. The East venerates age, while Western culture idolizes youth.

Upon our arrival at the girls' home, a five-story building decorated for the occasion, Rebecca and I separated to join our gender groups. Rebecca went and hung out with the women, whereas I walked up a few floors to visit with the men.

After a couple hours of meeting the country's power elite, a family member came, pulled me aside, and told me there had been a change of plans.

"Sir, you are wanted downstairs to join your wife."

Rebecca was already in the private room when I arrived. Forget the engagement, the event just turned into a wedding. After all, everyone who would be invited to the wedding was already there. Only the immediate families would attend the ceremony downstairs, but as the bride's teacher, an important role, my wife and I were included as honored guests.

An Imam, the Muslim religious leader, stood ready to perform the ceremony. The bride and groom sat next to each other, both looking down, with the bride wearing a veil covering her face. She held a mirror in her lap.

After a short ceremony, she raised her veil, and the bride and groom looked down in the mirror to see each other for the first time.

My wife and I congratulated the families, the newlyweds, and then excused ourselves. Approaching our car, I was surprised to see Alex standing next to it with a worried look on his face.

"Phil, are any of your American doctors in town?"

"I don't know. Why?"

"One of our Russian sailors was shot in a brothel down by the port, and he's in bad condition."

Rebecca drove home while I rode with Alex to our guest house. Fortunately, one of our senior doctors from our hospital down country was actually in town. The three of us continued to the hospital close by.

The Russian sailor, only eighteen, had suffered a gunshot wound to his abdomen. Our American doctor read the chart, talked to the Bangladeshi doctor, and examined the patient.

"The Bangladeshi doctor is doing all that can be done. A gunshot wound in the abdomen is a severe injury."

The eighteen-year-old sailor, overwhelmed with fear, couldn't understand English but could tell from our faces he was in real trouble. Alex explained to the sailor the gravity of his situation, tried to comfort him, and then we left. Outside, our American doctor told Alex it would be a miracle if the sailor made it through the night.

The next day Rebecca called me at the school office.

"Alex just told me the sailor boy died in the night. Now we have a dilemma. The body can't be shipped home on a plane unless it is in a hermetically sealed coffin, which the Russian embassy doesn't have right now. The American embassy is the only one in the country that has one, and the Russians don't want to ask. He's asked me to ask for them."

My wife turned into a temporary "diplomat" for an afternoon as she made several phone calls to our American embassy asking them to donate a "plane-worthy" casket. Between Rebecca and Alex, the coffin was delivered to the Russian embassy in a way as to not embarrass the Russians.

Alex was beyond grateful. "Détente" in this instance came down to an American expat interceding with her embassy to solve a diplomatic problem. All in an effort by an American mother to return home a young Russian sailor to his grieving family.

———————✳———————

From the day I hired him, our bearer Babul was my shadow. At times, it was almost hard to take because he constantly wanted to be around me. Always eager to please, one time he proudly brought me a pair of my shoes, freshly shined. He explained how happy he was because in only thirty minutes, he negotiated the traveling cobbler's fee from ten cents down to five cents. I never knew a more dedicated and loyal household worker.

Our cook quit yet I knew it wouldn't present a problem. Day in and day out, Babul assisted the cook, and by looking over his shoulder, he learned how to prepare meals. I noticed when the cook was home on *chuti,* his time off, Babul's cooking was excellent.

Now promoted as the new cook, Babul was in charge of the household. He always thought of ways to please me. It didn't take long for him to figure out the way to my heart was through my stomach. Every evening before leaving the house, he knocked on our bedroom door and with a cheerful smile handed me a bowl of fresh popcorn.

Whenever I pulled up to the gray gate of our house, the *darwan* usually opened the gate. If it was his tea time, then Babul covered. One day Babul opened the heavy metal gate with a huge smile on his face, happy to see us. While we waited for the gate to open, Rebecca looked over at me.

"You know, you are like a father figure to him. By hiring him, you saved him and his family from starvation. He really owes you his life."

"Never thought about it. Yeah, I guess I did save his life."

"More importantly, you trained a widow's son to become a man. Look at him. You've taught him life skills. We have to find him another job before we leave."

Our time in Bangladesh was coming to a close. It became almost impossible to fight the fungus growing in Nathan's ear canals. Every two months the doctors scraped out what looked like cottage cheese only to see the fungus returned. Our ENT specialist in the States urged us to return home. The clock was ticking one sure stroke at a time, and we knew it was time to leave for good.

I broke the news to Dr. Bipul that our time in Bangladesh was up. I reassured him we would time our departure after the new school's term finished. The school was operational, and the new president was more than capable of carrying on without me. After four years, our dream of starting the first private graduate school in our area to award a master's degree became a reality.

PRINCIPLE # 32: "Rome wasn't built in a day"
Creating meaningful project work in the developing world takes time, usually in a place where time isn't important.

Finding a job for Babul turned out to be quite easy. The guest house at the hospital compound needed a cook trained in preparing

American food. With a constant flow of American short-term doctors and nurses, he was right for the job. Plus, he could live at home in his Hindu village and take care of his widow mother.

For our other employee, it was more difficult. Rebecca had hired a Muslim woman, Amira, to watch our toddlers and help with the laundry. Our family of six lived in a humid environment that required a great deal of work. Clothes needed to be washed, dried, and ironed every day.

Amira was not her husband's first wife. In Islam, a man is allowed up to four wives, and there definitely was a pecking order among the wives. In Amira's case, her husband was too poor to marry more than two. But she got the dregs of her family because Wife Number One received priority from their husband.

Wife number one's four kids got to go to school. Amira's four kids didn't. After she started working for us, we paid for her kids to go to school. The fact that Amira had a good paying job with a foreign family only caused resentment from wife number one.

Rebecca couldn't find Amira another job, yet she knew her kids would have to drop out of school. It meant she would go back to extreme poverty, being neglected in her marriage and home. Amira was a woman at risk.

The last few weeks before our departure, Amira came up with a plan. She asked if we would buy her a sewing machine because she wanted to start her own business making *sari* blouses. We didn't know if spending a couple hundred dollars on a good sewing machine would empower Amira, but it was worth the chance.

A good sewing machine cost as much as eight months of wages. There was no way Amira could afford a sewing machine herself. Before our departure she learned to make quality blouses, and although shy and timid, she was desperate enough and had enough entrepreneurial spark to market them. A few sold and there was a glimmer of hope.

Our final weeks in Bangladesh required more "international downtime," meaning we spent our days packing, had a whole-house garage sale, and gave away many things. The day before we left, Babul came to me.

"*Sheib*, can I go with you to the airport? I've never seen an airplane or an airport."

As it turned out, he was the only one who saw us off. The driver of our NGO van dropped us off, I arranged for porters to carry our bags, and we walked into the airport. Babul walked between little Nate and Dani, holding their hands.

After checking in at the ticket counter, we made our way to security. Babul was speechless. I thought he was overwhelmed with the size of the terminal building and all the electronics. I was wrong. We were like family and about to leave, never to return as a family. He was overcome with emotion.

Not able to go any farther because of security, Babul hoisted each little tyke up on a table and proceeded to hug them both, sobbing and wailing as he tried to say goodbye. Nathan, patting Babul's back, kept saying in Bengali, "It will be all right, Uncle Babul."

The Bangladeshi passengers around us became utterly silent, surprised a young Bengali man had such an emotional attachment to two little American kids. Our children were often mocked by other American kids for speaking Bengali to adults in the honorific tense and calling adult Bangladeshis uncle or aunt.

Cleared through security, we made our way into the departure lounge. Through the glass partition, we all waved a final goodbye to Babul. He looked bewildered, as if the rug had just been pulled out from under him.

I might have saved Babul's life, but little did we know, seventeen years later he would help save Nathan's life. Spending a semester abroad as a college student, Nate became seriously ill with an infection while working at the Bangladesh hospital. Babul, the guest house manager, showed up at the hospital, fed, and cared for Nate as if he was his own child.

Our flight was delayed. Rebecca gave me a significant look, the kind I pay attention to because it usually is something profound.

"You thought you were here to help empower Dr. Bipul, but you ended up mentoring two other men as well. Babul is now on his own and will be working near his home. Alex is now a father to a beautiful baby girl."

"I know, can you believe it?"

"I don't think you realize the impact you have on people. Whether it's a poor, uneducated village boy learning to become a man, a dignified upper middle-class professor starting a school, or a young Russian diplomat learning to be a dad, their lives have been changed by your influence. I could keep going."

I didn't know what to say.

"Think about it. We have this unique role as educated Americans doing humanitarian work in a foreign country."

"How is it unique?" I asked.

"Because of our status as Americans, we have access to the power elite. Yet, because we also work with the poor, we bridge all social levels. We bridge diversity in a way most cultures don't let you. I grew up playing with illiterate village kids in the morning and then played with government officials' kids in the evening. Just like the time Nathan sat outside with the naked beggar kids, and then we flew to Dhaka the same day, and he played with the president's kids that evening."

"So, what are you saying?"

"If you don't take responsibility to embrace diversity and see who you can be to all kinds of people, you miss out on a lot of life over here."

"It's not easy, though. What do you think is the key to empowering culturally diverse people?"

"Cultural sensitivity is the core value that drives a cross-cultural relationship. Without it, you are just like an 'ugly American.'

Cultural sensitivity is so important in how you interact, whether the person is a villager, scholar, or diplomat. Most Westerners are clueless about how they offend people from different cultures. When they find out they made a mistake, most are too proud or embarrassed to admit it."

Her reference to the "ugly American" meant the stereotypical American abroad made famous by the 1958 bestselling novel by that name. It created such a reaction in America, the U.S. Peace Corp came about as a result. The concept later referred not only to Americans but any expat who is arrogant, demeaning, and ethnocentric around those in a host culture.

PRINCIPLE # 33: "Don't be like an ugly American"

Cultural sensitivity is the core value that drives a cross-cultural relationship. Without it, you are just like an ugly American. Develop cultural intelligence by learning proper ways of interacting, especially when very different from your own.

The airport loudspeaker came on and called our flight. Our kids put on their backpacks and all of us got in line. I leaned over to Rebecca.

"Well, I sure made a lot of mistakes these past few years."

"Yes, but you learned from them in how to relate to different kinds of people. That takes trust. Without trust there is no relationship. Think about all the cultural blunders we made with Alex and Lena. If we hadn't immediately apologized, we could have really blown our relationship."

"I never realized how suspicious Russians are of us and we are of them. It's kind of amazing we broke through that wall of suspicion."

"Did it ever occur to you that this last year we spent more time with Russians than with Bangladeshis?" Rebecca asked.

"Now that you say it, it does seem strange. We got a first-hand crash course on Russian culture, politics, and international affairs. I wonder why?"

Little did we know, all the time spent with our Russian diplomat friends in Bangladesh prepared us for our next foreign assignment.

CHAPTER 19

FOLLOW THE SILK ROAD

*If you have men who will only come if they know
there is a good road, I don't want them. I want men who will
come if there is no road at all.*
—David Livingston

MY FIRST TIME to see our new U.S. headquarters property, I was full of anticipation. I drove up the hill on a mile-long private lane wondering what my life stateside would be like. Before returning to America, I considered other job offers until our NGO president got wind of it and offered me an executive position.

Our move to the East Coast required selling our little house in Michigan and finding a place close to the office. Upon settling on a school district where our children would attend school, Rebecca and I built our first custom home. All those years of renting our home in Michigan while overseas allowed us to pay off our mortgage early and gave us a substantial down payment.

A Georgian two-story, with two white pillars and circle top windows, our new house was perfect for our family of six. Over the next several years our new house would serve as a *defacto* guest house for many friends and colleagues on home leave in the States.

A few miles from historic Gettysburg, our location provided close access to international airports in New York, Philadelphia, Baltimore, and Washington D.C. My new job would require substantial international travel.

Once the "newness" factor of my job wore off, I found myself in an office pushing paper. Those first two years at headquarters were perhaps the most monotonous years of my career. I soon realized I was the token "PhD." Although I chaired the board strategic planning committee, the bulk of my time I did research and planning, most of it ignored.

Overseas I was a doer, builder, and mentor. Now I was a desk jockey and became more frustrated with each passing month. All the politics of a large organization didn't help either. I started to think about finding another job.

Our in-house attorney learned of my despair and told our boss. The president, a former college basketball coach, always concerned about his team of executives, called me into his office. "Phil, I understand you are unhappy, and I want to know what you want to do."

"No offense, but we are an old organization working in the same countries, doing the same things, for decades. I would like to open up new countries and place teams of Americans."

"Where do you have in mind?"

"Now that the Soviet Union has collapsed, new countries have emerged and hardly any NGOs are working there. I'm especially interested in Central Asia, specifically Kazakhstan, Uzbekistan, and Tajikistan. Just north of Afghanistan and Pakistan."

Now that I had his attention, I laid out what I wanted to do.

"My research shows the Soviet Union didn't have much in the way of a charitable sector, so the concept of a nonprofit organization is new. Unfortunately, of the few foreign NGO groups working there, some have an agenda of political change. I don't think it's wise to try to register with a government as a traditional NGO. As an American, I don't want to be identified as having a political agenda."

"So, what do you recommend instead?"

"The best way to register would be as a foreign business. The concept of private ownership of businesses is new because during communism the state owned everything. But the laws have changed to support free enterprise, and Central Asian governments are encouraging it."

"I'm interested. Draw up a plan and let me noodle on it. We haven't done anything like this before."

Elated and energized, for the next several weeks I poured myself into creating a plan. A few days later I delivered it in person. He called me into his office to make my case.

"Tell me, what's the biggest challenge to your plan becoming a reality," he asked.

"Money. We are going to need a war chest to do this right. And, of course, the right people with business experience."

"Our organization doesn't have the funds for something like this, so the burden of raising a war chest will be up to you. I'm already raising millions a year to keep this headquarters afloat."

My heart sank. But like a good coach, he quickly gave me hope.

"If you are going to lead this new venture, then you need to take responsibility for funding it. But I tell you what. I will introduce you to a few of my rich business friends to serve on your board. I've already contacted them, particularly one who is on track to become a billionaire. They're fascinated by helping us do business over there that funds humanitarian work."

Long story short, the businessmen agreed to fund business operations and serve on the board. Once the men voted the board into existence, I was appointed Chief Executive Officer (CEO). My dream of leading an organization finally came to fruition in 1995. Now all I had to do was make it happen.

A young recruit heard I was planning to do business overseas and asked if he could join the new venture. Liam, born abroad to American parents, spoke three foreign languages and was a business major in college. Along with two other Americans, the four of us embarked on our first survey trip to Central Asia.

Several days in Kazakhstan, Kyrgyzstan, and Uzbekistan, it became clear Uzbekistan had the most potential. Home to the ancient Silk Road, the road traversed through Uzbekistan and once served as the main trade route connecting China with Europe. Cities like Samarkand, known for The Registan, an enormous Islamic theological Madrassa, and Bukhara, famous for their hand-woven rugs, were along the caravan route made famous by Marco Polo. A historic area known for trade now reopened thanks to the fall of the Soviet Union.

The majority of the population were ethnic Uzbeks and almost all Muslims. The ones educated in Soviet schools were Russified, meaning they were secular Muslims. Well dressed in European clothes, these Russified Uzbek professionals mainly spoke in Russian.

The traditional Uzbeks lived in rural areas, spoke the Uzbek language, and practiced Islam. Seventy years of atheistic communism did a real number on all practicing religions, especially Islam. Liam and I were used to majority Muslim countries where Islam dominated culture, speech, and norms. Not hearing the call to prayer and seeing only a few mosques was strange.

Market research revealed Uzbekistan had real needs in health care and food production, two sectors in which I had experienced American personnel anxious to join our team. A state-owned eye hospital in the capital, Tashkent, expressed interest in working with us to improve eye care.

The government eye hospital was dark yet clean. The hospital administrator, an older female doctor formerly from Tatarstan, was receptive and eager to know everything about us. Liam particularly hit it off with a young Uzbek surgeon.

Before our trip was over, the young surgeon introduced us to his older brother, a local businessman already doing international business. Somewhat wary, the older brother invited us to his house for dinner. After a delicious meal, his grilling commenced, mostly directed at me.

"My brother tells me you want to set up a business here?"

"Yes, our market research shows there is a lot of potential here."

"It is difficult to do business here and takes a lot of money. Are you the CIA?"

"No, we are not connected to the CIA. I have American investors who are interested in your country. One of my board members owns an investment firm and manages sixty billion dollars. He is only one of several interested in underwriting our business here."

A long pause ensued, and the expression on his face indicated he was somewhat miffed. I thought, here it comes, and braced myself.

"So, you Americans, with all your money are going to show us poor people how to run a business in a changing economic system you don't understand?"

Memories of our Bangladesh experience with Alex and Lena reminded me how proud and sensitive Russians were when it came to Americans offering to help. I knew to tread lightly.

"We understand the challenges, and on a practical level, you are right. We don't know how your economy works, nor do we know how to get things done with the communist bureaucracy. But we do know how important it is to have local partners who can navigate these challenges."

He began to soften, relieving tension in the room.

"What are you proposing?"

"If we introduce modern medical technology, both in equipment and techniques, your brother can be the first eye surgeon in Central Asia to offer world-class eye surgery. Our help will give him a competitive advantage, allowing him to grow his practice and profit personally. We have the technology, know-how, and money. But you know how to do it here. A good partnership is when both partners mutually need each other. We need someone like you."

The brothers looked at each other and communicated with their eyebrows.

"How would you structure the business?" the older brother asked.

"You and your brother register a local Uzbek business, and we invest in your business as foreign investors. Our new 50/50 joint venture would lease a wing of the government hospital for our exam rooms and offices, plus pay the hospital for the use of their operating rooms. Our American company would pay for remodeling the hospital wing, so it looks modern. Liam here would manage the office staff, and your brother would manage doctors and nurses. You would deal with the government bureaucracy."

Strategic planning and deal-making is a clarifying process. After a few more meetings, we struck a deal. Back in the States, Liam took a crash course in Russian and then moved his family to Tashkent.

Over the next year, my American team exported modern equipment, and our Uzbek team worked the system to clear it through the bureaucracy. Through a partnership with Ohio State University Medical School, we brought Uzbek eye surgeons for training in Columbus, Ohio. New surgery techniques learned in America would advance eye surgery in Central Asia by thirty years.

The fact our team was setting up the first privatized medical business drew local attention. All firms during the Soviet era were owned by the state. Individual investors owning a business was illegal. Now a new business would demonstrate how a privately held medical practice would function in a country of government-owned socialized medicine.

When it came time for our grand opening, Liam called me at my home in the States.

"Phil, as CEO it's really important that you come for the grand opening."

"I wouldn't miss it. Are we ready?"

"Yes, but can you bring over the eye surgeon from Ohio? Our opening will showcase our equipment and know-how. The hospital is lining up key patients, including free cataract surgery for World War II vets."

Fresh off a plane in Tashkent, I steamed the wrinkles out of my navy-blue suit. Our company car brought me to the clinic in time for the television interview. Broadcast live throughout Central Asia's population of fifty million people, it was our one shot to make a good impression.

Olga, our amazing translator, conveyed my remarks and made us look good. In another life, she easily could have been an actress or TV personality—she was that talented. After the TV interview, the hospital held a party celebrating our grand opening. Liam came over with a worried look on his face, let out a big sigh, and broke the news.

"I just found out the main patient for cataract surgery tomorrow is the widow of the former head of the Uzbekistan Communist Party."

"Wait a minute. You mean the wife of the former leader?" I asked.

"Yep, Gafurovna Rashidova, she's in her eighties, and everyone will be watching to see her surgical result, including her family."

Her husband, a hard-line communist dictator, ruled Uzbekistan with an iron fist during the Soviet era.

"If anything goes wrong with her surgery tomorrow, we are in a heap of trouble," I said.

"I have confidence in our American surgeon. He ranks as one of the best eye surgeons in the Eastern U.S."

"There will be hell to pay if anything goes wrong. I already have visions of spending time rotting in the *gulag.*"

Scheduled for the first surgery of the morning, the highly respected former leader's wife showed up with her bodyguards. A frail, thin lady, she oozed spunk, and acted like the "Queen Mum."

Because our American surgeon brought his equipment, replacing a cataract using the phacoemulsification procedure usually took a few minutes. But our surgical team operated on her longer than usual. The stakes couldn't be higher.

I sat alone in an empty exam room waiting for it to be over. Each passing minute seemed to go by in slow motion. The door opened, and Liam pulled down his surgical mask.

"Everything went well. Our patient sees better now than she has in fifty years."

I let out a vocal sigh of relief.

"I guess we get to go home now instead of the prison camp."

My gut told me we needed to start a second venture right away. It didn't seem wise to put all our hopes in the clinic succeeding. Starting two projects reduced our risk in case one failed. For a fee, the U.S. embassy's Gold Key Service found a suitable partner for our company to invest in a food-processing plant. Dollar for dollar, the Gold Key Service was the best investment in finding and vetting potential business partners in Central Asia.

Not long after sunrise on a chilly morning, Liam, Olga, and I left the urban bustle of Tashkent and visited an idle Soviet-era food-processing plant. Turned out, our rural destination was in an idyllic setting.

Shadowed by the stark majesty of the Tien Shan Mountains, part of the Western Himalayan range, I was stunned by the alpine beauty. The mountains surrounded a valley abundant in fruits and vegetables. Mountain streams flowed into the Chirchiq River, providing plentiful water for farming and food processing.

The owner of the plant property was a local Uzbek man with a long Muslim name. Somewhat overweight, this middle-aged, clean-shaven man exuded leadership and entrepreneurial passion. During Soviet times he was the manager of the food-processing plant. Like so many other state assets, during the Soviet breakup he ended up the owner.

More important to us, he knew the farmers, the mayor in a nearby town, and had experience processing food. His specialty was processing fruit jams and tomato paste. The robust flavor of the valley's fruits and vegetables was nothing I had ever experienced.

From an agricultural viewpoint, the growing seasons were ideal, water was abundant, and the fields fertile. The "bones" of the processing plant were good, but it would take a bit of remodeling, retooling, and sprucing up. After a tour of the plant and property, we sat around a table in his office.

Break time in our deliberations came. I stepped out of the plant and gazed up in awe at the towering, transcendent splendor of neighboring peaks. In front of them were rolling hills of carefully maintained orchards and crop fields, results of decades of collective farming.

Akin to the story of Rudyard Kipling's *The Man Who Would Be King*, it seemed as if we happened upon a lost, hidden agricultural paradise, cut off from the outside world. Store shelves in Uzbekistan's cities and towns were almost bare of any canned or jarred fruit.

Processed veggies didn't exist. Those empty shelves demonstrated a genuine market need but masked an even deeper strategic need for food security. Our talks resumed, and I said we might be interested in a partnership after we calculated the numbers.

Back in the States, I drafted a business plan. The plan was sent out to Liam, who explained it to our potential partner. My next trip back, Igor, the plant owner, was eager to make a deal. I contacted Olga.

"Hey, what do you know about business and negotiating deals?"

"I've interpreted treaty negotiations between countries, so I know how the game works."

Olga had interpreted for kings, heads of state, and countless diplomats. I already knew she had a photographic memory. Before Olga interpreted the first time for our eye surgeon, she stayed up all night and memorized a Russian-English medical dictionary. I figured she would do the same with a business dictionary. And she did.

Igor and I went through several rounds of negotiating. He could contribute land, the plant, offices, equipment, barns, know-how, and fruit left over from last season. Just as important, Igor had influential contacts in the government, knew local business practices, and could rehire the best former employees, all needing jobs.

My side could contribute money, technology, and modern know-how. Fortunately, I had recruited an American mechanical engineer who took early retirement from a Fortune 500 food company. A civil engineer who specialized in processed water also joined us, along with a marketing executive.

Our Joint Venture agreement signed, Olga informed me it was customary to celebrate. One of Igor's buddies owned a *dacha,* a small cabin, up in the mountains beyond the food plant. On the designated day, Igor drove to Tashkent and picked us up.

The drive up into the mountains was treacherous, but the exquisite views of the sun thrusting through towering granite peaks transported us into existential moments of timeless majesty. Warm hues of increasing yellow sunlight transfixed the countryside from darkish, vast walls of rock to bright, clear views of shimmering snow-capped peaks.

The vibrant blue sky above was completely devoid of clouds. Fresh mountain air flowed through the valley. Similar to Montana, around and above us was Central Asia's big sky country. The alpine scenery was stunningly unreal.

The dark wooden *dacha* hung on the side of a mountain like a giant birdhouse. A broad front porch dangled over a steep drop-off towards the slender Chirchiq valley below. Seated in a circle on a scarlet Bukhara rug, and reclining on cushions Uzbek style, the view of a gorgeous mountain peak out the window seemed like a picture hanging on the wall.

Thanks to a generous supply of vodka, by noon Igor and his Uzbek Muslim friends were happily telling jokes between endless toasts to good fortune. Typical of Central Asian hospitality, extravagant courses of delicious food kept coming. Before long, all of us dozed off.

A sharp crack of a rifle shot woke us. The sound echoed for several seconds as it rebounded off mountain walls. Less than a minute later, another rifle crack followed. Igor and his friends cheered with delight. Shouting "*Salud*" and holding shot glasses in the air, they arduously stood up and headed for the back door. I looked at Olga across the room.

"So, what's going on?"

"I have no idea. Let's go outside and see."

"When someone is shooting a gun outside?"

She looked over at Igor, who smiled, gesturing to come.

"Igor told me we are in for a big surprise."

Behind the *dacha* was a small corral, lined with local men sitting on the fence. Inside the corral were two giant gray mountain goats standing across from each other, restless and rearing for battle.

Each goat was held back by a stout man on each side, each handler gripping a horn of the powerful beast, with his bare feet planted forward. The rifle crack sound was, in fact, two goats butting heads, warming up for battle.

"Igor says he paid for two trained mountain goats be brought from Turkmenistan," Olga translated.

"Isn't Turkmenistan like hundreds of miles away?" I asked.

She raised her eyebrows, saw my growing disdain and with determined, piercing eyes, she got in my face.

"Listen, this man spent a lot of his money bringing these goats up here. Everyone will be watching you, so for his sake, you better act as if you enjoy it."

Although it felt like a scolding, I took to heart her counsel. Igor would lose face if I didn't act pleased.

"Olga, you are absolutely right. I'm sorry. I'll try to enjoy it."

PRINCIPLE # 34: "Eat humble pie"

The road to international success depends on humility, cultural sensitivity, and strong interpersonal relationships. Humble yourself, learn to take advice, admit cultural mistakes right away, and ask forgiveness.

Our entrance outside went unnoticed, as betting was already underway. Frankly, watching two huge brutes batter themselves senseless for two hours wasn't my idea of fun. But culturally, and for the sake of our new business relationship, I knew I had to act as if I enjoyed it.

All the locals' eyes were on the foreigner, an American no less. Cold war distrust still lingered. Most had never seen or met an American, so I needed to represent my country and our new company well.

By now, I learned to take Olga's advice, knowing she had my best interest in mind. Fortunately for me, she personified the concept of East meets West. Her European, Russian ancestry understood my Western mind-set, and her Uzbek ancestry understood my business partner's Central Asian, Eastern worldview. I learned to trust that bridge.

The time came when one of the mountain goats refused to back up for another round. Within a few seconds the exhausted beast fell over. Winners cheered while losers reluctantly paid up. I kept thinking how animal rights groups would be horrified by such an inhumane sport. I was appalled, but for Igor's sake I couldn't show it.

I sat in quiet introspection during our drive down the mountains. In the front seat, Olga and Igor carried on an extended discussion in Russian. After a contemplative time of silence, she turned around. This time her eyes were warm and soft, not daggers piercing through me.

"Igor wants to know when you are coming again."

"Not for a couple of months. Why?"

"He wants to know an exact date. He's inviting you to his only son's wedding and wants to schedule the date around your visit. There will be several days of feasting, but the first night he wants you to be there."

I knew from my wife who grew up in Asia that in this part of the world, they view it as a great honor to invite you to a family wedding. Turning down the invitation would never be forgotten. Those from the West don't often realize that feasting and food are a big deal in the East. I mean, a really big deal.

"Tell him I will be honored to come. I'll be back here the last week of July."

In town, Igor dropped me off at our American company's furnished apartment. He gave me a strong embrace, said goodbye, and then shook my hand with such enthusiasm I was beginning to feel like family.

CHAPTER 20

SUMMER OF '98

Twenty years from now you will be more disappointed by the
things that you didn't do than by the ones you did do. So throw
off the bowlines. Sail away from the safe harbor. Catch the trade
winds in your sails. Explore. Dream. Discover.
—Mark Twain

UNTIL OUR AMERICAN business teams relocated to Uzbekistan, every other month I traveled from the USA to Uzbekistan, nine time zones away. I lived in a state of jet lag for weeks at a time. The task of setting up two international businesses at the same time became all-consuming.

In any country, entrepreneurial startups become intense because right from the beginning both processes and people must become operational. Creating systems and controls, recruiting and training new personnel, and constant communications left one drained and spent.

Rebecca held the fort at home raising our four kids in my absence, which wasn't easy. Even the neighborhood kids wondered why I was gone so much.

"You want to hear what your boys said about you to their friends?" Rebecca asked.

"Sure," I said.

The gleam in her eye and the grin on her face prepared me for a dose of humiliation.

"One of the neighbor kids asked if you were a spy, like 007."

"What'd my boys say?"

"No, he's more like 00 nothing!"

I had to smile because anyone who knew me would agree I'd make a lousy spy. I always lost at games where you had to lie. Granted, I worked in an obscure part of the world unknown to most Americans.

But my boys were right. My work/life balance was out of whack. Summer was approaching, and Rebecca came up with an idea on how we could spend more time as a family.

"I think we should join you for your next trip to Uzbekistan in July. Summer camps will be over, and we're all anxious to see what you have going over there," she said.

"Babe, it will cost a fortune."

"I don't want our kids becoming too American. Matt and Mark are teenagers, and they need the summers from now on to be reminded of their international roots."

"Like I said, the tickets alone will be expensive."

"Don't worry about it. A donor wants us to spend more quality time together and offered to underwrite the whole trip."

I knew the kids were eager to go somewhere. After living through riots, a civil war, and charged by rhinos while riding elephants, life in the States was too predictable and benign. Five years had elapsed, and my kids were ready for an international adventure. And boy did they get one.

Our children now older, it made a big difference traveling as a family. Gone were strollers and diaper bags. Matt, now fifteen, and Mark, thirteen, were old enough to help with the luggage. Nate and Dani, eight and seven, were like twins and also capable of helping.

Across the pond, our first stop was Amsterdam. The streets filled with people, along came a tall, bearded man rollerblading with traffic. Rollerblading that is, wearing nothing but a small backpack and leather kneepads.

Shocked their little sister had to see naked body parts, my boys started chanting, "Wipeout. Wipeout." The rollerblader didn't fall, but to our relief, he disappeared behind a city bus.

The flight from the Netherlands to Almaty, Kazakhstan, arrived late in the evening. My fatherly duty included filling out all the arrival forms, tucking them inside our six passports, and handing them to the immigration officer.

The Kazak officer in the dingy, dark arrival hall kept staring at the visa stamps in our passports, and every few seconds, he glanced at his watch. His finger on the visa stamp, he shoved back my passport, tilted his head back, took off his reading glasses, then tapped his watch.

I looked at the date and realized that somehow we arrived an hour too early. Technically, we couldn't enter the country until after midnight.

He handed back all the passports and shouted in English the only word he knew: "Deport!" His long, skinny arm pointed to the sign over a door that read, "Deportation Lounge." I protested, saying we were only an hour early, but he kept shouting "Deport!" Immediately, security officers escorted us to the deportation lounge.

Rebecca and I both knew detaining us was a ploy for a bribe. A couple of hours passed, and I worried our luggage would disappear from baggage claim. My resourceful wife came up with a plan.

One by one our children went to the lady guarding the door and asked to use the restroom. She had to unlock the padlock holding the chain through double doors, let a kid out, relock the shackle, and escort each child down the hall to the restroom.

The test was on. An hour of this was all the lady could tolerate. Next thing we knew she was in an argument with the immigration officer. He conceded, then motioned us over and with a scowl stamped our passports.

Other than a fistfight outside the airport terminal between hungry taxi drivers wanting our business, we arrived safely at our hotel by four in the morning. After a few hours of sleep and a hearty breakfast, we returned to the airport and boarded a plane to Tashkent.

The wedding of Igor's son was a rich, cultural treat. Held in a large walled compound, 700 guests arrived on the evening of day one. An Uzbek Muslim wedding lasted four days, and unlike America, where the bride's father pays for most of the wedding, Igor, the groom's father, paid for the entire wedding.

Our table, situated on a wooden platform, was loaded with plates of colorful fresh fruit, piles of wedding pilaf, and bottles of Vodka. Lots and lots of bottles. Although Islam forbids alcoholic drinks, nevertheless it flowed. Never in all my days did I witness so many Muslim men drinking alcohol. I mean gallons of alcohol.

Hours went by without any sign of the groom, who was off at an all-day bachelor's party. Chatter soon spread through the crowd alerting everyone the bridegroom's procession was underway.

Decorated cars showed up and Igor's son, a recent law school graduate, was greeted at the gate by four men wearing thick purple robes. In unison, all four blew loud blasts from *karnays,* horns six-foot long.

The whole scene reminded us of what weddings were probably like during ancient Biblical times, especially the anticipated arrival of the bridegroom.

After a small ceremony, the couple sat in the middle of a long table, covered with gifts. Each wore a special wedding hat, and by tradition, the bride continued to wear hers every day for the first month. That special bridal hat announced to the public she was a new wife.

After the feast, dancing commenced. I noticed a seven-year-old girl dancing late into the night, her dress twirling in the moonlight, her blonde locks flowing in the air. Like a tiny Esmeralda, my daughter Dani danced her heart out. Our goal of connecting to her international roots was on.

PRINCIPLE # 35: "Be fascinated"

Attending special events gives insight into what is important in a culture. Weddings, funerals, rites of passage, and holidays all reveal embedded values.

Our teams of American families were soon to arrive and live in Tashkent, including children of high school age. Tashkent didn't have an international school, and other than homeschooling, the closest schooling option was Rebecca's old boarding school in Pakistan, on the other side of the mountains.

Twenty-five years had passed since her school days, and before recommending the school to our team, it was prudent to survey the old establishment. She was skeptical, recalling her unhappy, lonely days high in the Himalayans.

As a young teenage girl, she was surrounded by a Taliban mentality and because of the war between West and East Pakistan, cut off from her family.

The international school, perched at an elevation of seven thousand feet, was situated in an old Anglican Church compound.

Incredible views of contiguous snow-capped peaks, including majestic K-2, the second highest mountain on the planet, left us in awe.

However, a couple of days at the school revealed it was no longer a viable option for Americans, mainly due to changes away from an American curriculum. Another factor was the alarming change in the cultural shift back towards fundamental Islam, as many were sympathetic with the Taliban.

In public, anti-American feelings were clear and evident. My wife remembered enough Urdu to understand what people were saying about us. Now in 1998, their looks communicated a simple fact—we were not liked or wanted. A few years later, the boarding school would be attacked by an Al-Qaida cell and forced to close.

Time to go, we braced ourselves for the harrowing taxi ride down the mountains. Safety-wise, nothing had changed in twenty-five years. My precious cargo in tow, I gripped my seat and clenched my teeth at every hairpin turn.

At times, the van's tires slid on gravel towards the edge of the road. Guardrails were nonexistent. Over the edge, only air for thousands of feet meant a horrendous fall before certain death. After descending barren heights for nail-biting hours, our taxi delivered us to a hotel in the capital.

Our airline schedule kept us a couple of days in Islamabad, the capital of Pakistan. The Marriott Hotel was a welcome relief after bunking in dingy dorm rooms. My morning hotel ritual was to wake up early while everyone was asleep, eat a hearty buffet breakfast, and read a newspaper. This particular morning, tension filled the restaurant. Everyone acted on edge and seemed preoccupied.

Breakfast finished, I walked towards the door. An American man in his late forties approached me.

"You shouldn't be here."

A recurring phrase I had heard for decades, I wasn't buying it.

"Well, good morning to you too. What do you mean I shouldn't be here?"

"Too dangerous, things are about to happen."

"How do you know?"

He pulled out his press card and spoke in a soft voice.

"Look, I'm with CNN, and reliable sources tell me the U.S. military is about to launch a missile attack on Bin Laden's training camp over the border in Afghanistan. Some are wondering if Pakistan will be hit too because the targets are so close to the border. It's retaliation for the terrorist bombings in Kenya. I saw your family in the pool yesterday and thought you should know."

Two weeks earlier, Al-Qaida terrorists drove truck bombs into the U.S. embassies in Kenya and Tanzania, killing 224 people, including twelve Americans. The blasts wounded an astounding 4,085 people.

American embassies were on high alert. Islamabad, Pakistan's capital, was only 185 miles away from Al-Qaida's training camps over the border in Afghanistan. If missiles strayed from their mark, it was too close for comfort.

"When are the missiles being launched?" I asked.

"Anytime. I heard 7,000 foreigners are trying to get a flight out. Some countries are sending in chartered jumbo jets to get their people out. I hope you are leaving soon."

"Thanks for tipping me off."

Unnerved, I left the restaurant and headed for the elevators. In the lobby, two British men came up to me as I pushed the elevator button.

"Are you an American?"

"Yes, why do you ask?"

"Yesterday we saw your family in the pool and thought you should know something dangerous is about to happen. When are you leaving?"

"Scheduled to leave tomorrow on a PIA flight to Tashkent. What do you know?"

"We're here on an assignment to train Pakistani police but being recalled to London today."

"Is the U.S. attack happening?" I asked.

"We work for Scotland Yard, and our colleagues in British intelligence (MI-6) told us it's happening today or tomorrow. We're leaving for the airport in a few hours and you should too."

When three expats with credible intelligence suggest you get your family out of the country, it gives you pause. Their information explained the tension in the air and why people kept staring at me.

Rebecca and I felt we had to leave Islamabad that day. I spent five hours on the phone pleading with several layers of management at Pakistan International Airways (PIA), to move our flight up a day. A PIA manager finally took pity on us and reissued our tickets, all because I kept emphasizing my children were at risk.

Believe it or not, the only occupants in the hotel van that took us to the airport that afternoon were my family and the two officials from Scotland Yard. All of us sat in anxious silence, wondering if we would get out in time.

Our PIA aircraft landed in Tashkent at midnight. Happy to see us, Uzbek airport officials broke into applause, greeted us warmly, and treated us like sojourners who narrowly escaped a catastrophe.

The next day, August 20, 1998, the U.S. military launched 60–75 Tomahawk cruise missiles from ships in the Arabian Sea, destroying four Al-Qaeda training camps just inside the border of Afghanistan. I'm forever grateful to the CNN reporter and Scotland Yard officials who cared enough for my family's safety to warn us to leave.

And the Islamabad Marriott Hotel where my family stayed? Ten years later, a suicide truck bomb would demolish the hotel, killing 54 and injuring 266.

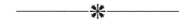

Project work and visits over, the first stop on our return to the States, was the country to the north, Kazakhstan. The coolness from

Almaty's high altitude was a welcome relief from the summer heat of Uzbekistan.

A brochure in our hotel advertised a Russian circus was in town. Years earlier, Rebecca and I attended one with U.S. diplomat friends and no one conducted a circus better than the Russians. Bareback Cossack riders at full gallop performed unbelievable acrobatic feats.

With the economy in terrible shape, I was able to afford front row seats at a great price. Inside a packed out circus tent, our seats placed us a few feet from a miniature ice rink. The game already started, giant Russian brown bears stood on ice skates and leaned on thick hockey sticks. With surprising accuracy, the bears passed the puck to each other. Just as we sat down, a bear scored a goal, and the crowd went wild.

One bear misbehaved, so the referee blew his whistle and directed the bear to the sidelines. The big bear refused. The ref blew his whistle again, pulled out a metal rod, and struck the bear hard on its nose.

Escorted off the rink, the whiny bear sat on a bench fussing and fuming, only four feet in front of us. It would have been less nerve-wracking if the bear wore a muzzle. A protective father, I couldn't watch the game. My eyes were glued to the gigantic brown bear with an attitude and long claws. I expected he would turn around at any moment and take out his aggression on us.

The hockey game over, clowns appeared. One clown pretended to lift a long inflatable log. He then searched the crowd for a volunteer to help him out. In a sea of dark-haired locals, it didn't take him long to select Matt, our redheaded teenager.

Matt walked over to the clown, who asked, "You speak Russian?"

Matt said, "No." The clown, already committed to his volunteer, whispered to him, "Okay. You do what I do."

My son played along, acting to lift the pole with the clown. Both stumbled around trying to balance it and then heaved it into the crowd. Those on the front few rows screamed as the log fell harmlessly on them. Best family Friday night ever.

Our fun and excitement were short-lived, however. The next morning, after my breakfast and newspaper ritual, I returned to our room of sleeping family members. I grabbed my handbag holding our tickets and without making a sound, closed the bathroom door. As I sat on the commode thumbing through our paper tickets, I made a horrifying discovery.

The top three tickets were scheduled for the Saturday morning KLM flight to Amsterdam, but the bottom three were for Friday morning. Throughout the trip, I only referenced the top ticket. It was Saturday morning, and I knew there was only one KLM flight every two weeks. Either we missed the flight, or we needed to leave immediately for the airport.

I called the airline only to discover the flight left the day before. But it got worse. Not only did we miss our flight, but our Kazak visas in our passports would expire Sunday night at midnight. The U.S. embassy duty manager, on call for the weekend, answered the phone.

"U.S. Embassy, how can I help you?"

"We're an American family traveling back to the States, and we missed our KLM flight yesterday. Our visa runs out tomorrow night at midnight. Do you have any suggestions?"

"Wow, they're strict here about visa violations."

A veteran traveler, I was too embarrassed to tell him about our detention in the deportation lounge several weeks earlier.

"What are our options?" I asked.

"Well, all the government offices are closed for the weekend, so you can't get your visa extended before it expires. All I can say is you better be out of the country before then, or they will detain you until the next international flight, which isn't until later this week on Lufthansa."

My next call was to Lufthansa. All the economy seats were taken, leaving business class seats at a price of $3,000 a ticket. There was no way my family would sit in jail all week and then pay a fortune to leave the country. Out of sheer desperation, I called Liam.

An hour later he called back with good news. A van with two drivers was already on their way from Tashkent. One driver would drive the twelve hours up to us, and the other driver would return us to Tashkent.

The waiting was torturous as each hour seemed like a day. The hotel personnel checked on us every couple hours, making sure we were really leaving. Otherwise, they would be in trouble with the authorities for harboring a family whose illegal visa status was *persona non grata*.

At last, our van appeared at the hotel and we loaded up for our escape. What we didn't calculate was the time required to go through a dozen police checkpoints. During the Soviet era, travelers needed a special visa to travel to another city, and the checkpoints every fifty miles allowed the authorities to monitor their whereabouts.

Our drivers asked us to act asleep when the police checked our passport pictures against our mugs. By the fifth checkpoint, our kids had difficulty not laughing while faking sleep. The heat of the day passed, and dusk was setting in as we drove parallel to a mountain range running along the flat, barren prairie.

After hours of not seeing any signs of life, our van came upon a lone yurt, a circular domed tent. The savory smell of rice pilaf emanating from the "yurt restaurant" called to us. Outside the yurt, we sat on a wooden platform and stuffed ourselves, watching a gorgeous red sun go down between the mountains.

On the road again, I couldn't sleep, either because the drivers were too intoxicated, or worried we wouldn't make it to the border before our visas ran out at midnight. The Kazak border police smiled as we passed through the gate five minutes before midnight.

But our escape wasn't over. A mile later we encountered another problem. The Uzbek border crossing was empty with no personnel in sight. Our drivers had no choice but to drive us to Tashkent.

Except now we were in Uzbekistan without any proof of how we entered the country. Now we were *persona non grata*.

Liam and Olga took over. Olga spent days at government offices explaining our situation and got them to recreate an Uzbekistan entry stamp in our passports. Meanwhile, Liam booked us on an Uzbek Air flight to Newark.

Before we left for the airport, Olga took Rebecca aside.

"You must understand going through Tashkent security and customs is treacherous. You need to hide your wedding ring in your bra. The officials are known for stealing foreign tourists' valuables."

Our plane landed in Newark and I breathed a huge sigh of relief. Our stressful summer voyage was finally over. Years later I asked Matt, now an adult, what he considered his favorite overseas memory.

"It was during our trip to escape deportation in Kazakhstan. As a family we ate rice pilaf at the yurt restaurant and watched the sun go down between the mountains. I was never happier."

As parents, traveling overseas was often stressful. But for our children, their experiences became wonderful memories. I mean, trained hockey-playing Russian bears? Really? What American family gets to experience anything like that?

CHAPTER 21

LOSS

Success consists of going from failure to failure
without loss of enthusiasm.
—Winston Churchill

ALTHOUGH I LIVED tired those days, I remained energized by the buoyant hope of growing our fledgling organization. Besides our two social enterprises in Uzbekistan, we
expanded traditional humanitarian work into other Asian countries, Eastern Europe, and Africa.

Recruits joined our new spinoff of the old NGO. Our passion
for helping local communities spread, not only with American
recruits but our local partners as well. The Uzbek doctors from our
medical clinic in Tashkent volunteered at the rural food-processing
plant and provided free medical care to our employees.

A young widowed school teacher joined our new NGO with
a desire to teach orphans in Eastern Europe. Another American
NGO was asked by the Albanian government to manage their

orphanage and our widow, Liz, went on loan and joined their team. Early on in her tenure, Rebecca and I visited her and her daughter.

I was surprised at the lawlessness rampant throughout the small country. The Albanian mafia controlled the international airport. Anyone who declared a large amount of currency at customs could count on getting robbed by affiliated mafia henchmen in the airport parking lot. It was the Wild West of Europe.

Liz's orphanage was a fortress, surrounded by barb wire, and manned by armed guards. An American couple managed the compound and faced danger every day. The husband carried a sidearm and at nights engaged in firefights from the orphanage building rooftop. He, along with his guards, shot down at mafia with automatic weapons who attempted to kidnap orphans.

The Albanian mafia trafficked stolen orphans to the Italian mob across the Adriatic Sea. In the evenings we heard the roar of mafia motor launches whisking away orphans from corrupt government orphanages.

The orphans were destined for the global black market of organ "donations," known as the red market. Usually organ donors ended up dead. The average person doesn't comprehend how evil the mafia can be.

Once the war in Kosovo was over, Liz left Albania and moved to Kosovo to assist a German NGO setting up a community center. Before recruiting a team to help her, Rebecca and I visited her work.

I wasn't surprised to see NATO peacekeeping troops still there, managing a truce that could have erupted into fighting any day.

Day and night persistent tension filled the air, even though a river separated the Serbs and Kosovars. On our end of the bridge, French peacekeepers occupied machine gun nests, always on guard. A cessation of fighting didn't end the anger and hatred.

The aftermath of the war caught me by surprise. First, fresh graves were everywhere. Some had new grave markers, yet many didn't. Second, the amount of construction and foreign aid pouring in was staggering.

At Liz's new community center project, semitrucks of food and clothes arrived from Germany every month, donated by either the German government or German church groups. Devastated by World War II, German generosity for rebuilding after the Kosovo war was understandable. But the sheer volume of their donated goods was striking.

With a team settled in Eastern Europe, our new organization was drawn to Africa. The AIDS epidemic ravishing East Africa sparked a response from some of my recruits to organize a team for East Africa.

One of the most critical parts of my job as an NGO professional was networking. I spent days talking to government officials, embassy officials, and civic or religious groups. All necessary for discovering strategic needs and how we could help.

The networking process always included a preliminary survey trip because only so much can be researched from afar. Completing research and doing it right required being on the ground. I took a couple of newbie American recruits with me to show how I opened up a new project in a new country. Our first stop was Kenya.

In Nairobi, we learned firsthand of the AIDS epidemic's impact on street children. The Kenyan government, local community organizations, and foreign organizations were doing their best to combat the scourge affecting youth, particularly homeless and parentless street kids.

One NGO project we visited was unlike any of the scores I had ever seen—a hospice for children dying of AIDS. An Italian Catholic priest operated the place. A stout man in his seventies, he graciously gave us a tour. When child patients arrived, first they were assigned to a cheerful room and allowed to play on the fun playground until they became too sick.

The second stage was the hospice itself, a large room of sick and dying children, their hospital beds attended by Kenyan workers. Here and there, the old priest gently held the hand of a child patient, gave a word of encouragement in Swahili, and then moved us ahead.

At the far end of the large room of patients were those nearing their end. Most were nonresponsive, but the humble priest continued to lovingly whisper to them, valuing their human worth and dignity.

Out the back door, the final stage was the cemetery. The priest held an internment service almost every day. The one from yesterday, the earth still fresh from burial, stopped us cold. The priest crossed himself while my team, all of us parents, fought back the tears. His mental fortitude, unconditional love, and tender compassion were unreal. None of us left that place the same.

On Tuesday morning, September 11, 2001, I turned on CNBC, the business news cable channel. I waited for Matt to finish packing for his first year of college at my old alma mater. The picture on the TV screen appeared as a telescopic view of one of the World Trade towers in New York City. Apparently, a commercial aircraft crashed into the building. Smoke billowed out of the tower.

"Hey, Matt, come see this plane crash."

Across the hall in his bedroom, he folded his last pair of jeans and walked into my room.

"Look at the strange bird in the foreground," I said.

He squinted at my daughter's small TV and edged up closer to get a better look.

"Dad, that's not a bird. It's another plane coming from behind."

"No, it can't be."

Seconds later an aircraft slammed into the second tower. Several moments elapsed as we mentally digested the horror. Speechless, I looked over at Matt the same second he looked over at me. Our eyes locked in disbelief. What we witnessed was surreal, unimaginable and unbelievable. Without saying a word, the two of us sat on Dani's bed staring at the television.

Over the next five minutes, our brains mentally digested this ghastly, unthinkable event. The act of Islamic jihadists flying commercial airliners into those towers revealed an orchestrated attack. Although hard to wrap our brains around such an atrocity, deep down we knew our world would never be the same.

I called Liam in Uzbekistan. Anxious to know if our team was all right, I was surprised by his response.

"Our team is okay, but right after the 9–11 attack, the thirty-five Muslim employees at the food plant assembled in front of our American engineers and expressed their condolences, and then asked us to tell our American friends back home they were sickened by the attack and condemned it. They wanted us to know the acts done in the name of Islam proved the terrorists were not true Muslims."

"What about our clinic people?" I asked.

"Told us the same thing. All the Muslim clinic doctors and their spouses put flowers in front of the U.S. embassy."

Upon my return from Matt's college, I sought out information on how the United States would react to the 9–11 terror attacks. The next Sunday morning, I walked out of the church and caught up with a friend in the parking lot. John, a retired Army Lieutenant

Colonel, with extensive overseas counterintelligence experience on loan to the CIA, was guarded but helpful.

"I can't say for sure because I no longer work for the government, but I can tell you this. An attack of this magnitude on U.S. soil requires a response of overwhelming force. From my experience, right now there are Special Forces either on their way or already on the ground in Afghanistan, preparing for an invasion to destroy the Taliban and kill Al-Qaida leaders."

"You know I have a team of NGO workers in Uzbekistan helping entrepreneurs. What precautions should I take?"

"How close are your people to an Al-Qaida training camp?"

"There's rumored to be a camp in the Fergana Valley about a couple hundred miles from our personnel in Tashkent."

The Fergana Valley was a hotbed of Islamic extremism where many supported Al-Qaida.

"If I were you, I would get on a plane, go over there, and give them a crash course on evacuation procedures. The U.N. has a good manual on that."

All good advice, but first I gave myself a crash course in evacuation procedures. Knowing I had other teams in politically unstable countries, I purchased a hundred copies of the insightful United Nations manual.

The ensuing weeks after the 9–11 attacks, a cloud of confusion and fear hung over America. Rebecca and I needed to reassure and love on our American team in Uzbekistan in person, but most of our headquarters colleagues, especially the president, advised us not to go.

Duty called, and after convincing my boss, Rebecca and I met our team in Chaing Mai, Thailand for several days of planning and training. The New York attacks rattled our team. All of us wrestled with the fact the attacks made our lives and careers difficult. The 9–11 attacks were a game changer.

PRINCIPLE # 36: "Stay calm and carry on"

As a leader, train yourself not to react every time you hear bad news in a crisis. Those under your leadership take their cues from you, so act as though it's no big deal. Unless it is.

After our evacuation training, Rebecca returned to the States while I flew down to Indonesia to check on a project. A small government university in Borneo asked for our help in their fledgling MBA program. Not knowing I was coming, the professors I always met with were out of town so I tracked down the university president at his home. He opened his front door and stepped back with disbelief.

"Dr. McDonald, what are you doing here?"

"I was in Thailand and thought I would drop down to see how things are going."

His body language demonstrated a combination of embarrassment and anxiety.

"I'm surprised you would come here, to a Muslim country, after what happened in New York City. All of us here assume every American hates us and you would stop helping us."

"Americans I work with don't hate Muslims; they hate terrorists who kill innocent people. You are my friend and we still want to help."

The terrorist attack of 9–11 was the straw that broke the back of my American team in Uzbekistan. A veteran used to living in challenging and bizarre overseas environments, I didn't realize how difficult it was for inexperienced Americans to live in Uzbekistan.

Despite all our training, life under a totalitarian state and adjusting to a new culture was difficult, but the fear of Muslim terrorists finally took its toll. On top of it, our businesses struggled because of the lack of normal free market mechanisms necessary for running a business.

For example, one year our food plant couldn't purchase sugar because the government-owned sugar supplier didn't order enough for the country. Another year there was a scarcity of jars, and we needed hundreds of thousands to fill our orders for stores and hotels.

The mayor of the town near our plant commandeered some of our employees to help harvest the city's wheat crop. The economy was part centrally planned and part free enterprise, making day-to-day business operations extra tricky.

On top of it, the country's foreign currency reserves were nil. The government blocked dollars from entering the country, requiring us to import and export material and products through barter.

Hyperinflation ate into our profitable earnings, and the local currency's devaluation turned our profit into a dollar loss. My American businessmen weren't accustomed to using barter instead of cash.

Igor couldn't comprehend how after our food plant made a 20% annual profit local currency, yet showed a loss in dollars. When local currency devalued 25% against the dollar, a 20% annual profit in local currency, equaled a 5% loss in dollars.

We had no choice but withdraw from our food joint venture. I was an emotional hot mess the night I told Igor. He sat and wept, begging us to reconsider. But due to the economic conditions and his unwillingness to modernize for us to be globally competitive, we had no choice.

The medical practice showed promise, but as Americans, we made a big mistake. Our American medical advisor assumed private practice in Uzbekistan would work the same way as in America. That business assumption almost sunk us.

Frustrated, we sold our interest to our Uzbek medical partner. Our team spent a year of tedious bureaucratic and legal work to be free from our joint ventures. The food plant permanently closed, but the clinic would go on to become a significant success.

In the meantime, south of the Uzbek border in Afghanistan, Osama Bin Laden put a $100,000 bounty on any American, dead or alive. Our American team was 400 miles away from the Afghanistan border and only 200 miles from terrorist camps inside Uzbekistan. Stress on my American staff grew to an unbelievable level. Our team and consequently our projects fell apart.

The only one to survive and stay was Liam. Although the youngest member of the team, Liam had more intercultural experience than the rest of his team combined. I put him on loan to another NGO doing relief work in Afghanistan.

From a risk management standpoint, I learned a valuable lesson. According to international business consultant Robert Porter Lynch, risks don't just add up but compound, increasing the overall risk immeasurably. I learned this lesson the hard way.

Our risks were off the chart. I put a new team of Americans who had never worked together in a new country, with a new language, new culture, new local partners, new markets, changing legal system, changing tax regulations and a broken financial system.

Conducting business ethically and legally in a dysfunctional, corrupt economic environment pressed my staff to the brink. The closeness of the chaos from Al-Qaida and the Taliban was unnerving. In my excitement to create social enterprises, I fell short in fully understanding the risks and enormous pressures it put on our American staff.

————— ✳ —————

As if my overseas problems weren't enough, back home at our NGO headquarters, storm clouds rolled in as well. After thirty years at the helm, our NGO president was retiring, and the board of trustees was looking for his replacement. During a board meeting break time, I headed towards my office.

At the center of our headquarters building was a large domed area connecting four wings. The rotunda's freshly polished marble floor gleamed and sparkled. On my way through, an older colleague stopped me. A former engineer, the tall, lean man had a curious look on his face.

"Phil, several board members want to know if you are interested in becoming the next president."

Caught by surprise, I knew my response needed to be measured, polite, and yet cautious.

"I'm honored, but I'm not interested. I'm busy opening new countries and starting up new projects."

I didn't have the heart to tell him why the top position didn't appeal to me. Already seventy years old, the organization had an entrenched corporate culture of "old school" thinking not amenable to change. Changing the corporate mind-set would require an immense effort.

There was another reason I wasn't interested in becoming the president. I knew one of my colleagues wanted the position in the worst way. His desire was known to us all. In the end, his relentless pursuit convinced the board, and he became the new president.

I knew I was in trouble because the new leader didn't agree with my philosophy of empowering through economic development. Furthermore, as an entrepreneur, I needed my freedom to mentor leaders and start social enterprises. That didn't go over well since my independent style nurtured by the past president didn't match with his hands-on style.

Many of the executives struggled under the new president. The previous president, a former coach, allowed us great freedom but always within bounds of the traditional corporate culture. As an athlete, I functioned well under my mentoring coach. He had been a true leader of leaders.

I realized my staying on wasn't a fit, but I didn't know what else to do or where else to go. The next two years would become the longest, most miserable years of my career. In hindsight, staying was a strategic error on my part. A very strategic error. If you have a philosophical disagreement with your boss, it's wise to cut your losses short and move on.

PRINCIPLE # 37: "Cut your losses"

If you have a philosophical disagreement at work, it's wise to cut your losses and move on.

On a spring afternoon, the new president summoned me to his office. A bit of small talk passed back and forth, and then he leaned back, folded his hands, and paused nervously.

"This isn't working out. Your services are no longer needed here at headquarters. Today you will resign all your executive positions and by this weekend your office will be cleaned out. If you want to stay with the organization, you can go back overseas and work with an existing team, but only with my approval."

Behind him, a large window framed a field of tall, green grass interspersed with large oak trees. Adrenalin surged through my body. In seconds the green grass became greener and the brown trees browner. My heart pounded and blood raced through my veins. It was difficult to breathe.

After decades of service, I couldn't believe what I just heard. The organization I led was the fastest growing arm of the entire NGO. I asked if I had done anything wrong. The answer was no.

"I will write your resignation letter to my own satisfaction and you will sign it. You aren't allowed to tell anyone I asked you to leave, including those under you."

"As long as I'm with the organization, I'll do that on one condition—I won't lie for you. If someone asks me point blank, I will tell what really went on here."

Later, when asked directly, I told the truth. A decade after I left, sadly the board forced the president out of his position.

PRINCIPLE # 38: "Watch out for self-interest"

Everyone has an agenda, whether they know it or not. Don't forget, you probably have one as well. Most people act out of self-interest.

That day I learned a valuable and practical lesson about leadership. A good leader doesn't control or micromanage. True leaders recruit, respect, trust, and empower capable people to shine. I determined never to treat those I led the way I was treated. Years later I would see my exit as a gift of sorts. I was set free to do what I could never have done if I had stayed.

Before I was dismissed, the president stood up and gave a final warning.

"If you try to take this to the board, I will put my armor on and destroy you!"

Stunned at what he said, I didn't doubt his threat for a second. I had zero interest in appealing to the trustee board. I gave no response and walked out of his office.

A burst of thoughts raced through my mind as I approached the rotunda. Soft rays of afternoon sunlight flooded through its glass dome, warming the marble floor. The circular rotunda was an open area, with the dome supported by tall white pillars. A wide band of ceiling curved inward up to the dome's curved glass windows.

A collage of pictures marched along the band beneath the dome's windows. An artist spent two years high up on a scaffold, most of the time on her back, and painted in exquisite detail a continuous mural of faces and landscapes from selected countries.

In no mood to greet someone, I glanced down the three other hallways leading into the rotunda. All were quiet, with no one around—except for one person.

In the center of the rotunda's marble floor was a visitor, a young quadriplegic man. He sat motionless in a wheelchair, his left hand resting on a joystick, staring up at the mural. The sight of his twisted, shriveled body was eclipsed by the look of sheer wonder on his face.

His joyful gaze struck like a dagger in my heart. Although my work at headquarters was done, at that moment I realized my career wasn't over. At age fifty, I still had a strong, healthy body capable of international travel. And I had the privilege of doing what this disabled young man could only dream about. I took it as a sign.

PRINCIPLE # 39: "Essence of Leadership"

True leaders cast a clear vision and convince others of the direction. Credible leaders trust and empower others to shine. Micromanagement of able leaders or managers causes resentment, distrust, and disillusionment. Treat those under you the way you want to be treated. People often forget what you say or do but rarely forget how you make them feel.

As destiny would have it, two days later I cleaned out my office on Good Friday, the day Jesus was crucified on a cross. I have to confess, it felt like a decade of my life's work had been crucified. Personal books and files all boxed up and stacked in my family's minivan, I started the vehicle for my last drive down the hill.

Ten years after driving up that winding lane, full of exuberant hope, I now drove down the hill in total despair, discouragement, and disillusionment. Years of growth and innovation were thrown away. Those I led, now like family, were left confused and abandoned. My career dreams lay shattered, like smashed, broken glass strewn on the side of the curvy lane.

Three weeks later, my father lost his battle with a rare form of cancer. In less than a month, my universe had altered, and as I reeled in a world of hurt, my mind resembled jumbled madness. I was distraught, confused, and rapidly losing hope. In a word, I was undone.

PART
IV
Unleashed Potential

Nothing ventured, nothing gained.

—Ancient Saying

CHAPTER 22

A Glimmer of Hope

*In the absence of real, objective reasons to think that
more time is going to help, it is probably time for
some type of necessary ending.*
—Henry Cloud

WITHIN TWO MONTHS of leaving the job on the hill, we sold our house and moved back to Michigan. Matt and Mark both in college, only four of us were left at home. After deciding on a compatible school district, we bought a house and settled in.

Over the next several months I wallowed in the dark night of the soul, daily battling depression as I grieved the loss of a dream and possibly my international career.

Many of my days I spent shoring up donors rattled by our transition. The other days I remodeled a room, complete with a wall of built-in bookshelves. I never dreamed woodworking skills from my furniture making days would play a role in my emotional healing.

A simple project working with your hands can go a long way in soothing a crushed spirit.

One day I got a phone call from a local businessman who wanted to build a hospital in South Sudan.

"Dr. McDonald, I understand you are between project assignments and wondered if you would help us. You know we have these lost boys from the Sudan who came here as refugees, and we need to do something about medical care for their families over there. I'll pay your way over if you join us on a survey trip."

Rebecca encouraged me to go, trusting it might help with my hopelessness and despair. In an emotionally dark place, I only considered going because she thought I should. I knew she deeply loved me, and as my soul mate, she was trying to protect me from myself.

She wouldn't let success go to my head, failure go to my heart, fear go to my confidence, nor loss go to my soul. I was grieving a "living" death, the death of a dream. Dreaming a dream is hallowed space, but living the dream is often harder than you can imagine, especially when your dream comes crashing down.

PRINCIPLE # 40: "Love protects"

A soul mate's love protects you from yourself, especially when your dreams fall apart.

When it came to adventure, the African bush was the best. I dug out my large atlas and studied East Africa. The country of Sudan, an immense landmass carved out by the British, was as large as the Eastern United States, east of the Mississippi River.

The lost boys were of the Dinkas, one of the tallest ethnic groups on the planet. Forty years of civil war with the Arab north left the Dinkas uneducated, living in extreme poverty, and their only expertise was survival.

Similar to those in Darfur to the northwest, the Dinkas suffered enormous war crimes perpetrated by the Sudanese Arabs in power. When I learned that, I called the businessman back and said I was in.

The powerful, single turboprop of our Cessna Caravan bush plane droned for hours in our quest to reach the small village in southern Sudan before nightfall. The pilot banked hard to the left and floated us down for a flyover of what appeared to be a landing strip.

Local villagers recognized the sound in the sky. By the time we circled for a landing, both sides of the landing strip were overflowing with cheering, waving Dinkas, a local population in desperate need of a hospital.

As I struggled with depression, I viewed everything negatively. Honestly, I wasn't excited about our lodging arrangements. Sleeping in a mud hut with a thatched roof was an exciting new experience for my comrades from Michigan. Myself, I already had my share of those types of living quarters in the developing world.

My days of camping ended with the Boy Scouts. Growing up in the jungle with no electricity, my wife's idea of camping was a chocolate mint on her pillow in a nice hotel. I couldn't have agreed more.

At least I had a mosquito net. Sure the net was to protect you from an array of diseases carried by miserable mosquitos, but the net also kept out spiders, scorpions, lizards, and bugs. And hopefully snakes. Snakes don't navigate the inside of a thatched roof very well. In fact, they have been known to fall on you in bed, as once happened to a colleague in Bangladesh.

Between the stale, earthy air inside our hut and wondering what lurked outside, time passed before I could drift off to sleep. The African bush came alive at night when large nocturnal cats roamed in search of food.

My American colleagues fell asleep in innocence, not knowing the dangers outside. Once you lie frozen in fear with a lion outside, you never forget it. I lay on my sleeping bag questioning what I was doing in such a remote and dangerous place.

In retrospect, it was a good thing I came along. The other Americans on my team had zero international work experience and no clue how to plan out and set up an NGO project. By the end of the trip, we earned the local leader's trust, and he arranged for a meeting with the township officials.

The dry season in full gear, dust from the military truck rolled into our small camp. Dressed in bush camouflage, twenty soldiers of the Sudan Liberation People's Army (SPLA) piled out, all armed with AK-47 assault rifles, their chests crisscrossed with cartridge belts.

Despite a cease-fire with the Sudanese Arab government, a perimeter was set up around our meeting place—under a big tree. Shade was precious in the heat of the day.

The rebel officers doubled as the town council. Nervous and edgy about the enemy, the conversation turned quickly to the subject at hand, building a hospital. Once explained, the councilmembers gave their blessing and commitment.

Then a call came in on a mobile device. The commander in charge said the cease-fire had failed, and his men were needed for battle.

Before leaving, the commander had one last request. He stood and asked if I would pray for them. I had prayed in public before, but this was the first and only time I prayed for elected officials who served in a rebel army, about to go into battle.

I was honored. Considering the atrocities and war crimes committed against the Dinka people by the same government responsible for Darfur, these soldiers deserved divine protection.

A month after returning to the States, I was asked to go back to Sudan. The second trip included a foursome: a retired British surgeon; an American surgeon from Louisiana; the Michigan businessman leading the project; and myself. Our mission was to visit two hospitals in Southern Sudan.

Our chartered bush plane flew us from Kenya to Western Sudan, and along the way, we landed on a desolate landing strip for a restroom stop. While others relieved themselves on the side of the strip, for some dumb reason, I chose to walk on a path into the bush. Almost out of sight, I heard the pilot shout, "Stay on the path!"

"What did you say?" I yelled.

"Stay on the path. There are landmines everywhere."

I stopped dead in my tracks. Stupid, how could I be so stupid? I knew it was a war zone. Looking down, I decided to get on with my business right in the middle of the path. I gingerly did an about-face and strode precisely in the middle of the curvy path back to the airstrip, one sure step at a time. Gave new meaning to "walking the straight and narrow."

After more hours in the air, our pilot descended low enough to recognize several villages.

"I'm pretty sure it's down there," he said as we listened in our headphones. Our destination was a rebel SPLA hospital. His voice resumed with a determined set of instructions.

"You need to know this is an active war zone. Once we land, you have thirty minutes before wheels up. While I'm waiting for you, I'm a sitting duck, so don't you dare be late."

Our plane rolled to a stop at the end of the airstrip. Seconds later, rebel soldiers in a camouflaged military vehicle pulled onto the landing strip. The four of us bolted out of the aircraft, jumped in, and within a minute arrived in a village.

Our vehicle came to a stop beside what looked like three large mud huts joined together. A Sudanese doctor came out dressed in light green scrubs.

"Welcome to our hospital. Please come inside."

To our amazement, the inside area of the contiguous mud huts was converted into a long operating room, completely enveloped in a rectangle of thick plastic. A wounded soldier was undergoing an operation.

"The Sudanese government bombed all our traditional hospitals, so we were forced to create these bush hospitals, camouflaging them to look like huts from the air," said the Dinka surgeon.

Like two machine guns, our visiting surgeons asked him medical questions rapid-fire, gaining as much knowledge as possible in twenty minutes. Soldiers interrupted, we jumped into the vehicle and hustled back to our plane. Ready for takeoff, as soon as we closed the door, the pilot raced down the bush strip and lifted off for our return across the Sudanese Sahel.

Halfway across the region, we landed in Rumbek, a town where several NGOs had set up humanitarian efforts, including a small hospital. Our medical team visited the hospital while the pilot and I checked our group into a tented camp close to the airstrip.

Operated by a Kenyan safari company, long-term NGO workers occupied the camp, but a few "hotel" tents were available for foreigners passing through. Each of us had a private safari tent with a wooden deck as a floor. The dining hall tent served fantastic food, and the local workers were well trained.

Before we left the next day, I was assigned by our team to visit the camp owner in Nairobi and find out what it would cost if they set up a similar camp at our hospital site.

Typical of many small businesses in the developing world at that time, the company's offices were in a house in a nice residential section of Nairobi. The two owners were white Kenyans, of British descent. After exchanging greetings, the owner in charge handed me a brochure.

"We specialize in setting up temporary tent camps in remote places and it's done quickly. We can set up a camp for a hundred workers anywhere within two weeks, complete with food service, showers, latrines, and security. What can we do for you?"

"We are planning on building a hospital near the Nile in South Sudan," I said.

The price quotes were ridiculously expensive, and I pivoted to my main concern, how a hospital in South Sudan could be locally sustainable. The other owner spoke up.

"I think you are missing something here. You are assuming peace will come and an economy will grow. I've lived my whole life in East Africa, and the war in Sudan has been going on for decades. There's no local economy because all the men are fighting, and the women and children are herding cows. When a cease-fire comes, local markets begin to take root, and then the U.N. planes, the "big birds in the sky," as the Sudanese call them, drop tons of food."

"What happens then?" I asked.

"The local markets collapse from the huge oversupply of relief food and goods. We've seen this cycle time and time again, so it's unreasonable to expect a hospital to support itself without outside funds. In a war zone, there simply isn't an economy around long enough to sustain a hospital."

The man was right. My assumptions were wrong. My Uzbekistan team made the same mistake, believing a change from a centrally planned economy would result in a robust market economy. In reality, the economy in Uzbekistan got worse, not better.

But here I was, the overly optimistic entrepreneur assuming the situation in southern Sudan would get better. I had overlooked a core premise of development economics. The businessman's distinction between a war zone and a normal third-world economy made perfect sense.

My assumptions about a hospital in a war zone becoming sustainable were incorrect. Sustainability works when there is a semblance of a working economy, where local people have a standard of living capable of paying for goods and services, such as medical care.

PRINCIPLE # 41: "Get it right"

Wrong beliefs and assumptions at the beginning of a project can destroy any chance of success. It's easy to get caught up with all the opportunity and overlook risks.

The overnight flight from Nairobi to Bangladesh arrived a day before I was to participate in a graduation ceremony at Dr. Bipul's school. I spent the day amazed at what Dr. Bipul had accomplished in the decade since I left. He set up a college to beef up the English proficiency of the students before entering his graduate school.

Outside of Chittagong, Dr. Bipul also started primary schools in remote areas as well as an orphanage and primary school in his city compound. His compound's buildings had doubled, and best of all, he did it all on his own. He was a nonprofit entrepreneur, starting new programs as needs arose.

PRINCIPLE # 42: "What is a nonprofit entrepreneur?"

Just like a for-profit entrepreneur builds a business by finding a need for a product or service in the marketplace, a nonprofit entrepreneur starts a program based on a social need in society.

That evening, after a famously delicious meal by Dr. Bipul's cook, our conversation over a cup of tea in the drawing room was interrupted by the *darwan*. A guest downstairs wanted to see me, a Muslim woman no less.

I followed the night watchman down the outside stairs and walked out to the gate. Standing there was an elegantly dressed woman in a beautiful green sari, standing by a car, not wearing a veiled burka. In addition to her driver, a bodyguard was also present.

The area near the gate was dimly lit, and I had difficulty seeing her face. But as soon as she greeted me I recognized her voice— it was Amira, my kids' nanny, for whom we bought the sewing machine to make and sell *shari* blouses.

Once a shy, timid woman, she now stood tall and addressed me with confidence. Fortunately, I remembered enough Bengali to carry on a conversation.

"I want to thank you and *Memsahib* (Rebecca) for helping me buy a sewing machine. I now own a tailoring business and specialize in embroidery. I have employees and own a house. I also own rice paddy land that I rent out. My children are receiving a fine education. *Allah* has been good to me."

I was overwhelmed. Beaming with pride, Amira handed me an expensive gift for my wife. Even though surrounded by other men, the longer we talked, the more awkward it became. A married Muslim woman shouldn't be talking to a foreign married man, especially in the shadows of the night. We hastily briefed each other on our families before saying farewell.

I walked alone up the stairs and realized you couldn't manufacture dignity. When you empower a person, dignity naturally follows. She wasn't the same person I knew ten years earlier. My initial surprise of seeing her and hearing her success had now turned into joy. I couldn't stop smiling.

PRINCIPLE # 43: "You go, girl"

Economic transformation for a disadvantaged person not only removes personal risk but replaces it with worth and dignity. And you can't buy dignity; it's earned by the one empowered.

The trip to Sudan and Bangladesh was a tonic that soothed my soul. The entrepreneurial growth in Dr. Bipul's nonprofit organization and Amira's for-profit business was rewarding to see. I couldn't wait to return home and share with Rebecca how we played a small part in launching their successes a decade earlier.

On the long flight home, I again reflected on my career options. With our children's continuing health problems, I knew we couldn't move back overseas. If we stayed in America, it meant either college teaching or working in a corporate executive position. Neither appealed to me.

Before giving up our relations with donors developed over the years, Rebecca and I met with most of them, explaining our career situation. One man, in particular, made an insightful comment.

"I don't care what you do next, but if you stay in international work, you should land in a position where you can maximize on all your years of training and experience. What you do is unique, so you should leverage that."

In time, it became apparent we needed to do just that. Rebecca and I should leverage our experience and put into practice our desire to empower entrepreneurs in developing societies.

Nate and Dani were actively engaged in sports and music in their middle school, had friends, and settled into their routines. The thought of uprooting them again was sickening. I either needed to organize a new nonprofit organization or take a position as a leader in a local one.

Rebecca picked me up at the airport. I briefed her on my trip and then she filled me in on a potential new job.

"He called again," Rebecca said.

"Who called?" I asked.

"Frank. He needs to retire and wants to recommend you to his board as his replacement."

Frank, a former youth camp director, had already retired once and lived in our hometown. Restless with retirement, he started a nonprofit organization to bring leaders from Myanmar to America for master's and doctoral degrees. I knew two of the five who came for their degrees and was impressed all five families returned to their country.

Frank's little nonprofit wasn't even a mom and pop organization. It was only him, with no staff, no office, and not even much of a budget, because most of his funding came from himself. By then, I had incorporated or registered over a dozen business or nonprofit entities around the world and could easily have done it again in America.

But Frank already had registered and set up a nonprofit, complete with an excellent board of directors, some I had known since college. I knew from experience that putting a good board together was a hard thing to do, especially finding the right mix of expertise and personalities.

Frank's board interviewed me a couple of times, made an offer, and I accepted. With a mixture of relief and regret, in September of 2004 I ended my relationship with the old NGO.

The doorbell rang. I opened the door. There stood Frank, a tall, strapping, seventy-eight-year-old man. He held a cardboard box of files, software, a few manuals, and a checkbook. He smiled as he gave it to me.

"Here is your organization," he grinned.

"So, what are you going to do now?" I asked.

"You know my wife has terminal cancer, so we sold our home and are moving to Florida."

"When are you moving?"

"Today."

Anxious to leave, he didn't stay long. I shook his hand, thanked him, and said goodbye. I closed the door and set the box down on our kitchen island. Rebecca came into the room.

"That's it?" she asked.

"Yep, here it is."

"It's funny. Compared to our old organization, this is a tiny thing."

I chuckled, knowing I had resigned from a large nonprofit that raised sixty million dollars a year. With American personnel in eighty countries, they were supported by a hundred headquarters staff. The finance department processed 9,000 donation checks a month.

I set the box on the dining room table and began to leaf through its contents.

"Here's what's happened to us," she said with a twinkle in her eye. "We left the ocean liner for a rowboat. But we've grown things before and we can do it again. It's you and me, baby. I love it!"

Just as Dr. Bipul set himself free from the old nonprofit with its colonialism, outdated methods, and old-school thinking, we had just liberated ourselves from the same institution.

As entrepreneurs, Rebecca and I were excited to finally build an overseas program without worrying about arcane rules and policies that controlled our lives for twenty-one years.

My new little "NGO in a box" did have a problem. It didn't have any money. Time was of the essence. A letter immediately went out informing our friends and donors about our transition. Although Rebecca and I took a step of faith, I would be lying if I said I wasn't anxious about the lack of money. We wanted to do big things in remote lands, and that would need sufficient startup capital.

My official start date for leading the "nonprofit in a box" came on a sunny fall day. The woods surrounding our house were alive in color. Leaves from red oaks and yellow maples glided to the ground. A slight wind gently pressed and pulled each leaf without making a sound.

In perfect silence, I walked down the quarter mile paved lane between two rows of tall, green spruce trees. At the end of the lane, I checked our new mailbox on the side of the country road.

On my stroll back, I opened a letter from a loyal friend. All it said was, "Congratulations on your new position. Here is something to get you started. Use it for economic development overseas and go build some sustainable programs!"

Enclosed was a check for $300,000.

CHAPTER 23

Starting Over

Change invokes simultaneous personal feelings of fear and hope,
anxiety and relief . . . threats to self-esteem and
challenges to master new situations.
—Noel Tichy and Mary Ann Devanna

THE HIMALAYAN MOUNTAINS, a furrowed, rocky mass of the earth's crust, rose off in the distance. Under a cloudless sky, I stretched for an early morning run. Here I was, back in Myanmar but this time near the China border, where the muddy Irrawaddy River begins its 1,373-mile meandering course to the Indian Ocean. Soft sunlight peeked over the horizon, and before humid, tropical heat replaced cool morning air, I took off down the road.

I was in Mychina, the capital of Kachin state, and home of the Kachin ethnic group. A century earlier, the Kachins were a mountain tribe of fierce fighters, known for their silent decapitation of an enemy.

At great peril, missionaries in the 1890s visited Kachin land and converted many to Christianity. By 1930, the less-advanced Kachins became modernized with schools, hospitals, and churches in the major towns.

Like most countries in Southeast Asia, the hilly border areas in Burma were home to several ethnic groups. These groups felt disenfranchised and after independence from British colonial rule, fighting broke out between persecuted ethnic minorities and the Burmese central government.

In the mountains before me were thousands of Kachin rebel troops living in jungle camps. Behind me to the southeast was the infamous Golden Triangle, notorious for trafficking of drugs, guns, and slaves.

I saw no one on the road. That was strange. Usually, a government agent kept track of my comings and goings. After decades of traveling through remote areas, I knew I was watched. I came to rely on a government agent acting as my personal bodyguard, or at least an early warning system.

Once in the hill tracts of Bangladesh, a government agent approached me out of a crowd, dressed in a tee shirt and flip-flops. Fighting between government forces and rebel forces was imminent. In perfect English, he told me that recurring phrase "You shouldn't be here." I thanked him and immediately left.

The other reason I liked having a government agent around was he would know for sure I wasn't a CIA agent. American intelligence agents were adept at posing as someone else, including an NGO worker like me.

My run over, I slowed to a walk for my cool down and reached the edge of town. An elderly Kachin man, dressed in a Burmese *lungi* and leather bomber jacket, stood on my side of the road, leaning on a cane. Before I passed him, his eyes got my attention. I stopped.

"Are you an American?" he asked in clear English.

"Yes, sir, why do you ask?"

"It's been a long time since I've seen an American in this town. I've lived here my whole life."

Decades earlier, Burmese authorities expelled all Western foreigners except Soviet advisors. From 1966 to 1986, foreigners were banned from entry.

"I'm forever grateful to America."

"Why? Because of the schools? Your English is excellent."

"I am thankful for my education, but I am more thankful for what your soldiers did for us during World War II. Our town was divided between Japanese troops on this side, right where we stand, and the other side of town where American and British forces protected a landing strip for Allied planes. The Japanese soldiers were cruel butchers."

The old man hesitated while he cleared his throat.

"All of my family escaped the Japanese except my sister. She arrived here at our ancestral home, not realizing we had left. She was stranded behind Japanese lines."

"What happened?"

"One night five American soldiers made a daring raid and rescued my sister. In the process, two American soldiers were killed crossing back through enemy lines. I want you to tell all of America how much we appreciate the sacrifice of those soldiers who helped my sister escape from the horrible Japanese soldiers. We love America."

Although the rescue of his sister happened sixty years earlier, the old man remembered as if it had happened yesterday. The sincerity in his voice and a firm handshake made me proud to be an American. What a great way to start my day.

Dr. Nyan, the college president and former doctoral student of mine, picked me up for our strategic planning meeting held in a classroom at the college. The small campus, part of an old church denomination, was home to 150 students and fifteen professors.

Present for our meeting were five leaders, including a wealthy Kachin lady whose husband was a gold and jade miner. I met her on a previous trip and was stunned by the jeweled necklace that hung around her neck. That necklace cost more than my entire net worth.

After introductions, which are so crucial in the developing world, I spent the morning teaching a simplified crash course in strategic planning. After lunch, we began our deliberations.

"Tell me, as an organization, what are your needs?" I asked the group.

Dead silence. All sat with a "deer in the headlights" frozen stare. Finally, the president spoke up.

"No foreigner has ever asked us what we think we should do."

A century of colonialism, where the white Savior, the great Sahib, big Bhawani, the patriarchal Father, and the one who made all the decisions, had instilled a mind-set of the foreigner being superior. Now, forty years after foreigners left, the ingrained subservience was still there. I couldn't believe the colonial attitude still existed. It made me mad.

"You should tell us what to do," one leader said.

"How can I do that when I don't live here, don't know your culture, and don't understand your needs? Only you can answer what your organizational needs are. I suggest you spend the rest of the day doing a needs assessment, while I go back to the hotel."

PRINCIPLE # 44: "It's all about what they need"

No one knows needs better than the local people who live day in and day out in their environment. All good development ideas emerge from a thorough needs assessment. Then projects are prioritized and planned, based on which ones are strategic and sustainable.

I wasn't worried if they could do a needs assessment. Back in the States during his graduate studies, Dr. Nyan took my doctoral course in strategic planning. Twenty-four hours later he showed up, said his group was ready with their answers and drove us back to the campus.

The group beamed with dignity and confidence as with the results of their needs assessment. Their needs were all listed in order on the chalkboard. The college facilities needed updating, the girls' dorm was overcrowded, and students were constantly sick from overusing the outhouses.

Price increases in the cost of rice and firewood made the college's food service bill exorbitant. The church denomination needed more headquarters space, and the overcrowded orphanage, located in a bad section of town, needed a better location. Human predators hung out near the orphanage, waiting to seduce lonely orphans.

My gut told me they had more needs than what was on the board. I dug deeper and found out their leaders and college professors often went five months without pay each year. While the few wealthy miners were generous with their donations, it still wasn't enough to meet budget.

Their faces sank when I told them my NGO didn't believe in monthly or annual handouts that could meet their operational shortfall. However, when I explained the concept of local sustainability, driven by for-profit ventures generating social impact, their faces turned to bewilderment.

"How can a nonprofit organization own a for-profit business?" a businessman asked.

"What's wrong with a nonprofit owning a business when the profits are used to meet your budget shortfall? Or generate money to expand current programs or start new programs?" I could see their minds mentally digest the new concept. Bewilderment eventually turned into excitement. I had to leave but knew we had a good start.

A needs assessment is foundational to a good strategic plan. A solid strategic plan gives direction to planning the right development projects. But the concept was new and I wanted to start small.

On the way to the airport, I brought up the concept again to Dr. Nyan. Although a college president and professor, I noticed a spark of entrepreneurial spirit in him.

"Before I leave, I need to tell you something," I said.

"What is it?"

"I want to demonstrate to your group how a sustainable project would work."

"But we don't have money to run operations, let alone a new project."

"I know, I know, but I need to tell you something else. I have money to help out here."

"Money for what?"

"Two kinds. First, I have funds to help immediately, like for new bathrooms and shower rooms for guys and girls, a generator for the campus, and books for the new vacant library your trustees just built. But second, I also have funds to capitalize new income-producing ventures out here."

"How can I help?"

"It would help us if you could find an income generating project to prove our sustainability concept. If your leaders could see how starting up a project can earn money, they would understand first-hand how my initial startup grant could keep on giving."

"Please give me an idea."

I paused for a moment and thought about their rural environment.

"You are in a rural area, so look for an opportunity in agriculture. An ag project could help feed your students and orphans, as well as generate money for your budget shortfall."

PRINCIPLE # 45: "Follow the leader"

A trusted local person with entrepreneurial passion serves as a champion because project success always comes down to leadership. Everything rises and falls on leadership.

Several weeks after I returned to the States, I got a call from Dr. Nyan.

"Dr. McDonald, I found a piece of property for sale. It is located about six miles out of town, has over one hundred acres cleared of jungle, and includes a barn and a pond. A previous owner was turning it into a rubber plantation but only planted six acres of rubber trees."

"Who owns it now?"

"A Chinese man bought it a few years ago. He wanted to help drug addicts learn to farm, but the government wouldn't permit him to run a drug abuse center there."

"How much is the property?"

"Almost nine thousand dollars."

"Buy it. Buy it right now from the college project funds I sent you, and I will reimburse you later. That's a great price for a property that close to town. We need to buy it before someone else snatches it up."

"Also, the wealthy lady in our meeting is willing to donate a 300-acre orange grove about forty miles from here. We could sell the fruit plus provide oranges to our students and orphans. But she wants you to see it first."

"I'll call you back tomorrow about the orange grove."

I hung up the phone realizing I didn't know anything about oranges. Time to call Carl, a retired rural economist, who worked forty years in thirty-six countries for the US Agency for International Development (USAID) and the Canadian International Development Agency (CIDA). He had been a great asset in helping us in Uzbekistan with the food plant and a textile mill.

Carl and I left a few weeks later. About the same age, height, and build of the British actor Sean Connery, known as 007 in the James Bond movies, Carl easily passed as his double. Passengers stopped and asked Carl for his autograph.

Here I was, "00 nothing" traveling with a "007 look alike." His resemblance to Connery was uncanny, and if fellow travelers didn't stop, they indeed starred or looked confused. I got a little taste of what it must be like for real celebrities.

Carl and I checked into the only hotel in Mychina. It was more of a guesthouse, and breakfast was served on the top floor. The menu was the same each day—two fried eggs and a piece of toast. By midmorning, our car arrived with Dr. Nyan and "Jade Momma."

The dusty road to the orange grove required passing through several police checkpoints. We were the first Americans to travel in the area for decades, so the police took extra time checking our documents. Our vehicle turned off the main road and drove through high grass. From there we hiked. The orange grove was on a hillside, and after inspecting the fruit, Carl gave us bad news.

"I've never seen this variety of orange before. They are like wild oranges if there is such a thing. You can't sell them commercially, and to do it right you would need to bulldoze them all out of here and plant new trees. That would take a long time before harvest, especially if you need money now."

Our wealthy lady understood it wasn't feasible. The world over, business is business. It didn't make financial sense to pursue her idea.

Carl's expertise was impressive. Give him a day or two in a town, and he could give you a complete overview of how the local economy worked. Using his networking skills, he could figure out supply chains to each business niche and then came up with where the new business opportunities existed.

Upon our return to Mychina, we worked on the rubber plantation project. In two days Carl wrote up a full thirty-page business plan, complete with financials and procurement lists. I learned a great deal from that man, a real expert. Carl would forget more about rural development than I would ever know.

The business plan for the rubber plantation was sobering. Tree crops are a long-term play, taking years for trees to mature before bearing product. In the case of rubber, our trees required seven growing years before producing latex, the gooey white sap-like substance drained from cuts in the bark.

The local leaders approved the business plan and I deployed funds to start the project. The project manager, a former government rice expert, bought a tractor and built two staff homes on opposite ends of the plantation. Each house was strategically placed for security. Our team of Kachin employees spent four years planting an additional 6,200 rubber trees.

PRINCIPLE # 46: "Strike while the iron is hot"

Progressive improvement is better than delayed perfection. Fifty percent of something is better than one hundred percent of nothing. When a good opportunity presents itself, commit to it and make it happen.

Desperate for operating cash, we tried fish farming, raised livestock, anything to generate money while waiting for the rubber trees to grow. Our plantation even started a nursery, growing rubber seedlings for sale to other plantations.

Another project started up, one able to generate benefits right away. We bought rice paddies. With two growing seasons a year, our harvested rice helped feed orphans and students along with selling the extra rice to subsidize the plantation's budget shortfall.

One plantation project didn't work out. Apparently, when you stock a small pond with 35,000 fish, there's not enough oxygen to support them all. Think of that. Disease set in and decimated our stock.

PRINCIPLE # 47: "Don't put all your eggs in one basket"

As a social entrepreneur, your overall goal is to become sustainable. A way to lower your project risk is by investing in several small projects under the umbrella of a larger project. If you have the resources, another way is starting up two or more projects in different industries at the same time, hoping one will succeed.

Early one morning Dr. Nyan called me at my home office in the States. The entrepreneur in him came up with another project idea.

"My wife wants to start a school. Because our kids studied so many years in America while I finished my education, they need to continue their education in English. Since we've been back, we have homeschooled our kids using American curriculum. But now so many relatives and neighbors want their kids to study under my wife. No school here teaches in English."

"So, who would own and fund the school?"

"I don't know. The church denomination doesn't have enough money for its current budget."

Until our new ventures generated income, shortfalls in funding would continue. I knew his salary as college president was seventy-five dollars a month, except for the months he didn't get paid at all. A thought occurred to me. There could be another way to skin this cat.

"Have you ever heard of a for-profit charter school?" I asked.

"I heard the term used in the States, but don't know what it means."

I spent the next several minutes explaining the concept of a privately owned, for-profit school. Before we hung up, he pointed out a potential hiccup.

"I'm not allowed to work another job while college president."

"Does that apply to your wife? Couldn't she be the owner and headmistress of the school?"

"Yes, that would work."

In a developing society, carefully deploying a lot of money takes hard work. My list of projects growing, I felt overwhelmed, especially basing out of the States. I needed an experienced person who lived in Asia, saving me from circling the globe on a regular basis. One who could train, provide accountability, and help solve problems.

Believe it or not, around this time I got an email from Liam, saying he was fed up with the old NGO and wanted to join my little rowboat NGO. He would continue living in Uzbekistan, not too far from Myanmar. His timing couldn't have been more perfect.

When I left the old NGO, I didn't want anyone to accuse me of "cherry-picking" or poaching top talent. But Liam's nickname was "Mr. Spreadsheet," and I needed his skills. And he had come to me, not the other way around.

After joining us, his first assignment was to help me with the charter school project. A few weeks later, we met up in Myanmar and I introduced him to our Kachin partners. The wealthy lady from the gold and jade mining family was best friends with Dr. Nyan's wife.

This "Jade Momma," as we called her, wanted to be part of the for-profit educational venture and owned a building where the charter school could start. The wife of the college's vice-president also became a charter owner.

Liam wrote a good business plan that proved the school needed sixty pupils to "break even" and become financially sustainable. Once building renovations were complete and a few teachers hired, the new administration scheduled the start date and enrollment began.

Word got out about our new English-medium school, and without any formal marketing, the school accepted 175 students. Tuition paid up front made the school project profitable from day one.

Upon my return to the States, Rebecca picked me up at the airport.

"So, how was your trip?"

"Good. With Liam's help, we're cranking out business plans for our social enterprise ventures."

"Well, I have some interesting news. I got a call from a foundation while you were gone."

"Is it good news or bad?"

"Both. Although the foundation director said they like what we are doing overseas, the bad news is we present a risk to them."

"What did he mean?"

"We are too small, and if anything were to happen to you and me, their investment, meaning their donations, could be a lost cause."

"Did you tell them our costs are low with no office, no office employees, and little overhead?"

"I did. Apparently, we are too small."

"Huh. I didn't know you could be too small. So, what's the good news?"

"The good news is they want to give us a transformational grant to make us bigger."

The grant was almost a million dollars. A few miles from our house, I found office space and Rebecca went on a careful spending spree, purchasing office furnishings as only she could do. She also had a knack for getting supplies donated and found a warehouse full of used office equipment.

I hired an accountant, fundraiser, and receptionist. Our "rowboat" office operations in our house moved to the office. In two years, Frank's little cardboard box became a legitimate office.

As serial entrepreneurs, Rebecca and I couldn't have been happier. The growth in overseas projects, coupled with a new stateside office, made our small nonprofit no longer feel like a rowboat. I liked to think we moved up to the speedboat stage.

What happened next was unforeseen. I should have seen it coming, but didn't.

CHAPTER 24

"The Stars Are Lined Up"

Not all who wander are lost.
—J.R.R. Tolkien

OUR FOUR-HOUR DRIVE to Chicago consisted of long periods of silence punctuated with bursts of questions.

"What am I going to do with the rest of my life?" Rebecca asked.

Sounded more like a rhetorical question, and I decided to let her process her thoughts out loud without my feedback. By this time I'd attended "husband school" for almost thirty years and knew a thing or two. Sometimes just letting your spouse talk out loud clarifies things.

"I mean, what am I going to do once Dani is done with high school and goes to college? The last twenty years I've poured myself into our kids and the women's programs of your work. What am I going to do once the last one leaves home?"

I continued to drive, staring ahead without comment. More thoughts poured out.

"As your office gets more sophisticated with hired help, you will need me less. And you and I don't recruit Americans much anymore to go overseas as we used to. Your overseas partners don't need me to help them in their own lands like American recruits needed me to help get them acclimated to a new culture."

A rite of passage refers to a transition in life. Passing from one stage of life to another is part of the human experience. In our case, the transition from active parenting to becoming "empty nesters" was hitting home. My wife was too driven to sit at home and do nothing. Of all days for me to be my wife's astute confidant, I didn't know what to say. So I punted.

"I don't know. Let's talk about your options on the drive back," I said.

From time to time, civic organizations, churches, schools, and universities asked us to speak about our overseas work. The small church in a western suburb of Chicago had invited us to come. On Sunday morning before the worship service, the minister gave each of us an hour for our presentations. In separate rooms, I spoke to the men while my wife addressed the ladies.

My presentation complete, I walked with the other men down the hall towards the sanctuary. On the way, I could see into a large room of at least 100 women, some weeping and the rest in tears. I stopped, peaked inside, and the speaker was Rebecca. I was dumbfounded.

A few minutes later she sat down next to me in the long wooden pew. I whispered in her ear.

"What on earth did you tell those ladies that made them so upset?" I asked.

"I didn't make them upset. That's how they responded."

"What did you say?"

"I just shared all the horrible ways women are treated around the world, what I've done about it for years and the growing need here. I'm telling you, women in America are fed up with all the abuse and discrimination. There's a movement starting among women and it crosses all generations, races, and social ranking."

The drive back to Michigan was an eye opener, and I realized the "movement" she described would soon become a tsunami of an outcry. Always the planner, I felt I needed to make a suggestion.

"From what I saw in that room of ladies, and from what you're telling me, you can only advocate so much before women will want to get involved in a solution."

"It's already happening. Women are lining up, wanting to sign up, and asking how they can help fight this injustice. Furthermore, this new generation wants nontraditional, significant ways from the sanctity of their homes to be involved in an on-going way. Traditional methods aren't going to work."

"Then we need to start a program under our NGO that makes a way to do that."

"I've already thought of that. I'm not terribly excited to be the head of something. I've searched for a group already doing what I've learned. I'd rather help behind the scenes."

"Why haven't you found another organization that does what you want to be done?"

"The problem is American organizations are not holistic in how they approach their overseas programs. Everyone here specializes in meeting a need instead of meeting all the needs of a victim. Sure, victims need aftercare like counseling, medical treatment, and a safe place. But they need training and job skills, so they aren't at further risk. I'd rather stay hiding in your organization where I can just do what I love. I don't know. . . ."

"I get it. Immediate aftercare is only half the problem. So then how do you reduce continued risk?"

"The reason women are at risk around the world is they aren't valued. What I learned from helping Amira in Bangladesh was her husband stopped abusing her when I helped her add economic value to her family. She became the goose who laid the golden egg. Her husband valued her because of her income from clothing sales."

"That's fascinating, go on."

"Really, it's what I've done for women in your programs from day one. Goats for war widows in Sudan. Orphan and widow care in Burma and Kosovo. Women's needs in former communist countries. The list is endless and growing even here in the U.S."

"So, what do you want to call the program?"

"*Women At Risk*, because the initials create the acronym *WAR*. Women are going to join me in a war against those putting women and children at risk. My guess is it will include some men and certainly boys."

Word spread about Rebecca's new program, and a wealthy friend gave a generous grant for conducting an overseas needs assessment. I joined Rebecca for a month to interview friends in Nepal, India, and Thailand. Our last stop in Asia was Bangladesh. Over dinner in the hotel restaurant, I asked what she had learned thus far on the trip.

"Everywhere I visit I hear the same theme. At-risk poor women make products to sell on the market, so they don't end up in prostitution. But even with foreign tourists, the local markets aren't big enough to generate the sales needed for them to survive, let alone expand. They say if I want to help, I should sell their products in America."

"So, what's wrong with that?"

"I'm not a widget person. I've spent my whole life in the nonprofit environment. Now you're talking about importing products and selling them."

"But you know how to do it. Think of all the times through the years we've seen a unique product overseas, and you would say, 'now that would sell in America,' only to see it three years later in

American catalogs. I don't know anyone better at understanding how the developing world works and at the same time is classy and shrewd enough to understand consumer tastes in America. If you import and sell their products, especially jewelry, think of the impact it will have in empowering them."

"I don't know. I hardly ever wear jewelry."

After a few bites of curry and a slug of Fanta Orange, the concept clarified in my mind. I put my fork down. It was my turn to give my soul mate some perspective.

"Sounds like this is a major solution. At-risk women overseas need help in selling their products. Women in America could help wounded women by buying their overseas products imported to the States. The stars are lined up, and you're the only person I know who can make East meet West."

"But it will take extra training because a lot of the local stuff made here won't sell in America, either because of a selection of colors Americans don't like or poor quality."

"That's where your lady volunteers come in. Bring them over and train."

"I also don't want Americans to buy out of pity. I can sell a "pity buy" once, but it will end up in a garage sale. I would only want to import quality stuff, like what's in Macy's or on Fifth Avenue."

"Well then, let's start searching markets and bazaars for high-quality products."

"You know me; I'm risk averse when it comes to money. And the products have to be made from raw materials available in their local markets to be really sustainable."

"Let's just find some quality products, test the market back home, and see where it leads."

The next day Rebecca visited the markets in Dhaka, the same ones she shopped during our time in Bangladesh two decades earlier. One shop caught her fancy. A man was stringing pink pearls onto a necklace.

She knew all the natural pink pearls in the world only came from the Bay of Bengal. Iron particles from the rocky Himalayans washed down into rivers and ended up in the bay. The pearls in the bay had a slight pinkish hue from rust-colored sea water.

"Sir, can I buy what you are making?" she asked in Bengali.

"Yes, but I'm only half finished."

"No, what you have done so far is perfect. I'll take it as is. The style right now in the US is pearls that appear to float as if on the sea."

PRINCIPLE # 48: "The global marketplace is brutal"

For a social enterprise to compete in a global marketplace, it must minimize costs. Products made in the developing world need to be high quality, made with local components, and correctly priced. Then market the story of how buying the product helps fight injustice.

Cairo, Egypt, was our next stop in her search for unique products. Each day we combed the markets long and hard to find something original, unique, and high quality. A shop owner in the historic *Khan el-Khalili Souk,* the famous bazaar in the Islamic district, had on display a few hand-blown glass perfume bottles. Rebecca was captivated.

Ancient Egyptians believed aromatic scent was the sweat of the sun god Ra. Egyptian hand-blown glass had a long tradition going back thousands of years. Not wanting the English-speaking shop owner to understand, she whispered to me in Bengali.

"Phil, these would sell in America."

I enticed the shop owner by telling him I would buy all his perfume bottles if he would take us to his wholesale supplier. He hesitated until I pulled out a crisp, brand-new, one hundred dollar bill.

This man led us down dark alleys and from time to time we stopped, wondering if we should continue. A safety principle in traveling overseas is never let a stranger take you "somewhere" by leading you down alleys, promising you a better place to shop. Often, it's a ruse for getting you alone to rob you or worse. Against our better judgment, we nervously followed.

Hidden at the back of the alley was a dark stairway with steep steps. After a demanding climb to the top, the three of us came upon a small warehouse. A group of men sat on the floor, sewing up burlap bags of wholesale merchandise for the owner's retail clients.

Stepping over and between the workers, we made our way to a small showroom in the back of the building. In addition to a variety of perfume bottles, Rebecca was mesmerized by hand-blown glass Christmas tree ornaments.

Once outside the warehouse, she asked our retailer guide if he would take us to a glass supplier. By now he understood we needed to cut out the middlemen. He rolled his eyes, and it took another crisp one hundred dollar bill for him to lead us to the glass manufacturer.

A ten-minute walk later, we climbed up a steep, rickety staircase to another second-story shop. Inside was a small showroom with exquisite samples of hand-blown glass products.

The owner couldn't speak English. A few minutes later his operations manager appeared. In excellent English, he explained the process of glassmaking.

"Glassblowing is an ancient craft with skills passed down from father to son. Sadly, the industry is dying because the artisans depend on the tourists to buy their products. Because of the bombings by radical Islamists, the tourist trade has slowed and it hurts our sales."

In his early thirties, Hasan was more than a manager; he was a good salesman. Rebecca leaned close and again whispered in Bengali.

"Do you trust this guy?"

"I do. Seems like a quality person, and he knows his stuff."

One of the five pillars of Islam is *zakat,* the giving of alms to the poor. From his deep faith in Islam, Hasan responded with compassion to Rebecca's goal of helping poor, at-risk women.

"Based on how he responded to our potential profits going to help at-risk women, he seems like a good Muslim," she whispered.

For a small beta test of the American market, Rebecca placed an order for a variety of glass products, including ninety glass Christmas tree ornaments. Hasan assured us the box of ornaments would arrive in time for Christmas.

A couple months later a FedEx truck pulled up to our office, and the driver wheeled in a big cardboard box from Egypt. I was convinced half the ornaments would arrive broken. I was wrong. All but one came intact, each carefully wrapped in bubble wrap, held together by a rubber band.

The timing couldn't have been better. I put up an extra Christmas tree in our home, and Rebecca hung the ninety glass ornaments in time for a Christmas party of close friends.

Awestruck with the ornaments, our friends fought over the different designs. Within fifteen minutes all ninety sold. The little market test of glass tree ornaments revealed Rebecca's foray into the American retail market could have real promise.

After the holidays, Rebecca's mind went into planning mode, thinking about the next Christmas.

"We need to go back to Egypt and order more ornaments for this year's Christmas. Hasan said he needed several months to make large quantities. But I need to see if the workshops have good working conditions. I don't want to buy anything made in a sweatshop."

In strict Islamic culture, she wouldn't visit the workshops alone. I would have to accompany her. But she was already way ahead of me, with a much better idea.

"You know how family-oriented Arabs are, and if we bring along our college kids, we'll look like an American family. Otherwise, the workers will only perceive me as an American, or a woman, not a mom. I need to be a mom to them as well."

"Sure, let's plan the trip during their college spring break and use frequent flyer miles for their tickets."

PRINCIPLE # 49: "Build a bridge"

Knowing their culture creates the right impression on locals who may fear foreigners or have biases against them.

In March, Nate and Dani met us in the Cairo airport. Hasan arrived to take us to our hotel in his recently purchased late model car. As he left the airport terminal, he pulled into bumper-to-bumper traffic, normal for a city of twenty-five million people. Yet he seemed unsure of himself.

"Hasan, when did you get your car?" I asked.

"Yesterday."

"What did you drive before?"

"I didn't. I just got my driver's license the day before."

My heart rate jumped at least twenty beats a minute, but fortunately, the traffic slugged along at a snail's pace. It was rush hour, and there wasn't much danger. Before we visited the glass factories, we told Hasan we needed a few days to show our kids Egypt.

One can't visit Egypt without taking in the history. A visit to the Pyramids and riding camels was a delight. In the evening, the four of us cuddled up on a blanket and watched a fantastic outdoor light and sound show. Lasers lit up the pyramids and sphinx, while a booming recorded voice explained the eras of Egyptian history.

Dinner at a fancy restaurant outside the pyramids included live music in English, the Egyptian singer crooning all-time Western favorites. During the song request time, Dani, on a vocal music scholarship at college, requested an unfamiliar song. She jogged his memory by singing a line or two, and he insisted on her singing with him.

The two sang several songs against a backdrop of a two-story wall of glass. The profile of three dark pyramids cut gigantic triangles against the setting sun of an auburn sky. The stunning view, coupled with hearing our daughter sing, made the evening seem all the more surreal.

Our visit to the glassblowing workshops the next day quickly brought us back to reality. Located in a poor section of Cairo, Rebecca and I both felt we entered a place dominated by Islamic fanaticism. The Muslim Brotherhood and Al-Qaida terrorist organizations held strong support among poor, conservative Muslims. The first workshop visit confirmed our concern.

All the artisans worked in quiet diligence listening to a loud Islamic sermon on the radio. Islamic inscriptions hung on the wall. Rebecca was relieved to find no child workers, plus the place was clean and dry. She became more at home by the minute.

Their hateful, suspicious glares dwindled when our two college kids entered the workshop. The American businesswoman was a mother who brought her family, a cherished value in the developing world. During our tour of the shop, the heavy feeling of stern fundamentalist Islam changed to smiles and excitement.

Without a doubt, the workers had never met Americans, citizens of the Great Satan country. All they knew of us infidels was from the daily anti-American rhetoric of the Islamic radio programs.

Hasan introduced us to each worker, explained what he was doing, and the race was on to make a special glass-blown item with Nate or Dani's name inscribed in the glass. By the time we left, the Islamic radio station was switched off. Our college kids were a hit, walking out as celebrities, bearing personalized hand-blown glass mementos.

The second workshop met us with the same wariness, but now Rebecca became bolder. She wanted to know the names of their wives and daughters. In Islam, a man is allowed to have up to four wives.

Hasan pulled her aside. "It's improper for me to ask out loud the names of their wives and daughters. It's too personal."

"Tell them the money from my selling their glass products will help women and children around the world, including their women. If they need any medical care or help to pay their daughter's school bills, I have resources. Tell them I'm only buying from them because I care about the women in their lives, not them," Rebecca said with a smirk.

"I still can't ask them to say their names out loud," Hasan said.

"Okay. Have them write their names down on my pad, so you and others don't hear their names."

Once Rebecca's intent was explained, names were written down. Well, except for one man who refused to list his wife number two.

"Why won't you list your second wife?" Rebecca asked.

"I don't like her anymore," said the worker.

"Well, if you don't like her, I don't like you!" she tartly replied.

The room erupted in laughter. The ice was broken. My wife's interest in their wives cemented in their minds that the American woman, who would become their largest customer, was for real.

Before the list was complete, one man quietly enquired if Rebecca could do anything for his wife. The new bride couldn't get pregnant. Rebecca knew infertility was a divorceable offense.

On the spot she offered to help and gave Hasan money for the new wife to see a doctor, knowing she was a woman at risk. If her husband divorced her and her father didn't take her back, she would probably end up on the street as a prostitute.

PRINCIPLE # 50: "Knowledge is power"

The goal of every social entrepreneur should be changing lives for the better. The more a social entrepreneur understands the culture, the better the social impact.

Because Rebecca understood Islamic culture, her specialty of creating a social program out of thin air took place in a matter of minutes. After a couple of visits to an OBGYN specialist, the worker's new wife became pregnant. Years later Rebecca and the new mother finally met, hugged, and connected as only moms can.

CHAPTER 25

The House of WAR

*A social entrepreneur is someone who designs and implements
an intervention, product, or service that improves the well-being
of marginalized individuals and populations.
A social enterprise is an organization . . . that is formed
to meet a social or environmental challenge.*
—Teresa Chahine

NEPAL IS KNOWN for Mt. Everest, Indiana Jones fighting Nazis in a bar, and the Hindu living goddess known as the *Kumari*. Most people think of the whole country as mountainous, but few know about a great little game park in the Chitwan valley on the southern border with India.

Populated with 400 rhinos, herds of deer, and eighty tigers, tourists rode high up on an elephant, sitting on a large wooden platform. At dawn, my family rode through the nature preserve on elephant back when two rhinos charged us for being too close to their young.

You haven't lived until you are sitting on an elephant, a toddler in one arm, a video camera in the other, and then your elephant rears up on his hind legs as if he's in a three-ring circus. Our *mahouts* shouted commands, and the three elephants in our group counter-charged the rhinos.

The elephants trumpeted with ear-piercing blasts as they bore down on the charging rhinos. At the last second, the rhinos veered off from their game of chicken. My kids wrote about it for school reports only to have their American teachers not believe them. I had to come to class and show the video.

This time, Rebecca and I weren't in Nepal for sightseeing. Anjuli, a new partner, had opened a café in Katmandu and was interested in expanding her social programs. Rebecca helped her qualify for a grant to start a bakery that employed abandoned or abused women. But the bakery had two problems.

When the municipal electricity was off, the bakery shut down. So, Rebecca brought an American jeweler to teach the bakery employees to make jewelry by hand during bakery downtime. Every revenue stream was vital for helping the ladies. Even still, all their efforts didn't produce enough money.

The second problem was bread sold for too low a price for the bakery to become sustainable. My wife recruited an Australian volunteer, a professional cake decorator, who taught the Nepalese ladies to decorate cakes, each cake selling thirty times more than a loaf of bread. This level of baking required a generator. Hotels, embassies, and expats snatched up their cakes. Word spread among the locals, and the bakery became a thriving business employing at-risk women.

PRINCIPLE # 51: "Hunt fat rabbits, not skinny ones"

A startup social enterprise should generate the most profit for the time and money invested. If possible, find a high-margin business model that can provide a cushion to absorb inevitable mistakes that will cost money until you are well established in your market. The key is to become profitable before running out of startup capital.

But Anjuli had a bigger problem. Young women were going missing. I didn't understand why.

"What do you mean they're going missing?" I asked Rebecca.

"Human traffickers are kidnapping or scamming young girls and selling them in India, either chained to a bed in brothels, or they end up on a slab having their organs removed and sold on the black market, commonly known as the red market."

"You mean they become sex slaves or killed for their organs?"

"That's exactly what's happening. According to a United Nations Report, hundreds of thousands of people each year are sold against their will as slaves, most of them women and children used as sex slaves. Not just in India, all over the world."

"Who are these traffickers in this region?"

"Believe it or not, they are little old ladies with silver buns who scam poor parents into thinking their daughters will get a high-paying job in the city."

"Wow, that's pure evil."

"Trafficking isn't about sex or gender. It's about money and greed."

By this time, Rebecca's *Women At Risk* program had identified fourteen risk issues women around the world faced. Issues such as physical abuse, honor killings, and female circumcision, just to name a few, were making her overseas programs grow.

Human trafficking had become the fastest-growing arm of the criminal underworld and became the main priority for Rebecca's personal war to help rescue, restore, and protect the helpless.

But now I had a problem. Every day DHL, UPS, or FedEx trucks dropped off boxes of goods imported from overseas at-risk women. Female volunteers sat on our office floor sorting and tagging products while customers milled around. Our parking lot was jammed with people coming and going. My office had turned into a zoo.

I returned home from overseas to find our basement filled with 300 wedding dresses and ball gowns, all donated to be shipped to a project in the Caribbean where dresses were fitted and rented, with the proceeds underwriting an anti-trafficking shelter. Besides my office, now my house was filling up with goods.

"Hey, we need to talk about our growing programs," I said to my entrepreneurial wife.

"What do you mean?"

"We're running out of space, and I don't have enough employees to handle your side of our organization. I think we need to spin you off as a separate nonprofit organization because I underestimated the power of women getting behind a cause like yours."

"So, what are you saying? You're shoving me out on a limb, and now you're going to cut the limb off saying, 'Fly, birdie fly?'"

I had to grin at her analogy, as if I ever would abandon her.

"Yep, that's what I'm saying. But don't worry. When I saw off the limb I'll be on it too, and we can learn to fly together!"

"How's that going to work?"

"Look, you know I've started up eighteen organizations and companies around the world. You've devoted your whole life to helping me help others. The least I can do is help you with a startup. I'll assist you in forming a governing board, organize legal documents, and then once the board is seated and votes WAR into existence, you lead it. I believe in you. You're a natural leader and you were meant for this."

The missions of our organizations were similar, as both addressed social and economic injustice. My staff and I were into empowering entrepreneurs who created jobs and generated funds within their community. We didn't believe our field partners should be dependent on foreign funds.

The new *Women At Risk* organization was about helping traumatized women and children heal. By creating safe circles of protection, WAR's aftercare programs helped victims rebuilt their stolen lives, adding worth and value. Even men were being rescued and helped.

Aftercare was more than just teaching how to make products. As a victim of a heinous crime, a wounded person also needed health care, trauma counseling, housing, child care, legal advice, career training, formal schooling, and leadership development. Rebecca was all about "wraparound services."

The financial crisis of 2007–2008 hit the global economy like a sonic boom. Some called it the perfect financial storm. For me, it was two perfect storms colliding. The recession came just as my three-year startup grant ran out.

Headquartered in especially hard-hit Michigan didn't help either. Whole supply chains for the auto and truck industry vanished into bankruptcy. On one dismal Friday alone, 37,000 auto employees in Detroit lost their jobs.

For several years, Michigan's economy was ranked the worst state in America. Many of my larger donors were located there, and their companies held on for dear life. Most were unable to make donations.

By some accounts, the financial crisis caused hundreds of smaller nonprofits in America to either go bankrupt or disappear. Donations to my organization were decreasing. I had to dissolve an Internet company my organization started that was to be an added revenue stream.

PRINCIPLE # 52: "Give yourself grace"

While it's paramount to evaluate risks and have plans to mitigate them, unknowns can't be predicted. A new enterprise in the developing world can face up to ninety risks. Don't beat yourself up if your risk management plan is derailed by an unpredictable event, for unknowns are out of your control.

———————————

I was fortunate my board had the foresight to set aside a rainy day fund for lean years. That rainy day fund lasted five long years, and somehow I stayed afloat, albeit much smaller. My speedboat became a floating rowboat again, this time bobbing around in the waves of financial distress, without strong oars of support to keep me going.

In the meantime, Rebecca's organization appeared to be immune to the economic downturn. I learned never to underestimate the power of women getting behind a cause. WAR took off like a rocket.

Thanks to her dual revenue streams of donations and sales, her organization grew 50–100% a year. Throughout the global financial crisis, some of her overseas partners increased their programs by 500% a year. In a short period of time, imported goods distributed by WAR sold in all fifty States.

It was the best of times for her and the worst for me. Word got back to me that some male acquaintances I knew were asking, "What's wrong with Phil's organization? Rebecca's is growing and he seems to have fallen off the map." When I heard these comments, it didn't help my ego at all.

Rebecca's fight against international sex trafficking took on a whole new dimension when she discovered Americans were being sold into sex slavery, right here in the land of the free. Homeland Security called her, and she ventured into rescuing American slaves.

A gifted speaker, almost every month Rebecca was interviewed on radio and television. Her travel schedule became insane as she spoke hundreds of times a year. Both of us were so busy that at times I forgot her location. One day my cell phone rang, and Rebecca's number showed on the little screen.

"Hey, what are you doing?" she asked all chipper.

"I'm back at the office after my noon workout at the gym."

"Do you know where I am?"

"I'm sorry, I don't remember. Are you in D.C. today?"

"I'm at a White House-sponsored anti-trafficking seminar. President Bush and Secretary Powell are standing across the room from me. Anything you want me to tell them?"

"Uh . . . sure. Tell them thanks for all they do in fighting terrorism because it impacts what we do."

"Okay. Hey, it looks like another session is starting. Got to go. Love you."

I switched off the mobile phone and stood next to my car for a few minutes, vexed with mixed emotions. In one sense, I was extremely proud of her accomplishments. In only a few short years she landed an invitation to a White House sponsored meeting for nonprofits.

At the same time, I had a personal sense of drowning in a deep hole. I felt worthless. The harder I worked, I thought I was stuck on a hamster wheel, going nowhere. My organization continued to decline.

As it turned out, my landlord sold his building, and I had to move my office into the big building WAR purchased on the other end of town. It all felt like I was going backwards.

In my mind, I knew why she was at such a noble meeting with the White House administration. Rebecca was the right person, in the right place, at the right time, fighting for the right cause. Yet, as I wallowed in self-pity, my mind was disconnected from my heart. I'm sad to say, I was jealous.

Upon her return home, she knew something was wrong.

"So, what's up with you? It seems like you are moping."

"I'm not moping. I'm brooding."

"Same thing. Come on, what's going on?"

"I had lunch with an old friend who said I should just close down my organization and work for you. It felt like a sucker punch to the gut."

Our conversation grew quiet as she handled the reason why I was demoralized.

"He has no idea what you are accomplishing overseas," she said.

"Yeah, well, he sees me as part of a dying organization and yours just booming. It's an obvious, visible comparison."

"It's not about size, revenue, or space. It's about impact. My organization is big in America because we carry products that take up space. Human trafficking is the hot button right now. You're comparing apples with oranges. You don't need to be big on this side of the ocean. Besides, your organization is probably the leanest nonprofit in America with the biggest global impact. I don't nearly have the depth and quality of leadership you have."

"What do you mean? I'm down to only three other American guys."

"Look, it will take me years to get where you are. Retail is a curse. I have ladies in Timbuktu dependent on the fickle US retail sector. We're sure to enter murky waters at some point. Our growth rate isn't sustainable. We're dependent upon something you aren't— sales income to run safe houses and to pay salaries. You don't have that fear. Our growth rate is scary, and I keep warning it won't continue. By the way, how many advanced degrees do you guys have?"

"We all have master's and two of us have earned doctorates."

"How many years of cross-cultural experience do you have?"

I thought for a minute, calculating my team's total years of experience.

"About 135 years, but that's because two of them grew up overseas."

"How many foreign languages do you four guys speak?"

"Eleven."

"Eleven?

"Well, we spoke them at some point in our lives, not all now."

If you don't use a language, you forget it. But I could see where she was going with the conversation.

"How many overseas projects have you done in the last ten years?"

"Over 100 in twenty-one countries."

"How many successful?"

"Most of them. But sometimes we have several smaller projects with the same field partner."

"Oh. My. Gosh. Phil, listen to yourself. I would kill for my staff to have the depth of education and experience you have. It's not about quantity. It's about quality. Phil, it's about relationships, not just accomplishments. It's about making a difference in people's lives, and you have."

Rebecca did it again. My wife, so grounded, so logical, with so much common sense. She righted my ship, and rightly so, because I needed to hear it. I had lost all perspective. But my best friend, my soul mate, was again there to protect me from myself.

PRINCIPLE # 53: "Man up"

A real man doesn't fear vulnerability because being vulnerable is what makes him real. Learn to express your feelings and listen to those close to you, especially in times of difficulty. They may give you a perspective you may not see.

What happened next in my life was totally unexpected and nothing short of unreal.

CHAPTER 26

Beyond Sustainability

Life can only be understood backwards;
but it must be lived forward.
—Soren Kierkegaard

T HE PHONE RANG and it was Liam, calling from Asia.

"Hey, are you sitting down?" he asked.

"Is it bad news or good news?"

"It's unbelievable news. I just got back from Myanmar. Remember the piece of property we helped our partners buy for a commercial printing company?"

"I do. That was the project we did four revisions of a business plan, and it didn't make economic sense. But didn't our partners put a building on it?"

"With our help, they built a two-story building. The bottom level they rented out retail space to four shops and used the income to help keep the rubber plantation going all these years. The top level they used for their organizational offices."

"I think we had put in around a hundred thousand dollars for the property and building. So, what happened to their property?"

"They just sold it for 1.3 million."

"I don't understand. You mean in Burmese Kyat?"

"No, in US dollars."

I sat astounded at the news.

"Phil, are you still there?"

"Yes, just trying to process what you just said."

"There's more. All the project properties we helped them with are worth millions, including the school, rubber plantation, orphanage, and women's training center."

"That's unbelievable. So, what are they going to do with all the money from the sale?"

"They took part of the money and immediately bought forty-four acres on the edge of town. A week later someone offered double what they paid for, but they turned the offer down."

"What happened that caused the property values to go up so much?"

"Myanmar is opening up. Asian investors are pouring in and buying up property."

"Wow, and our critics told us it was too risky to invest in Myanmar. Good thing we didn't listen."

"Hey, it's late here so I'm going to bed. Thought you would want to know right away."

I hung up the phone. For thirty minutes I sat and digested the news. I remembered the American donor who underwrote the printing project saying the property had to be worth something, which is why we turned it into a real estate project. But none of us would have predicted a thirteen-fold return on investment in our lifetime, let alone in seven years.

Our next trip to Myanmar, Liam and I took a couple of close friends. The two American businessmen had heard our stories, believed in what we were doing and wanted to see our projects in person. Both in sales, one was trained as an accountant and the other an engineer.

After meeting with a few partners in Yangon, formerly known as Rangoon, our team headed up north 800 miles to see our original projects in Kachin land. The growth in projects even amazed me.

The small school started a few years earlier now had 600 students and forty teachers. Dr. Nyan's wife, Win, the headmistress, beamed with joy. Though it was wintertime and she was sick with a cold, she wore a dark ski hat that covered her black locks, but her face was radiant.

A thick coat and scarf hid her tall slimness as she gave us a royal tour of the school. Plans were already in the works to purchase a large property for an even bigger school. Local investors lined up to underwrite millions of dollars for the school expansion. In other words, the school not only was self-sustaining but now able to grow without outside, foreign funds.

Site visits to the other projects around town were also impressive. Our final meeting was held with organizational leaders at the rubber plantation. In our open-air meeting under the rubber trees, our American guests listened as Liam and I discussed several issues with the leadership related to our projects.

At break time, I stood and looked around at over 6,000 rubber trees. Endless rows of tall, skinny trees stood far as the eye could see. I walked over to the smoking barn where the rubber was processed and then hung outside to dry. Like clothes hanging from a clothesline, dozens of lines held latex sheets drying in the sun. The American engineer joined me.

"So, what do you think of our projects?" I asked.

"Hard to believe all this happened in the last seven years."

"I know, every year for the next four years, hundreds of more rubber trees will reach maturity and come online with latex sap. Is this what you expected to see?"

"I really didn't know what to expect. I've gone on mission trips where I took a hammer, and we ended up building something. Here it's different."

"No, we started out here as mentors and now are advisors. We train and mentor leaders as well as empower entrepreneurs. As an engineer you understand project management. That's what we do. We are nonprofit project managers helping others help themselves."

"Well, the Kachins have done a lot in a few short years."

"You know, it's not been easy for the Kachins. They've suffered political and religious persecution at the hands of the Burmese. They've had to deal with the "3 C's" of corruption, collusion, and cronyism of government officials. In spite of that, they've prospered.

Compared to the easy life I have in America, sometimes I don't feel worthy sitting in our partners' presence."

"It must feel good though to see what's happened here."

"I have to tell you, it's a great feeling when one project is sustainable. But when all our projects become sustainable and then grow on their own, it totally feels unreal."

On our way back from Myanmar, we stopped in Bangkok, Thailand, the regional airline hub for Southeast Asia. A massive, modern airport, thousands of passengers moved through it each day. The four of us stood and looked at the big screen listing flights to cities all over the world.

Out of the corner of my eye, I noticed an Asian man walking towards me. I turned and it was Dr. Zin, my former doctoral student and one of the three families who owned the school in Kachin land. I walked over to greet him, asked about his family, and then asked why he was in Bangkok.

"I'm part of a government delegation. The governor of Kachin State appointed Dr. Nyan and me to be advisors on setting up the first public university."

"How did this happen?"

"Many of the government officials had their kids enrolled in our school and knew the two of us had doctorates from America. Between the quality of their kids' education, and knowing both of us have served as president of the college, the governor wants us involved."

"That's tremendous! So, where are you going today?"

"We are headed to Japan to visit some universities. I'm sorry, sir, but they are motioning to me for us to catch our flight. It was nice to see you. Goodbye."

Dr. Zin briskly walked away, yet it seemed like he was moving in slow motion. My role in his and other Kachins' lives was over. Not only were they financially independent, but now their leaders, who Liam and I had mentored, were the experts, hired by their own government to serve future generations of university students in their state.

His slender frame became smaller before he finally walked out of sight. In a way, seeing Dr. Zin disappear was symbolic. His ethnic group no longer needed our help. And I was okay with that. Our goal was to work ourselves out of a job. After ten years of working together, we had accomplished just that, yet it seemed strange to be done. At the same time, it felt profoundly rewarding.

PRINCIPLE # 54: "Time to move on"

Building solid, sustainable programs and projects in the developing world can take years. Besides knowing the culture, it requires quality local champions, sufficient startup and growth capital, training, and coaching. When your work is done, it's time to move on.

The clinical psychologist sat across from me in my office. Home for a few weeks, he specialized in trauma counseling of war victims. When he wasn't doing that, he traveled the world treating Americans learning to cope with the enormous stress of living in another culture.

With years of living and working overseas, he understood first-hand what it was like to be in the trenches. But today, visiting in my office, he caught me off guard.

"Last time I was here, Phil, you wondered if you were suffering from compassion fatigue. Did you take the online test for that?" he asked.

"I did. I don't have compassion fatigue."

Compassion fatigue is burnout of those in helping professions, who suffer exhaustion from intensely helping others.

"So, what do you think is your problem?"

"I think it's career fatigue. When I'm sitting behind a desk here in the States, I get bored and feel useless. I don't know ... maybe I'm an adrenaline addict and spoiled by so many overseas adventures."

"You aren't an adrenaline addict. You're an adventure seeker. Clinically, there is a big difference. Maybe you should do less administration and set up an overseas project on your own for a change. Maybe it will renew your passion?"

"That's a great idea. I know the rush I feel when I help someone set up a project."

The two of us sat in contemplation. I wasn't prepared at all for his additional advice.

"And another thing. You should probably take better care of yourself. You need to think about self-care."

"What do you mean? I work out at a gym three times a week, and if I have time to train, I compete as a sprinter at Masters' level national track meets. At sixty-three, I feel in great shape."

"Phil, I don't mean physically. I mean emotionally."

"I don't understand?"

"You tend to be too hard on yourself, thinking you never do enough to help people. The older you get, you need to take care of Phil first, so you have energy to help others."

PRINCIPLE # 55: "Take it easy"

Learn to manage and regulate expectations of yourself, so you are physically, mentally, and psychologically capable of building into the lives of others.

Self-care. I had heard of soul care but not emotional self-care. Reminded me of the first year in Bangladesh when I lost thirty-six pounds due to illness. I was so sick I could hardly stand before the bank teller.

An old American gentleman banking next to me looked over and told me if I was planning on living there, I had to take better care of my body. I took it to heart, since he survived living in Dhaka for forty years, first when it was British India, then East Pakistan, and later Bangladesh.

Perhaps having a new foreign project would help my state of mind. I remembered a WAR partner in Uganda Rebecca asked me to visit for her a couple years earlier. A group of fifty ladies became widows when their husbands died of AIDS and left them with HIV.

The widows formed a cooperative. A steady income from magazine jewelry, as well as beautiful items made from paper-mache, made them and their village prosperous. WAR sent so many orders that they had to hire all their relatives and neighbors to fill their orders on time.

On that previous trip when Rebecca couldn't join me, the widows honored WAR with a big celebration. After a big feast and group pictures, I was seated on a platform. As if I was the big American chief, I listened as co-op members took turns coming before me and explained how their lives were changed, all because WAR sold their jewelry in America.

The last person to stand before me was a nicely dressed young woman. She became emotional. The audience turned silent.

"Sir, please go back and tell the women of WAR how they saved my life. Before my mother made jewelry, her family disowned us because she had HIV. We were on the brink of homelessness. I was destined to become a prostitute."

She fell to her knees and began to wail. Tears filled my eyes. A minute later she crawled over to the platform, grabbed my ankles, and looked up, her eyes swollen from weeping.

"Because of WAR selling my mom's jewelry, I'm finishing a university degree and already have a promise of a job when I graduate. Please thank everyone in the US because they changed my life forever."

I leaned down and whispered, "I certainly will tell them."

Before I left, Jayde and Candace, both sisters and leaders of the widows' cooperative, gave me a business plan to bring back to my wife. Candace, a former assistant bank manager, felt the widows' co-op needed to diversify and not be dependent on one kind of jewelry. Her knowledge of the risk-averse banking industry gave her cause for alarm.

I silently entered Rebecca's office as she finished up a radio interview on the phone. Phone interview completed, she swung around in her office chair.

"Hey, whatever happened to that business plan I brought back from Uganda a couple years ago?" I asked.

Rebecca let out a sigh before responding.

"I assigned it to a volunteer businesswoman in Cincinnati, who never followed up with the widows because she got married."

"Oh, but these are an amazing, hardworking group of widows. Do you mind if I pick up their project with the business plan?"

"Go for it. WAR now has over 200 projects and programs in fifty-two countries. We can't keep up."

Uganda. Winston Churchill called it the "Pearl of Africa." A small landlocked country, its southern border rested high on the rim of an extinct volcano, filled with a body of fresh water known as Lake Victoria. On the north rim, water spilled over and became the source of the Nile River.

At 4,000 feet above sea level, the lush green vegetation rooted in fertile volcanic soil made southern Uganda the breadbasket of East Africa. Perfect for tea and coffee plantations, this area of Uganda was the only place in the tropics I knew where red raspberries grew next to bananas.

From the Entebbe airport, my route took me through a vast plantation comprising two million acres, its rolling hills dotted by tea pickers plucking the valuable leaves.

But there was trouble in paradise. Candace's fear of being dependent on only one kind of jewelry made her a seer. On this second visit, I couldn't believe the change in attitude in her village.

In two short years, their jubilant celebration and prosperity had turned to gloom and despair, all because the world market became saturated with newspaper jewelry. The co-op's orders were down, and the widows were back to living like most of sub-Saharan Africa—on less than a dollar a day.

There is a reason a money manager doesn't buy only one stock but instead spreads his risk by building a portfolio of securities.

Diversification lowers risk, not just in money management, but in all kinds of areas.

——————————

PRINCIPLE # 56: "Entrepreneur beware"

The highest risk to any business or organization is relying on only one source. Whenever you are dependent on one customer, supplier, product, donor, or service, and that source dries up, you are at tremendous risk for survival.

——————————

Candace's business plan for branching into products made from large horns from butchered cows was still relevant. Not only could jewelry be made, but close to eighty other products also could be manufactured, providing one had the right equipment.

Over several months, Liam and I helped the co-op research the cow horn market, set up and equipped a small manufacturing workshop, bought a truck to transport raw horns, and hired a Ugandan man with many years of experience in manufacturing cow horn products to train the women.

Things went well the first year. But then the market changed. China's demand for carved items from an insufficient supply of ivory spilled over into the market for raw cow horns. The price for unprocessed horns increased tenfold, raising the cost of production to unsustainable levels.

Out of desperation, we tried adding other products to our business model, including dabbling in charcoal and timber. Neither panned out, but the brave widows wouldn't give up and continued to search for a business solution.

PRINCIPLE # 57: "Another way to skin the cat"

In the absence of quality market research, you can lower your risk by testing the market with seed money to see if another way is viable. By diversifying the product or service mix, sometimes you find a combination that works, without spending a lot of money.

It came to our attention that the older widows struggled to carry water to their home, sometimes walking two miles to the river. When Rebecca heard how these women had once collected rainwater in plastic baggies with straws and sold them as drinking water, she went into overdrive. These ladies were precisely the kind of people she wanted to empower—women who would work for anything honest to feed their families.

From its widow's fund, WAR provided 500-gallon black plastic cisterns that collected rainwater off the widows' metal roofs into plastic gutters that drained into the above-ground containers.

Instead of spending time walking to fetch water to run their household, they were able to plant gardens to feed themselves and earn income by selling the excess produce. WAR also provided them with goats, which, in turn, added organic fertilizer to their gardens. The meat and milk from goats, along with extra produce, all sold for cash.

While the co-op sought a sustainable business model for its social enterprise, humanitarian help in the way of clean water and livestock gave widows some hope. A combination of business and humanitarian aid demonstrated the power of a holistic approach to projects.

_____

PRINCIPLE # 58: "Look at the big picture"

An integrated, holistic approach to meeting needs is more strategic in the long run.

_____

CHAPTER 27

Around the World . . . Eighty Times

Life's most persistent and urgent question is,
"What are you doing for others?"
—Martin Luther King, Jr.

I CROSS BORDERS for a living. Whenever I accumulate a million miles with an airline, a sobering thought comes to mind. A million miles is equivalent to flying around the world forty times. I've flown over a million miles with Delta Airlines alone.

Of course, that's not counting the miles I've traveled on fifty-four other airlines, most of them overseas. Nor the thousands of miles in private, chartered bush planes. Safe to say, I've probably flown close to eighty times around the world.

Despite weary travel, I never tire at the grand magnificence of our planet. Around our world lightning strikes 100 times a second. At any time of day, 1,800 thunderstorms rage and rumble. Somewhere on earth, 1,370 earthquakes daily move seismic dials. I've experienced the tremors of earthquakes in the Philippines, seen the destruction of a Tsunami in Thailand, and experienced the aftermath of a cyclone in Bangladesh.

I stood in awe next to a volcano about to explode in Guatemala. The ground shook, and from a mile away I heard lava gurgle like a giant cauldron. Red hot chunks of lava, the size of cars, spat out hundreds of feet over the rim.

One can only marvel at the power of the earth. Yet still, while the earth groans, there is a darker side to nature—the senseless injustice of man against man. What energizes me is to empower leaders to rise above hurdles and face challenges head on.

Most people get up in the morning and go to work. Rebecca and I do as well. But several times a year one of us gets up in the morning, flies to another country, and goes to work. Many people equate flying with going on a vacation, because that's the only time they fly.

Those who travel internationally for a living know it's anything but a vacation. Long, boring hours sitting on a plane, crossing time zones until your body and mind are numb, deposits you weary in a faraway place. Then you go to work, despite your screwed up circadian rhythms that leave you dull, drowsy, and, at times, disoriented.

The Amish seek a plain life, celebrities have a fairy-tale life, and Rebecca and I live an unreal life. When either of us returns from a foreign trip, we brief each other on the progress and problems of our respective field partners. More often than not, we have at least one bizarre story to share and often say to each other, "You know, we live a weird life."

———————— ✳ ————————

In early August of 2016, I drove once more to the little airport in our Michigan hometown. Except this time, I wasn't flying. I was to pick up a foreign guest. Inside the airport, the digital sign disclosed the flight had arrived and I waited outside of security. Soon he came into view.

Dr. Bipul, a dignified, well-dressed man at age seventy-one, walked tired. The luggage carousel dumped his bag onto the belt, I grabbed it, and the two of us made our way to the parking garage. He seemed weary and stressed. I figured it was from jet lag. I was wrong. It was much more.

"Phil, it's so good to be in a country where you can walk freely."

His comment sounded very unlike him. I hesitated before turning on my car's ignition.

"What do you mean, walk freely?"

"Oh, you haven't heard?"

"Heard what?"

"The Islamic State, ISIS, is giving us the hard time in Bangladesh."

"Yeah, I know about ISIS."

"What you probably don't know is now they are targeting leaders of non-Muslim minorities for execution."

The Bangladesh population of 163 million was ninety percent Muslim, nine percent Hindu, one-half percent Buddhist, and Christians, like Dr. Bipul, were less than one-half percent.

"A few months ago...one of my best friends was beheaded by ISIS."

The news hit me like a rock. Adrenaline flowed into my body, and my hands gripped the steering wheel. My eyes stared straight ahead while my eyelids blinked in disbelief. I couldn't believe my ears.

"He was out taking his morning walk when three ISIS men came up behind him on a motorbike. Two got off and pushed him on the ground. One held him down and the other used a large machete. It was all over in thirty seconds."

"Bipul, I'm so, so sorry," I finally uttered.

"The next day I received a text message telling me I was next on their list and should prepare to die."

I let out a gasp.

"Oh my gosh, what did you do?"

"I contacted the police, and they assigned members of their *Rapid Action Battalion* to watch me. I have been confined to my compound for the last three months. That's why it is so good to be here and to walk freely."

I had heard about the terrorist attack on a restaurant in Dhaka the month before, on July 1, 2016. Swat teams killed the militants in a raid to free remaining hostages, but by the time it was over, twenty-nine people died, including eighteen foreigners. The Islamic State claimed responsibility.

"The police made me buy a closed-circuit TV security system to monitor our property. I can't leave the compound unless I call the authorities who give me the permission. ISIS is watching my compound, looking for an opportunity to kill me. My walking group in the morning asked me to stop walking for my own safety."

For years, the southeast part of Bangladesh where Dr. Bipul lived was a hot bed for Islamic extremism. The fact Al-Qaida and ISIS had training camps near Chittagong was common knowledge.

A question we often hear is, "Is what you do dangerous?" Unless a nation is at war, most countries have safe and unsafe places. You quickly learn where to go and not go. Even still, in unstable, unpredictable environments, danger comes with the territory.

Like the time in southeast Bangladesh, when a riot devastated a Christian village without warning. One Bengali family, the husband a schoolmaster, and his wife, a woman who grew up with my wife, lived in a nice home on the edge of the village.

Upon hearing the commotion, they ventured outside. Teenage boys running by called out to him, "*Sheib*, you need to run into the jungle now. A mob is coming to kill community leaders."

The school principal ran into the jungle and found safety by submerging himself in a muddy, leach-infested creek. A hollow reed served as a snorkel while he stayed under water for four hours until dark.

Meanwhile, his wife, knowing Muslim men might beat her but wouldn't kill her, stayed behind to protect their home. She kept throwing buckets of water onto fires started by rioters who attempted to burn her house down.

Later, after she told this story to my wife, Rebecca came to me and said, "If rioters come to our house and you take off while I stay behind to protect our house, you better just keep on running and never come back!"

Huh, how scintillating. I was given the splendid choice of being killed by rioters or never come back. Oh, the spark and wonder of an intense wife. On the day of this writing, after forty years, eight months and twenty-seven days of marriage, my soul mate, my intercultural coach, not only loves me but continues to help me be my best. Of course, I pray I never have to run for my life.

PRINCIPLE # 59: "Are you all in?"

A key to a good marriage in an overseas career is flexibility. Conflict arises when you insist on having your own way. A solid marriage is a committed love relationship built on a set of mutually shared values and goals. Remember, any weakness in a marriage, or any relationship, will be magnified under the duress of cross-cultural stress.

Then there's the big question: "Why do you do it?" I identify with poet Robert Frost who wrote, "I took the road less traveled by, and that has made all the difference." That less traveled road I chose decades ago wasn't only from a thirst for adventure, a chance to travel, and an escape from boredom.

The more important reason I followed the less-traveled road is quite simple—making a difference in people's lives. Great personal satisfaction comes by empowering people. Lives transformed from despair to hope give meaning to my life.

However, that is only one side of the coin. My life has been filled with people I hoped to change, who instead changed me forever. People who materially have very little are content to live a happy life. They focus on things that matter, such as survival and a better life for their children.

For example, I received an email from Dr. Bipul, asking if I would come back and lecture in his graduate school. I would teach the same class I taught on strategic leadership twenty-five years earlier. Except now, in early 2018, I would train a new generation of leaders.

Security was still tight when I arrived at his compound in Chittagong. I stayed on the ground floor of the main building in one of his guest rooms for visiting professors. In the morning I taught and spent the afternoon in my quarters.

One afternoon the clouds parted, and a warm shaft of sunlight entered my bedroom window. I looked out the thief bars, as I had for decades, and realized the bars now made my room seem more like a jail cell. ISIS could be watching and waiting for an opportunity.

Although the Bangladesh government had made gains against the jihadists, my freedom to go outside the compound and walk down the street to buy a tube of toothpaste was gone. Times change, people change, and things were not the same.

However, some things don't change. Every society needs an education system. At dinner, I gave Bipul a list of students from my class twenty-five years earlier and asked what happened to them. He went down the list. "These two passed away, these three went on for more education, this one received a PhD from Australia, and these three all stayed here because their employment was in Chittagong."

"I remember all three here in Chittagong. Two of them were Bengali, but Jahnu was from a minority ethnic group in the hill tracts. What happened to him?"

"He got his master's degree from us, worked several more years, and now is retired. He lives in town here with his daughter who is a medical doctor."

Memories of Jahnu rushed into my mind. I remembered my wife saying she knew Jahnu's family. His father wore a loincloth, was illiterate, and lived in a remote village up in the jungle Hill Tracts. I also remembered Jahnu was the first person from his ethnic group to get a master's degree. Now Jahnu's daughter was a medical doctor, a female doctor in an Islamic culture no less.

In three generations, a family went from living in an isolated jungle village to living in the city, with the son, my student, earning a master's degree and his daughter becoming a medical doctor. As the son's professor, I had a small part in his family's transformation, and I'm not the same.

The foundation of empowerment is training, especially formal education. Never underestimate the power of education in developing societies, for its impact is truly amazing.

PRINCIPLE # 60: "Systemic, generational change"
Never underestimate the transformative power of education, for it is the foundation that can change the trajectory of a family's hope for a future.

When I started to write what you hold in your hands, I didn't know how I would reach back through all the stories and select the right ones that would make sense of it all. How to relate the ups and downs, the failures and victories, in a continuous story form.

In what manner could I explain lessons from so many cultures in a way that's understandable to others who may never experience my family's journey.

Furthermore, to what extent could I explain the sights, sounds, and smells? In what way could I describe the vibrant cultures, the incredible people, and the tapestry of lives we set out to change, who also changed us?

I could wander through our house and point out the scraps and pieces of our story, the visible artifacts that somehow made it around the world and ended up in our home. On the walls and shelves are objects that authenticate our global journey—from the most remote corner of Borneo to the palaces of Middle East royalty.

To this day, our children and their friends call our home a museum. What is a museum anyway? A display of articles of value, a collection that holds memories deep inside. Pictures and maps adorn our walls, books rest silent on our library shelves, and exotic weapons once hung on my boys' bedroom walls before they grew up and moved away.

Throughout our marriage, wherever we lived, Rebecca loved to decorate our houses using local materials and items for decor. For her, it was intentional decorating and had a mantra to go with it.

"When you move a lot, you get sick of stuff. Simple memories are the best. Every culture has inherent beauty, art, and meaning. I've wanted our children to internalize those values as world citizens and focus on the good, not the dark. I love watching them walk our home and tell others the stories memorialized in simple treasures."

One morning over breakfast, I asked Rebecca to show me her favorite item we brought home from overseas. She didn't hesitate. In our living room, perched on a shelf of the white bookcase built into the wall next to the fireplace, was a small, gold picture frame.

"What is it?" I asked.

"This is the only time I framed a paper banknote. You brought it back from Hungary after the fall of the Soviet Union."

"Right, the one and only time I visited Budapest."

The small, rectangular frame, with the cropped oval picture surrounded by a burgundy mat, disguised the fact it was actually a picture on the back of a large Hungarian 100 Forint note. The small picture was a miniature copy of the painting "Flight from the Thunderstorm" by artist Károly Lotz.

Professor Lotz was known for painting romantic landscapes during the latter half of the nineteenth century. The oval picture on the banknote revealed in exquisite detail a young couple fleeing a storm across a prairie in a horse-drawn hay wagon, against a backdrop of black thunderclouds.

"I love storms. They're a reminder that life is wildly alive, and you must accept and respect things you can't control. Where I grew up in the jungle, after a storm passed through, the rains washed the world fresh and clean again. Sunlight sparkled on the jungle path before you," she said.

"After all these years, I never knew you liked storms. So, why is this your favorite thing in our house?"

"The couple in the picture represent us, boldly fleeing the storms of life on a journey to places unknown. The look on their faces isn't fear but adventure, the two clinging to each other, and hanging on to wherever the road leads them. That's been our life. I find it romantic," she said.

I studied the small picture. The scene of two fleeing a thunderstorm truly represented our journey together.

"When you face a future with passion and purpose together, the storms are worth it. A storm is just a storm. It will go away and the sun will rise again. If you don't follow your passion, but huddle in a corner, or shoot for nothing, then you'll hit it every time. To me, that's not a legacy. I'd rather venture out and dance in the rain with you," she said.

Our life together has been mundane and extraordinary, commonplace and dangerous, deeply rewarding yet costing much. Most of all, the journey has been sacred, all because of meeting inspiring people, the real treasure we found along the way.

I don't regret giving up the prestigious jobs, big money, safety, and ease of life in America. I'm into counting lives, those empowered through education and sustainable development, for I sought the hidden path and happened upon an unimaginable life.

Time and again, people ask, "So, how did you get into this line of work?"

My answer is straightforward. "It happened a long time ago in college when a coach asked me to take a team to Central Africa. My life was never the same, and to this day I continue to live an unreal life. No matter how many times I circle the earth, I wouldn't trade it for the world."

In Search of Meaning

Gratitude bestows reverence, allowing us to encounter everyday epiphanies, those transcendent moments of awe that change forever how we experience life in the world.
—Sarah Van Breathnach

I TRUST MY STORIES and life lessons inspired you to ask yourself critical yet straightforward questions. *First, what is your passion, what energizes you?* Not everyone needs a PhD in international development to make a difference. I've known mechanics, carpenters, teachers, and doctors who helped out overseas, either career or for a short time, influencing lives with their skills and passion.

For a young person, with your whole life before you, consider this: after reading my real-life stories, are you cut out for a career of dodging risks yet enjoying the intrinsic rewards of helping others less fortunate?

Perhaps a life overseas is not for you, as my college friend found out on our trip to the Central African Republic, and that's all right.

To my surprise, I was attracted to international work. But neither of us would have known if we hadn't gone.

If you are not sure, then go overseas for a time and see if it's a life for you. Discover what causes you are passionate about and volunteer for a few weeks. Always follow your passion, not someone else's, because enthusiasm without strong commitment is not enough. In fact, to weather the hardships, it should be a calling.

Second, *if you knew you couldn't fail, what do you dream of doing?* Will you have regrets if you don't fulfill the dream? What is holding you back? The answer to this last question will reveal the risks and fears that are keeping you from stepping out into the deep.

At any age, whether overseas or in your home community, helping others by volunteering can change your life. Many nonprofits provide opportunities to get involved as a volunteer.

For instance, Rebecca's organization, *Women At Risk International (WAR)* and their merchant arm, *Warchest Boutique,* have what they call "a banquet of thirty-nine ways" for people to get involved in significant, ongoing ways from all walks of life. Volunteers include writers, artists, athletes, newscasters, jewelers, retirees, and attorneys, just to name a few.

A practical way of getting involved is purchasing *WARCHEST* products made by rescued slaves and those at risk of slavery. Each sale helps lift them to a life of dignity. Host a *WARCHEST* product party, donate, or attend a *Civilian First Responders (CFR)* seminar.

A CFR seminar teaches you how to identify the fifteen demographics, twenty-one signs, and twenty-two lures of human trafficking in your community. This is only one of the thirty-nine ways a person can get involved with a nonprofit organization.

And it's never too late to give back. While leaving Bangladesh after teaching, I met an American couple and the husband, a retired doctor, was pushing eighty years of age.

Here he was, at the airport flinging large bags of medical supplies into the airport X-ray machine. The couple was on their way to help with a severe refugee crisis on the border with Myanmar. It was his fourteenth trip to rural Bangladesh since retirement.

Whatever career you are in, consider using your free time to help others. Opportunities abound for helping those less fortunate. Whether you are home or abroad, if you are a person of religious faith, then put your faith into practice. Fight for social justice and care for the less fortunate.

Regardless of your personal worldview, my call to action is to remember the words attributed to John Dewey, who said, "It's not enough for a man to be good, he must be good for something." So join a cause and fight against any form of injustice and bring hope.

I hear a common theme—a search for meaning and significance in life. Many find meaning in their family, their possessions, and their careers. Others find meaning by volunteering at civic organizations and places of worship.

For some, life may seem meaningless, a "chasing after the wind" (Ecclesiastes) or "the mass of men living quiet lives of desperation" (Henry David Thoreau).

For me, meaning doesn't come from the number of zeros in bank accounts, or the degrees hanging on the wall, or the size of the organization or business that one builds. It doesn't even come from NGO project outcomes.

I find meaning in a personal relationship with the God of my faith, my family, and my friends around the world. From my theistic worldview, I believe everything happens for a reason, and the only thing I can take with me when I die are relationships I had on this earth. Meaning comes from lives touched, changed, and those who changed me.

Mother Teresa once said, "I alone cannot change the world, but I can cast a stone across the water to create many ripples." Each ripple for me is a changed life.

At the end of the day, what you do in life is all about risk and reward. The financial investment principle of "greater reward requires greater risk" is true in life as well. An unreal life requires taking risks. I was fortunate to find a soul mate who shared this view towards risk. Along the way, we met incredible people who lived in difficult places under extreme circumstances, as chronicled in this book.

For you to be fulfilled, what risks are you willing to take? I say, face your fears, give up your small ambitions and journey out into the deep. Almost a century ago, G. T. Shedd wrote, "A ship is safe in harbor, but that's not what ships are for." Everyone knows ships are made for the sea and that is their purpose.

Outside the harbor, and far away in the deep, there are risks. Herman Melville, in his classic novel *Moby Dick,* revealed the deceptive nature of the deep: "When beholding the tranquil beauty and brilliancy of the ocean's skin, one forgets the tiger heart that pants beneath it."

Mariners of old called the sea a fickle friend, whose calm serenity could quickly change into formidable fury. Lumbering, lazy waves can turn into heaving swells that unleash wrath that takes your breath away. I know that from my experience of surviving a cyclone on a wooden ship in the Bay of Bengal.

Like life, the sea has secrets, stories to tell, is gentle yet mean. The deep is not for the faint of heart. Not surprising, at those times of fury, when the ocean roars, you crave the safety of the shore, the protection of the harbor.

But remember this: the open sea marvels with translucent beauty and depending on the day, can bring forth a rich kaleidoscope of colors: deep blue, lavender, pink, and turquoise. A horizon of a disappearing red sunset seamlessly brings a dark blue sea to meet the light blue sky.

Beneath the ocean surface lies another world of beauty, variety, and pageantry, where drama unfolds under royal blue waves. A display of vibrant colors swims and drifts among the reefs. In the sea, diversity of life reigns.

So too, diverse cultures of the world await your discovery. Pursue them, or an orchestration of beauty and adventure will pass you by. The deep is a constant changing of the guard, a color fest of sights and sounds. The rewards are immense, ever-changing, deeply satisfying.

The sea cycles between peace and anger. The same is true in life, as living in the deep will test and try a person. That's when you find out who you really are, what you are made of, and what you believe. Adversity reveals character and then builds character. Embrace adversity, don't flee, for that is how you mature.

I ask the question: what will you do with the rest of your life? J.R.R. Tolkien gave a simple answer that was crystal clear, "All we have to decide is what to do with the time that is given us."

Choose wisely.

Acknowledgments

The most challenging experience in my life has been writing this book. It was a journey in itself. Fortunately, I had tremendous help along the way from many accomplished people.

My first thanks belongs to a former U.S. ambassador, Jonathan Addleton, PhD, who analyzed my manuscript and graciously wrote the Foreword. His decades of development work, notably serving as a USAID Mission Director over India, Pakistan, Cambodia, and Central Asia, provided excellent insights. A published author, his comments strengthened this book.

I appreciate the insights from actress, director, producer, and author, Nancy Stafford, who early on introduced me to the importance of themes that gave structure to so many stories. Nancy understands the power of scenes threaded by themes. A veteran star, she is most known as Andy Griffith's law partner on the Matlock TV series.

Many thanks to publishing coach Tim Beals, who connected me to author Latayne Scott, PhD. Latayne converted me from a textbook author into a storyteller. Her highly valued efforts went way beyond the scope of a content editor, for first she instructed me how to write a story and write it boldly.

Amy Louise Shane's amazing line editing ability brought laser focus and attention to detail that the manuscript sorely needed.

A special thanks go to several early readers for their remarkable editorial advice: Jasmine Linabary, PhD; Diana Osipsov, PhD candidate (ABD); Donna Anders; Mary Elizabeth Medawar; Alan Carter, PhD; James Sandberg; Mike Shane; and Jim Anders.

A further note of thanks goes to the staff of North Loop Books, who worked as a great team to produce this book.

I am grateful to my past and present staff, board members, and donors who believed in the vision of sustainable growth for the developing world.

As to my own family, their love and support made this book possible. My 100-year-old mother, Helen McDonald, provided correspondence and memories going back almost a half century. Our children, Matthew, Sheridan Mark, Nathan, and Danielle, gave unique insight and perspective, by reflecting on their memories of the many experiences we shared together.

I am most thankful for my wife, Rebecca, the love of my life, whose memory and amazing insights into our life together enhanced the book immensely. Without a doubt, she is the most incredible and extraordinary person I have ever known.